The Parent Track

The Parent Track

Timing, Balance, and Choice in Academia

Christina DeRoche and Ellie Berger, editors

WILFRID LAURIER
UNIVERSITY PRESS
www.wlupress.wlu.ca

Wilfrid Laurier University Press acknowledges the support of the Canada Council for the Arts for our publishing program. We acknowledge the financial support of the Government of Canada through the Canada Book Fund for our publishing activities. This work was supported by the Research Support Fund.

Library and Archives Canada Cataloguing in Publication

The parent track : timing, balance, and choice within academia / Christina DeRoche and Ellie D. Berger, editors.

Includes bibliographical references and index.

Issued in print and electronic formats.

ISBN 978-1-77112-241-2 (paperback).—ISBN 978-1-77112-263-4 (pdf).—ISBN 978-1-77112-264-1 (epub)

1. College teachers—Family relationships. 2. Work and family. 3. Work–life balance. 4. Women in higher education. I. DeRoche, Christina, 1980–, editor II. Berger, Ellie D., 1973–, editor

LB2331.7.P37 2016   378.1'1   C2016-904923-X
                                            C2016-904924-8

Cover illustration and design by Angela Booth Malleau, designbooth.ca. Text design by Angela Booth Malleau.

Preface originally published in *University Affairs* (Ottawa), 19 September 2012.

This book is printed on FSC® certified paper and is certified Ecologo. It contains post-consumer fibre, is processed chlorine free, and is manufactured using biogas energy.

Printed in Canada

We would like to dedicate this book to our children, Alessandra, Gabriella, and Joel; to our parents, Rosanna, David, and Frank and Eveline and Sam; and to our partners, Michael and Rob. Lastly, this book is also dedicated to the countless other academics and aspiring academics struggling to achieve work–life balance.

Contents

xi   Foreword | On Overlaps and Bleeds
Amber E. Kinser

xv   Preface | Pregnant Publications Pause: Pursuing Motherhood and the Tenure track
Elizabeth Koblyk

1   Introduction | Parenting as a Choice or Dilemma
Christina DeRoche and Ellie D. Berger

Part One | Foundational Narratives

11   Unanswered and Lingering Questions
Christina DeRoche

23   Work–Family Balance? | A Challenging Yet Rewarding Journey Through Gendered Academia
Ellie D. Berger

Part Two |Making the Big Decision

31   Conversations with Women | Mothers and Academics
Erin Careless

41   Academia, My Mother, and Me | Reflections on Intergenerational Emotional Geographies of Academic Parenting
Sara L. Jackson

55   Patchwork Academia
Sarah Milmine

65   Motherhood and Graduate Studies | The Untold Stories of
     Summer Residency
     Melissa Corrente

77   I've Been to Me
     Jennifer Barnett

Part Three | Parenting within Academia: Friend or Foe?

87   Fatherhood and the PhD | Time Management, Perfectionism,
     and the Question of Value
     Geoff Salomons

95   Going In and Coming Out | Understanding Ourselves
     as Mama Scholars
     Lisa J. Starr and Kathleen M. Bortolin

109 Longing to Belong | Parenting and Self-Realization
     within Academia
     Ilka Luyt

117 "Dad and Mom Do Not Want to Get Zeroes" |
     Parenting in Academia
     Mildred Tsitsi Masimira

125 Of Diapers and Comprehensives | A Feminist Exploration
     of Graduate-Student-Mothering in the Academy
     Anita Jack-Davies

135 He Told Me "Babies Sleep" | Expectations and Realities about
     Maternity Leave Productivity
     Tarah Brookfield

149 Legacy and Vulnerability | Queer Parenting in the Academy
     Sarah R. Pickett

163 Surviving Parenthood and Academia | Two Professionals
     Striving to Maintain Work–Life Balance
     Rose Ricciardelli and Stephen Czarnuch

185 Parent-Student, Student-Parent | A Tale of Two Roles
     Kevin Black

Part Four | Ongoing Negotiation in Academia

203   Navigating Role Conflict in Pursuit of an Academic Career |
      A.k.a. "You will get used to it"
      Jane E. Barker

213   Engaging Academia as the Nest Empties
      Timothy Sibbald

223   Juggling Fatherhood, Child Disability, and Academia
      John Beaton

233   Hopeful Intrusions | Moments as Both a Dad and a Professor
      David Long

247   A Bridge Too Far? The Elephant in the Ivory Tower |
      Parenting and the Tenure Track
      John Hoben

257   Baby Step by Baby Step | That Was the Way to Do It!
      Michelann Parr

267   About the Authors

273   Index

On Overlaps and Bleeds
A Foreword

Amber E. Kinser

Life in the academy is characterized by what can feel at times like a flexible, self-determined schedule, with its long breaks and short days at the office, and with the academic's ability to break up the day to accommodate appointments and family demands, relative to the workaday grind of much full-time, on-site employment. For all its "flexibility," the workload itself, of course, is not actually lighter but is instead broken up, deferred, and dispersed. Such workload, or work–life, or work-life circumstances challenge what I believe to be a mythical notion of "balance" and complicate the faculty members' ability to create any notable space or time that is exclusively or sacredly family. Academe is exploitive of the already blurred boundaries between home and work that are its trademark, with its student assignments created and evaluated off-campus, its research and writing appearing to non-academics as *not*-work, because they're not done *at* work. With its activity that goes on in places where home or family or solitude are supposed to happen—at the kitchen table, in the car, at the park. With its activity that looks suspiciously like leisure to outsiders but that is done on behalf of work—holiday gatherings, intramural games, university concerts or plays, meetings over lunch, fundraising over dinner, community activism or engagement or schmoozing on the weekends. Ever crossing and living between these blurred boundaries, where summers are ravenously consumed by research or guilt over the lack of it, where "temporary" work takes on an undercompensated permanence, academic parents probably have to push harder than many against the occupational intrusions into self and family identity.

My own experience, as an academic, a parent, a professor of family communication, a motherhood studies scholar, and an administrator, is a case in point, even if my circumstances are particularly challenging. Recently, I sat in the audience of a theatre production at my university thinking about the

overlaps of academic and parental life. The exigencies and contingencies of
these overlaps are a salient part of my identity, and particularly so given my
current work–life setup. I am the chairperson of a department; my partner
is a head of a program in my department. My daughter has been a major for
the last four years in the program my partner, her stepfather, heads, and she
is a fine- and performing-arts student in the honours program my partner
also heads. Our teenage son attends high school at the University School on
campus that is part of my university's College of Education, and he is planning to "dual enroll" in a course in my department to earn both high school
and college credit next semester; he is dating a student who is a major in my
department. Even as someone who values and works to embody the third wave
feminist sensibility of embracing contradiction and messiness, I find the ways
my family life and my academic life bleed into each other to be more than I
can take at times.

    When my daughter hit a rough patch in her education—the patch that
so many of my students have hit and from which a number of them never
bounced back—I was exhausted from the mental, and even spiritual, contor-
tions I was doing not only to help her, despite my feelings of powerlessness,
but also to keep myself from reading her struggle as evidence of my failure as
a mother and my inadequacies as an academic and teacher. Was I so wrapped
up in running the department, in focusing on the graduation rates of other
parents' children, that I didn't attend to my own daughter's academic success?
Was I being too professorial when I encouraged her to get an apartment alone
so that she could avoid roommate drama and its impact on studies, and not
enough aware of her need for companionship and peer support? Did I push
her to opt for the living situation I wished I'd had in college? Why was my
academic experience not helping me to rescue her from this moment? How
were her professors—my colleagues—reading any of it? How dare I think of
collegial perceptions of me at a time like this?

    In the theatre production I was watching, my daughter was in a starring role
onstage and my parents were sitting in the audience with me, having driven
into town to see the production. I read through the program in which she
mentioned me in her cast member bio. I moved between being—as mother—
immeasurably proud of her on the verge of graduation and sad that my partner was missing it for his research sabbatical, and being—as chair—annoyed
that the ushers were allowing people to enter late and making a mental note
to do something about that, curious about whether the department should
be spending so much money on the program I was reading, and wondering
whether "we" should have made other choices about a couple of the costumes.
If my recent evening at the theatre were an anomaly, if this moment in which

myriad home-life matters and work-life matters seemed to create a bit of a "bloodbath" stood out in contrast to what I experience every day, I might have run screaming from theatre. But I sat there familiar with the conflict and discomfort. I sat there, in fact, enjoying my daughter's craft and thinking about how to write the experience into this foreword.

If I had been asked to use these pages to offer some insights on achieving work–family balance or affirming family boundaries, I'm afraid I'd have little to offer. What I can provide is confirmation of the themes explored in this collection: university life is both flexible and unyielding to families, responsive to and disregarding of reproductive life cycles, open and restrictive to the variety of family forms and circumstances, welcoming and dismissive of children, employing and exploitive of women's labour. It is a complex equation that academic parents are positioned to solve and, in addition to becoming highly educated experts in their fields, if they are to flourish, or even just survive in those fields, they also must acquire, on behalf of their families and in service to their own identities, a set of improvisational problem-solving skills and an ongoing ability to adjust and accommodate and innovate.

Pregnant Publications Pause
Pursuing Motherhood and the Tenure Track

Liz Koblyk

McMaster University professor Lorraine York was putting together her tenure package when she became pregnant. She received notice of tenure two days after giving birth. Luckily, the timing of her pregnancy had minimal impact on her tenure bid, as she already had a strong publications record.

Like other women who have had a child while preparing for an academic career, though, she has felt the pressure of balancing motherhood with research. While systemic barriers cannot be overcome by individual actions, this article shares advice from mother-mentors like Dr. York on planning to have a child and pursue an academic job.

In the twenty-one years since Dr. York had her child, she has served on numerous hiring committees. When asked whether candidates should openly address motherhood in their CVs, she offers an emphatic yes, even though Canadian employers cannot legally ask whether candidates are parents. To best address the publications gap that typically results from parenthood, Dr. York advises candidates to write, "in an unapologetic manner, 'Between this date and this date, I was a primary caregiver.'" Such statements can reassure hiring committees that candidates' future research output will exceed their current output.

During pregnancy and early child-rearing years, choose research projects strategically, says Dr. York. Forget about book reviews. They are manageable in terms of time commitment and level of analysis required but count for little with hiring committees. Delay starting new projects in favour of building on conference papers. Collaborative work may be useful, but make sure your department values it before you commit to projects.

Meanwhile one sessional instructor (who doesn't want her name used) says that when her first child was three, she received a tenure-track offer but turned it down because of the challenge of handling "two demanding jobs simultaneously"—academia and parenthood.

Even academic interviews can be a challenge for mothers, this instructor points out. For her first academic interview, she chose to disclose her status as mother: she asked for (and received) breaks in the planned twelve-hour day, so she could nurse.

Dr. York adds a few more suggestions for academic interviews. Before interviews, a designated person within the department or university could review fair hiring practices with the committee, to make members aware of what they can and can't ask, and to remind them that publication numbers alone may not accurately predict research potential.

Another academic mother who prefers to remain anonymous focused her suggestions on institutional change, citing the need for more spaces at university daycare centres, and daycare as a standard feature of academic conferences. Her own wait for a university daycare space lasted two years—years in which she could have been more productive in her research.

More radically, universities could introduce more flexible tenure-track positions where new parents might work half or three-quarters time at a reduced rate of pay for a number of years while raising their families, proposes this mother.

If you're in a department that's not particularly supportive, Dr. York suggests finding "the one person who is most sympathetic. Say it's the admin assistant. Go through them to get what you need," even if it's minor assistance, such as putting up a cancellation notice on your classroom if you're home taking care of an ill child.

Whatever steps you take to plan for parenthood, and however family-friendly your department is, York says, "get ready for the guilt that you will inevitably feel. Don't assume you'll be the magic person who makes it look easy."

While research and parenthood are both rewarding, each is challenging in its own right. In concert, the two demand planning, determination, and the support of friends and family, if not the institution itself.

INTRODUCTION

Parenting as a Choice or Dilemma

Christina DeRoche and Ellie D. Berger

During the entirety of our academic careers, we have been faced with many life-changing decisions regarding school, work, and family. Both of us continue to be highly affected by these ongoing decisions and realize through talking to others in our field that we are not alone. This book is based on our belief that by sharing these difficult yet often rewarding challenges that we have faced as a collective, others pursuing an academic career will benefit immensely. In fact, Clandining and Connelly (2000) also acknowledge how such qualitative inquiry is essential in that "stories lived and told educate the self and others, including the young and those such as researchers who are new to their communities" (p. xxvi). Further, Shields (2005) elaborates that sharing stories helps "connect us across time and place" and emphasizes the importance of "restructuring stories from the past in the light of present knowledge" (p. 180). Thus, we firmly believe that sharing our experiences and those that the authors in this book have so generously shared will help others who are negotiating similar experiences in their own personal journeys. This book, therefore, is a collection of narratives and experiences that are related but at times quite different. They represent the variability in experiences that individuals have in pursuing all levels of academia but also the many similarities between them. Thus, the main purpose of this book is to highlight the ongoing challenges of negotiating a work–family balance amid the unique pressures of academia. Throughout this book, you will find many common themes that emerge: struggling with the decision to become a parent within the delayed biological context of academia, facing the challenges of trying to negotiate a balance between work and family, managing the pressures we feel from "outsiders," dealing with the guilt we feel almost constantly when family time turns into work time, and acknowledging that this is an ongoing process that we encounter at varying points throughout our careers.

1

Anne-Marie Slaughter made this conversation and the gruesome and tiring tug-of-war for working mothers apparent in her article "Why Women Can't Have It All" (2012), where she stipulated that as women we need to stop thinking we can have it all as successful working mothers, as the economic and political structure of North America does not allow for it. This is not to dissuade women and men from thinking it is possible but rather to face and target the real reasoning behind this consistent and old debate. Time and time again, we have encountered numerous research studies that have shown that having active involvement from both mothers and fathers is beneficial to child development, as well as to each other's well-being (Goldberg & Perry-Jenkins, 2004). Given this finding, it would be logical to assume that the political and economic structure would change to reflect this, but unfortunately, it has not.

This book is a tribute to these work–family struggles from a variety of perspectives and aims to highlight how structurally we are still so very behind. Structurally, there is an inherent myth that coincides with what Slaughter is really talking about in her article, the myth of having it all. As Slaughter explains, we cannot begin to imagine having it all, men or women, without first acknowledging how the economic and political structure of our businesses and corporations hinders movement within and encouragement of parenting in families. Second, once we acknowledge this reality, we can then begin to discuss how to change it.

Research on Mothering and Fathering and "The Myth"

So what do we know? We can draw from two areas here: motherhood and fatherhood. Research on motherhood is abundant and reveals that it comprises separate spheres: that of work and home. Each one comes with various demands and, most of the time, incompatible expectations (Springer, Parker, & Leviten-Reid, 2009). Research on women in academia proves undoubtedly that despite the number of women entering academia in unprecedented numbers, they are not occupying levels of tenure as expected (Expert Panel on Women in University Research, 2012). What is left is a male-dominated profession where silence reigns on the matter of family and negotiating balance within the profession. With the increased number of women in post-secondary institutions, many believe that equity between the sexes has been achieved, but Coward (1992) states (and we agree) that this equity is a fallacy and that women now more than ever encounter challenges and problems.

What about fathers, you ask? As Dowd (2000) states, more than ever before fathers are intensely involved in the rearing of their children; as a result, narratives and research have been emerging on the experiences of men pursuing parenthood. More recently, Marotte, Martin Reynolds, and Savarese (2011) state that fatherhood in academia is not characterized in the same fashion as motherhood in academia; fathers are presumed to not experience the same tug-of-war between parenting and academia as mothers do (Wilson, 2003). With the new fatherhood emerging, the social sentiment seems to be positive in comparison to the experience of mothers in academia; that is, society tends to look more positively on a father who is trying to be a good and nurturing parent than a woman who is trying to do the same.

So where does this challenging journey begin? What are the sources of the problem in maintaining the work–family balance? There are three main areas of tension through the various levels of academia for women in juggling family and work: the demands of home, the demands of work, and cultural expectations (Jacobs & Winslow, 2004). Both family and work require that women submit themselves wholeheartedly to the exclusion of one over the other (Edwards, 1993). This responsibility of being successful at both, more often than not, rests on women (Mason & Goulden, 2004). Being good at both constitutes being a superwoman, and this often entails women sacrificing one domain for the other. This struggle is often silent and goes unrecognized in academia (Leonard & Malina, 1994), something that Hoschild describes as a "cultural cover-up" (Hoschild & Machung, 1989). Swanson and Johnston (2003) comment that academic mothers struggle to have their role identified and feel that the motherhood role is not valued. Further, Coward (1992) states that while society has progressed in allowing for equity in the education of both men and women, there has been a new-found expectation that women should be good mothers in addition to excelling at their jobs, yet not be allowed to vent their frustrations in any way.

In fact, many women enter academia under the false impression that it is a flexible career choice (Comer & Stites-Doe, 2006). But this idea of flexibility is layered within fallacies of equity itself. The academic world is still largely dominated by men and male ideals (Evans & Grant, 2009), and having children is often seen as career suicide (Wilson, 2003). The flexibility of academia entices women since often professors do not have to be on campus to work (Evans & Grant, 2009). However, many seem to forget that working at home does not mean that work is put off altogether—it only means that work time can be slightly more flexible, which also means that it more often than not seeps into family time. How, then, is motherhood experienced by women at various levels? What does it mean to be a mother and a graduate student or professor, for example?

At the graduate level, Springer et al. (2009) state that the complexities of graduate school, with coursework, comprehensive exams, and dissertation work, can further complicate the work–family balance. With these complexities, women are increasingly postponing motherhood, especially if they are enrolled in a post-graduate degree (Kuperberg, 2009). This pattern of postponement is based on one primary reason: many women in academia view children as a hindrance to their careers and to the advancement opportunities within them (Kuperberg, 2009; Leonard & Malina, 1994). Edwards (1993) elaborates on the struggles that mature female graduate students have in balancing their families and graduate studies. She herself was one of these women and admitted that she did not want one to affect the other. Her participants also elaborated that they did not want their family lives to be affected but the tension between each was prevalent throughout their time in graduate school; however, they generally managed to find ways of coping with these pressures (Edwards, 1993). For these participants, the tension between family and education was a "process of constant negotiation" (Edwards, 1993, p. 13).

Edwards' (1993) participants consistently cited time as being of the utmost importance and a continual problem. Because the job of being a graduate student and the job of being a mother both require intense time and energy, they had times of stress, joy, guilt, and even physical and emotional exhaustion (Edwards, 1993). In fact, women reported that time spent with family was seen as time not spent on work, and conversely, time spent on work was seen as time not spent with family (Edwards, 1993). Most of these women did try to find ways of negotiating the two roles and discovered some type of a happy medium (Edwards, 1993).

But the key issue that makes academia distinct from many other professions is that for many women who enter graduate school or their first academic position, the timing of these events usually coincides with the ideal timing for motherhood. For most women entering graduate school, having children during their studies can be appealing for reasons already mentioned. There is a common perception that many women *choose* to take time off to be mothers, but this perception presumes that there is actually a choice involved (Springer et al., 2009). Further, many worry about how this decision will interfere with their career advancement (Kuperberg, 2009). But as Springer et al. (2009) point out, most academics are slaves to their work and the idea of publishing or perishing is ingrained in us early in our careers.

Women who wait until they have secured an academic job to have children do not differ in their feelings of conflict between work and family. Many female academics still see motherhood as a barrier to their career development in attaining tenure (Comer & Stites-Doe, 2006). Kittlestrom (2010) comments on the discrimination that most women face in academia, noting that fewer women than men attain tenure, and often they are relegated to a second tier of academia. Women without children are far more likely to attain tenure than women with children (Mason & Goulden, 2004). And because the brunt of the responsibility for child-rearing falls on women, men usually attain tenure at the expense of their female partners (Kittlestrom, 2010). So, for women in academia who decide to become mothers, role negotiation pervades much of their lives. Role negotiation for women means balancing the demands of career with the demands of family life. This role balancing is defined by Comer and Stites-Doe (2006) as "the process of experiencing greater interrole facilitation than interrole conflict and depletion" (p. 496).

Achieving complete harmony between both spheres is often a struggle for women and usually entails establishing conditions within a woman's life that are ideal for allowing her to have children and a career at the same time (Comer & Stites-Doe, 2006). In discovering why it is that women still have to accept this, Coward (1992) states that women's identities rest on something more profound than just social conditioning: they are programmed to expect breaks in their career paths because of the cultural expectation that they are to be mothers. Subsequently, if women choose not to have children, they are often viewed negatively by their peers:

> But there is still an assumption that something must be wrong with you if you don't have kids: you are seriously, perhaps pathologically, career driven; you are inherently selfish or obsessed with material things that you don't want to sacrifice; you are too unattractive to get laid; or you have biological "problems" that prevent you from fulfilling your biological destiny. (Warner, 2009, p. 9)

Kittlestrom (2010) echoes this sentiment when she states that "for every successful academic mother, there are a good dozen women who have either sacrificed their family plans for their careers or sacrificed their careers for their children" (p. 5). So why does it have to be one or the other?

Furthermore, all of this does not address the source of such problems. Douglas and Michaels (2004) explain that women have been under the false impression that motherhood is the penultimate goal of the woman's sphere, attributing this misconception to unattainable ideals set out by media and propaganda. This "new momism" comprises powerful ideals and at first glance celebrates motherhood, but "we buy into these absurd ideals at the same time that we resent them and think they are utterly ridiculous and oppressive" (Douglas & Michaels, 2004, p. 4). Furthermore, although the feminist movement has proven that women have choices and are active agents in their decision whether or not to become mothers (Slaughter, 2012), "the only true enlightened choice to make as a woman, the one that proves, first, that you are a 'real' woman, and second, that you are a decent, worthy one, is to become a 'real' mom" (Douglas & Michaels, 2004, p. 5). This is the myth of motherhood: women must buy into the notion of an ideal motherhood that is filled only with joys, but at the same time there are so many "choices" and decisions that leave women with enormous amounts of guilt along the way. This myth is the underlying premise and source of this research: Are women at every stage of their academic careers buying into this ideal notion of motherhood? How do they deal with the feelings associated with these conflicting demands—do they experience discord and are they led to believe it is their fault? It is a myth that has resonated throughout literature over time but has not been adequately addressed in previous research.

Recent research has shown that women in academia have made slow gains in achieving harmony between work and family, but this delicate act is negotiated by several propositions (Comer & Stites-Doe, 2006). Having pre-school-aged children at the same time as working toward tenure complicates the balance; however, having a supportive partner and working at a university with adequate childcare facilities can aid in achieving this balance. For women, greater career satisfaction, overall, comes from balancing these two spheres and contributes, largely, to the overall success in academia and in tenure and promotion, specifically. So perhaps the myth of motherhood can be aided by the addition of support from all ends: spousal, familial, and institutional.

Our Final Message and Organization of the Book

Despite what research tells us, we believe in change and in creating more awareness for ourselves and for others like us and unlike us. Our frustrations and experiences in pursuing academic careers prompted the creation of this book and ignited a deep desire for understanding the variability within academic experiences and the compatibility of academia with family life. After several work–family balance conversations, we realized that we both felt strongly about this topic and we decided to pursue this venture. In our casual conversations and advice seeking from peers, we found that women and men in academia have faced difficulties, and in an effort to help others we felt compelled to share some of these struggles. This book is an attempt to provide a venue for the individual authors to share their experiences, but it is also our hope that it provides a detailed means of understanding, comfort, and especially guidance for the upcoming generations of academics. This book aims to be inclusive of all in academia, men and women, those with and without children, and those who are single or in heterosexual or same-sex relationships. In allowing for such inclusion, this book answers a largely ignored aspect of intersection: parental status, gender, age, timing, marital status, and sexual orientation. There is a lack of literature pertaining to the experience of same-sex academic couples in the quest for parenting or in the decision to not become a parent. Marsiglio, Day, and Lamb (2000) state that conversations of parenting and academia often encompass the typified heterosexual, married couple. We want to break this mould and add to the conversation of parenting in academia. In an effort to be inclusive we have found several themes within the submissions and have organized the book to reflect the different stages in academic and family-life history. While we received many submissions from students and junior academics, we also wanted to include narratives from more senior full professors. We even actively sought out several senior faculty members nationally, who we thought would make excellent contributors to this book; however, intriguingly, none ended up submitting narratives, generally because they had "too much on their plate." This further highlights to us how truly busy life for academics is (particularly female ones with children), and we can only hope that this book will begin to break down some of the issues that we face daily and make the work–family balance less challenging in the future.

This book has been organized into four main sections based on the entries we received and selected. Part One contains two foundational narratives written by DeRoche and Berger, which present many unanswered questions and challenges that we both continue to face in our academic journey. Part Two contains narratives that examine the decision to become a parent, written by those who are childless by choice or otherwise, or by those who are contemplating parenthood in academia. This section provides a detailed account of why some have decided to remain childless, such as Barnett, who describes her experience in loving children but also wanting to be herself. In her account she explains how her sexuality and the heteronormative nature of academia contradicted her decision. This section also depicts the factors negotiated in making the decision to become a parent in academia; Jackson's piece is unique here, as it reflects on her mother's experience and now hers in becoming a parent in academia, while Careless, Milmine, and Corrente describe their own personal sacrifices and rewards in delaying their decisions. For example, Careless uses her research on the experiences of female academics to reflect on her own decisions and describes how these experiences affected some of the barriers she encountered as well.

Part Three focuses on the constant negotiation and tribulations that family life and academia can present. This section contains contributions from individuals who come from various levels in academia, including graduate students and tenure-track professors. In this section you will find a range of experiences from both men and women who are parents and who were misguided in many ways about what parenting would entail, such as Brookfield's experience of being told that "babies will sleep" and that she would have time for her academic duties. The incompatibility of academia and parenting is obvious in this section, but what is also apparent is how rewarding each can be to the other. Take Starr and Bortolin's experiences in separating their identities as mothers and academics and discovering that this was no easy task, and that one without the other would be inconceivable. Another interesting piece in this section is the narrative written by Ricciardelli and Czarnuch, a couple in different stages of their academic careers, comparing their experiences as husband and wife and in different academic areas. Black's experience summarizes the feeling of this section best by stating that "every day I am exquisitely aware—sometimes painfully so—that this is the life that *I* am choosing. And that, for me, makes all the difference." Pickett's narrative on queer parenting is a welcome addition to the heteronormative literature on academia, and Salomons' piece highlights some of the challenges of combining fatherhood and PhD studies. Finally, the three narratives by Luyt, Masimira, and Jack-Davies bring a diverse array of reflections on parenting within academia.

Part Four contains the narratives of academics who are further along in their careers and have reflected upon their experiences. Barker does an excellent job in portraying how sacrifices have to be made in work and in family life and describes telling her children on countless occasions "you will get used to it" when work conflicts arise. Sibbald describes his path from being a graduate student to entering the world of online courses and telework in order to make family life work, and the many conflicts he dealt with along the way. The narratives written by Beaton, Long, and Hoben provide rare and enlightening views on the meaning and negotiation of fatherhood within academic life. Finally, Parr sums it up for many of us in academia: it is not about sacrificing what we love in academia, but making what we want work for both family and career fulfillment. And that is the final message of this book, that despite our marital status, parental status, sexuality, gender, and point on the academic road, we all make sacrifices and continue to actively negotiate; however, this does not mean that we lose something. What we have discovered and hope others discover by reading this book is a deeper understanding of what it means to "have it all" and a deeper understanding of who we are and who we want to become in the process.

References

Clandinning, D. J., & Connelly, F. M. (2000). *Narrative inquiry: Experience and story in qualitative research.* Toronto, ON: Wiley–Jossey Bass.

Comer, D. R., & Stites-Doe, S. (2006). Antecedents and consequences of faculty women's academic-parental role balancing. *Journal of Family Economic Issues, 27,* 495–512.

Coward, R. (1992). *Our treacherous hearts: Why women let men get their way.* Boston, MA: Faber & Faber.

Douglas, S. J., & Michaels, M. W. (2004). *The mommy myth: The idealization of motherhood and how it has undermined women.* Toronto, ON: Free Press.

Dowd, N. E. (2000). *Redefining fatherhood.* New York: New York University Press.

Edwards, R. (1993). *Mature women students: Separating or connecting family and education.* Washington, DC: Taylor & Francis.

Evans, E., & Grant, C. (2009). Introduction. In E. Evans & C. Grant (Eds.), *Mama PhD: Women write about motherhood and academic life* (pp. xvii–xxv). Piscataway, NJ: Rutgers University Press.

Expert Panel on Women in University Research. (2012). *Strengthening Canada's research capacity: The gender dimension.* Ottawa, ON: Council of Canadian Academies.

Goldberg, A. E., & Perry-Jenkins, M. (2004). Division of labour and working-class women's well-being across the transition to parenthood. *Journal of Family Psychology, 18*(1), 225–236.

Hoschild, A., & Machung, A. (1989). *The second shift.* Toronto, ON: Penguin Books.

Jacobs, J. A., & Winslow, S. E. (2004). Overworked faculty: Job stressed and family demands. *Annals of the American Academy of Political and Social Sciences, 596,* 104–129.

Kittlestrom, A. (2010, February 12). The academic-mother handicap. *Chronicle of Higher Education.* Retrieved from http://chronicle.com/article/The -Academic-Motherhood/64073/

Kuperberg, A. (2009). Motherhood and graduate education: 1970–2000. *Population Research and Policy Review, 28,* 473–504.

Legard, R., Keegan, J., & Ward, K. (2003). In-depth interviews. In J. Ritchie & J. Lewis (Eds.), *Qualitative research practice: A guide for social science students and researchers* (pp. 138–169). London: Sage.

Leonard, P., & Malina, D. (1994). Caught between two worlds: Mothers as academics. In S. Davies, C. Lubelska, & J. Quinn (Eds.), *Changing the subject: Women in higher education* (pp. 29–41). London, England: Taylor & Francis.

Marotte, M. R., Martin Reynolds, P., & Savarese, R. J. (2011). *Papa PhD: Essays on fatherhood by men in the academy.* Piscataway, NJ: Rutgers University Press.

Marsiglio, W., Day, R. D., & Lamb, M. E. (2000). Exploring fatherhood diversity: Implications for conceptualizing father involvement. *Marriage and Family Review, 29*(4): 269–293.

Mason, M. A., & Goulden, M. (2004). Marriage and baby blues: Redefining gender equity in the academy. *Annals of the American Academy of Political and Social Sciences, 596,* 86–103.

Mason, M. A., & Mason Ekman, E. (2007). *Mothers on the fast track: How a new generation can balance family and careers.* Toronto, ON: Oxford University Press.

Shields, C. (2005). Using narrative inquiry to inform and guide our (re) interpretations of educative experience. *McGill Journal of Education, 40*(1), 179–188.

Slaughter, A.-M. (2012, July/August). Why women still can't have it all. *The Atlantic*. Retrieved from http://www.theatlantic.com/magazine/archive/2012/07/why-women-still-cant-have-it-all/309020/

Smartt Gullion, J. (2009). Scholar, negated. In E. Evans & C. Grant (Eds.), *Mama PhD: Women write about motherhood and academic life* (pp. 16–19). Piscataway, NJ: Rutgers University Press.

Springer, K. W., Parker, B. K., & Leviten-Reid, C. (2009). Making space for graduate student parents: Practice and politics. *Journal of Family Issues, 30,* 435–457.

Swanson, D. H., & Johnston, D. D. (2003). Mothering in the ivy tower: Interviews with academic mothers. *Journal of the Association for Research on Mothering, 5*(2), 1–10.

Warner, J. (2009). The conversation. In E. Evans & C. Grant (Eds.), *Mama PhD: Women write about motherhood and academic life* (pp. 3–10). Piscataway, NJ: Rutgers University Press.

Warren, C. A. B. (2001). Qualitative interviewing. In J. F. Gubrium & J. A. Holstein (Eds.), *Handbook of interview research: Context and method* (pp. 83–101). Thousands Oaks, CA: Sage.

Wilson, R. (2003, December 5). How babies alter careers for academics. *Chronicle of Higher Education: The Faculty*. Retrieved from http://chronicle.com/weekly/v50/i15/15a00101.htm

PART ONE
Foundational Narratives

Unanswered and Lingering Questions

Christina DeRoche

In the pursuit of comparing my own experience with that of other women in academics, I was challenged in one of my graduate courses to conduct my own research in this area. Informed by my own struggles as a more mature graduate student (I laugh as I say this because I was twenty-nine when I started, still quite young), I felt I had to justify to my family members and my spouse the decision to enter into a PhD at an age that was ripe for child-bearing. My husband and I had been married for about four years at that time and had already been receiving looks and lectures on how we should think about having children. In fact, I believe by the next year people had just given up hope! And this conflict I contended with throughout graduate school, on top of trying to do well in my courses and get my comprehensives done, was the nagging issue in the back of my brain. My husband was and is a most supportive partner and eased some of my concerns. I felt shafted, though—no one tells you that you might sacrifice your career for parenting. After all, I should be able to have it all, or at least that was what society told me. I am now thirty-three and pregnant with our first child and on the brink of completing my PhD—perfect timing, as those in the academic world would say. But I am still worried and concerned. Am I going to be able to do this parenting thing and be a fabulous and well-known academic? I have my doubts.

So in pursuance of affirming my own struggles I interviewed nine women from various disciplines, stages within their academic careers, and ages and stages of the family cycle. After analyzing the data, I found in fact some of what had already been alluded to in my previous research, but also some variability in responses and experiences. More importantly, there were variables not accounted for by my previous research that needed to be addressed.

Finances, Spousal Support, and Job Security

In negotiating the role of being a mother, participants elaborated on three areas of key importance, those things that would help in making the proactive decision to be a mother: finances, spousal support, and job security. Courtney, despite not having children, states that "money and time are the two big ones [factors] for me, and my partner's view on it; these were the big three factors for me ... the sheer demand of childcare costs a lot of money. The costs of childcare for those years when you are at work but your child cannot go into school yet are enormous." Elizabeth says, "It [finances] definitely came up. My husband and I asked ourselves questions like, can we afford it? But I have always heard that somehow you make do with things whether it's that you get by on less or it's whatever." Finally, Robin mentions, "I guess I waited until there was a point of financial stability, so having a tenure-track position was important to me. Especially since my husband was a student and so long as one of us had a job and we lived within our means it was okay."

For other women in this study, making the decision to be a mother had less to do with their jobs as academics and more to do with other factors: "Well, I think for some women it has little to do with academia but more so their life circumstances. Do they feel economically stable? Do they have a house or place to live? For me it was more about finishing my field work, because I didn't want to be in the field while pregnant" (Christine). And Jen highlights that it also has to do with the husband's economic stability: "You can have a spouse who is very supportive of having children, which is a huge influencing factor ... there are other things that have to do with your husband such as his career, his income, these all have to be weighed out when you are thinking of becoming a mother."

For most of these women, becoming a mother either involved finishing their graduate work or finding an optimal time when they could be graduate students and mothers at the same time: "Finishing my PhD and getting a job, those were important. That was priority one, I must admit. And that is the case for a lot of academic women I am sure. You want to get through that big first big hurdle and then find a job with security" (Leslie). Even graduate students mention the prospect of being finished and attaining a job: "I think it depends on the person and not just the job ... some [women] have pushed back motherhood because of the job and security. Some people have started their PhDs and had kids, so having kids during the degree can sometimes not be a big deal. It really depends on your situation going into graduate school or into the job" (Sarah). Karla mentions,

For me one of the big factors in making the decision, where I got the green light, was when I got the tenure-track position. So for me if I had been in a contract position still then it would have been a no go because of the lack of job security and maternity leave benefits. If you don't have stability and you are just working contract to contract that is a huge barrier.

Job security equated to financial security for these women because of the benefits in a tenure-track position. Jen states this well when she says, "There are a lot of barriers including financial; financially it is very difficult to take a year off, and I chose not to with my first child because we couldn't afford it at the time." Sarah states that these barriers are also created by her spouse's financial situation: "Part of my worry comes out of what my husband is doing also, what his finances and job prospects are like. And if he was making more than I do, like a substantial amount more, then I might choose to have children as soon as possible." So financial concerns were integrated with job security for both the participants and their partners, and were also tied into the stage of the participant's career. This leads into another major area of research concerning the biological and tenure clock.

Biological and Tenure Clock

All these women commented on the pressure to perform and prove they were serious academics in the face of a ticking biological clock. This was often difficult for them for various reasons: "When you get out of your PhD as a woman you are just before the age of 30, usually about 28 or 29 for most women. And then you finish and now you are working on your tenure. So at this stage where you may want to be a mother you have this conflict of attaining tenure" (Elizabeth). Leslie elaborates on this conflict: "There is a time clock, as they call it. That's why I think so many of us are having our babies later on.... You can read lots of literature on how women are panicked by not getting their tenure and they are also trying to have a family. And there is kind of a conflict there, a conflict of the tenure clock and the biological clock." Christine mentions her view on this conflict:

> What typically happens is that women are ready to graduate with their PhDs, they are usually in their late twenties, so you have this collision. I mean a coinciding of women who are getting ready to enter into tenure-track positions presumably at the same time they are really thinking about having children. Because they really have only ten more years to be able to do that. So as an academic you have to wait until you are done graduate school with its requirements and then be able to at least build up your career somewhat.

Some of these women negotiated with themselves on becoming a mother by a certain age and interweaving such with their academic output: "I had it in my head that [it would happen] by age thirty or whenever my data collection was finished, whichever came first in my life" (Karla). Karla also mentions the public reaction to having another child from her peers and the administration:

> How am I going to be looked at if I want another child? There is an inherent barrier there because people start to question your motivation in getting your career going. And you know, another barrier then is that there is only a limited amount of time and engagement that you have: you can't be in your late forties trying to have a baby, it doesn't work biologically.

Karla summarizes the conflict best, stating that

> Focusing on their career from the mid to late thirties and then trying to have a baby is not compatible; biologically they just can't.... We are lucky in academia, in the ivory tower. As long as I find time in the evening or on weekends to do my publications and my research, you are okay. It's hard with the tenure thing and I think about that on a regular basis; I ask myself, am I good enough to get tenure? You are constantly negotiating the conflict between doing enough to get tenure and being there for your child.

Despite all these competing forces within motherhood and academics, participants commented on the advantages of being in academia.

Advantages to Academia: Flexibility of Time and Enrichment

Most of the respondents had more than enough to say on the advantages of academia, with particular emphasis on the flexibility of academia and time required and the enrichment that it provided to their families and vice versa—how families enriched their work. Most of the participants commented on how academia was one of the best jobs for flexibility, which was so necessary in being a parent:

> I remember one professor that I had in my undergraduate saying that she thought this was the best profession to have kids. She was saying you get the most flexibility. I can take a day off, or if my child is sick I can take off if I am not teaching. It is easier for me to take that time and if I have to do work I wait until they go to bed or sometimes you do work on weekends. That is a big deal because at least I have the flexibility to be with my child. (Elizabeth)

All the mothers commented on this fact and highlighted how the job was not a regular type of job for this reason: "In some ways it is good because you don't have the nine-to-five job … in the academic work you have a bit of flexibility" (Elizabeth); even the non-mothers commented on the flexibility of time and how it was an attractive quality of the profession: "Our job is so much more flexible than 90 percent of the jobs out there" (Sarah).

Even though they had this option of adjustable hours, most of the participants felt that the work never left: "There is flexibility in time … and with that flexibility I can take an afternoon off or any other time if I need to, if I become a mother. The work is still there" (Courtney); "I think to some extent we have that flexibility but also our job is, as a grad student or as a professor, to get the work done" (Sarah). Thus flexibility was an attractive and important component in academics and in being a successful parent, but they also acknowledged that the work does not just disappear. It is a process of negotiating flexibility, in time needed with family versus time spent on work. Leslie puts it best when she states that "it's flexible in some ways but not in all. It's flexible in the sense that you have a longer summer break or research term, whatever you want to call it. So you can work it around family life that way, you can fit it in." With this flexibility, participants were adamant in highlighting how academics and motherhood would enrich their lives.

Although academics is all encompassing, and though there is flexibility in how this work is accomplished, most of the participants who were mothers commented on how academics provided enrichment for their families, but also their families enriched their academics. Take for instance Leslie's comment: "I mean it enriches only in the sense of education in general. I sometimes share what I am doing in class and encourage my kids to think about it. It helps us engage us in some discussion or debate." Christine even voiced that "I love being a mother and an academic, and I love when these things can come together. Being in field work and bringing my child to the field has been a great experience." Being both a mother and an academic allowed the participants to relate to their students better and enriched their lecture material: "The only thing I have found is that when I lecture I can't keep out family experiences or tidbits about my kids. I approach things differently as a professor to a degree" (Robin).

Experiencing and Negotiating Work–Family Conflict

Despite all their efforts to mention the advantages of academia, participants detailed more conflict between work and family and on occasion noted how they would negotiate such conflicts. Julie speaks about her inherent conflict in deciding whether to go back to graduate school while being a mother: "The most difficult part was negotiating whether to go back to school or not as my children were in their formative years. The demand I felt from them was consistent, even with childcare and my partner's support." She explains that returning to her PhD was very different: "Having grown children who were in high school was a very qualitatively different experience in going back to complete a graduate degree. It was difficult still but very different from when they were younger." For Julie, negotiating her role as a mother was dependent on having a supportive partner and the stage at which her children were in their developmental years; this was the case for most of the women in my study.

In addition, participants consistently mentioned that they felt guilty for leaving their children and/or their work: "You know every day my kids have phoned me and said, 'Come home early, Mommy,' and every day I say I will try … but at the same time if I come home early I might want that time to myself, to go to the gym, or use it for something else" (Robin). Even Jen mentions her feelings of guilt as both an internal and external force:

> There are negative voices or negative feelings implied by some individuals; like why aren't you spending more time at the university, or are you doing more research, … you know? And all of those things are drawing you away from your kids, physically and mentally, and there is this underlying feeling of guilt for spending time with your kids. I don't want to feel guilty for spending time with my kids.

Other women commented on how the balance was impossible:

> The balance is like impossible if you ask me. I have not been able to do the real academic work since having my two children. I find some time in between things with the kids to do it. I get home from work and I am the one who gets them ready for dinner, gets them to bed, etc. I can't get to my work until eight or so and by that point I am too tired and there is only about an hour and a bit left. (Robin)

Other participants commented on how this conflict was difficult but they negotiated it in some way or became used to it: "You can become incredibly efficient when you have a child because you become extremely focused; but there is always that guilt factor" (Karla).

For Elizabeth, part of this conflict involved accepting the fact that work might have to be completed outside of normal working hours. "When I am out of town, I wish I was at home with my children. I couldn't imagine them being at home and doing work; that just doesn't work very well. But when they are at home I am with them, and then if I have to do more at night, I have to do more at night." Leslie comments that "there are times when they [the kids] just have to understand that sometimes there are times when Mom just has to do work." Contrast this to Robin's feelings on the conflict experienced in her roles: "So I sit down [after becoming angry or frustrated with my kids] and think about what is wrong here? Work is driving the horse here. It's been affecting my family life and my ability to relate to my children. To learn to let that go is really hard and sometimes I can't." Jen summarizes this conflict best:

> There are times in my job when I need to work evenings and/or weekends and that has affected my childcare, time with my family, and interactions with them.... I also found that in academia it often means that I have a computer at home with me and that I am often working when I am not working; it is the pressure to succeed in academia that drives that. You know that the requisite hours mean nothing to an academic—it is whether you get your job done. So that means that sometimes I find that it lowers the quality of time spent with my family.... So I find that being in this kind of profession lowers the quality of time I have with my kids and sadly the quantity of time I have my kids.

Institutional and Structural Barriers

Many of the women, during the interview, mentioned various structural and institutional factors that were barriers to making the active choice to become a mother. One highly mentioned factor was maternity and parental leaves, as well as top-ups: "My current institution provides a four-month top-up to maternity leave, but that's it. So more would have been a little more helpful. And I was fortunate that my partner was working, but if he wasn't, I might have taken only those four months" (Elizabeth). "Maternity leave is good but nowhere near what it should be and is in other places ... some women have managed to extend the paid, topped-off leave, but in my circumstances I couldn't because of the finances" (Leslie). Finally, Robin reiterates the sentiments of graduate students:

> I had the great fortune of having a top-up, but as a student or as a grant student? You get to write to the granting institution and say you are on maternity leave and all they do is defer your payments. You don't get payments for the duration of your maternity leave. It's a ridiculous system; there is no support or even recognition that doctoral students are adults with lives.

Other women discussed not only the parental leaves but also the ambience of the department and institution as deciding factors:

> I think there is a definite fear ... that if you are willing or considering having children that you will not get hired. That they will think that you don't have

the commitment to academia. Completing my master's at one institution that was very well known by women that if they were thinking of being mothers, they wouldn't be considered serious academics … contrast that to where I did my PhD; faculty there had young kids and that made a huge difference because I felt like then I was able to have children. (Christine)

Jen comments on how the feelings about the administration have affected not only her choice but that of others around her: "I get the feeling that administration feels that maternity leaves are inconvenient and that they are not supportive. They have been made to be more supportive I think today than in past but only because parental leave is viewed as being an important aspect of a person's life." This impression of the administration carried through to the idea that academics are to publish or perish, something which also coincided with the ticking of the biological and tenure clock mentioned earlier.

Sarah mentions, "I think the institution puts a lot of pressure to publish or perish. At the same time I do think they are supportive of those people who want to be parents, but that depends on the department and the institution." Karla describes her experience with this pressure to produce: "I was evaluated by my superior while I was on maternity leave; you know how we have to submit reports every year based on teaching, researching, and service, well she went into my file and found my old CV and responded to that. I found it ironic since I was on leave and hadn't submitted anything to her because of that." For most of these women in academia, having children seem to be a risky move, and Robin describes how it can also be of benefit: "I have a friend who finished her PhD and would desperately like a tenure-track position but there aren't any. I think that having a baby during that time would be a good excuse for the time away on a CV—it explains the gap from finishing her PhD to getting a tenure-track position."

For the graduate students in this study, gaining a job was of the utmost importance, but so too were the supports in that institution; Sarah mentions that "one of the tricks a friend of mine taught me when I do get a tenure-track position is to talk to your union and to really figure out how the maternity leave and benefits work and how top-up works. And with that she structured her maternity leaves accordingly." Jen mentions that this support can also come on a more informal basis: "On a more positive note, I have found that faculty are extremely supportive of motherhood, and usually these people are mothers themselves or are partners of somebody who is a mother and is in an academic type of profession." Courtney states that "being in an environment where people don't have many kids and certainly don't have them early has certainly affected my decision and view of what is normal." She goes to describe an experience of a friend of hers who hasn't had any children: "I have some friends who are in different professions who are practically obligated to have children, because parents or others won't respect them if they don't ... my one friend is in a profession where being childless is seen as taboo."

Thus, for these women, having children or not having children were definitely affected by the administration and institutional atmosphere; it governed much of their decision making from financial resources available from the institution to their marked absence from the field.

In the End ...

At the conclusion of my research, which was fuelled by my own interest and experience, my sentiments have remained unchanged. I still often feel angry, isolated, confused, and cognitively aware of my disillusionment (that I might be able to change things). The one thing that has changed is my feelings of family: whether academia supports my choice or not, I will be a mother sometime in the near future. I just wish there were a more hopeful expectation of this academic world and my work that came with that decision. In the end, the decision has still left a bitter taste in my mouth, as well as lingering questions that have yet to be answered.

Work–Family Balance?
A Challenging Yet Rewarding Journey through Gendered Academia

Ellie D. Berger

I cannot count the number of times that I have been faced with issues around work–family balance in my career as an academic. I am currently an associate professor in the Department of Sociology at Nipissing University and I am married with two incredible children, but arriving at this point in my life was not particularly easy psychologically and physically. Being a gerontologist, I am very familiar with gendered ageism in the workplace—both near the beginning (despite the legality of the issue, I was asked in several job interviews whether I had kids or had plans to have them) and at the end of one's career (see for example McMullin & Berger, 2006). While I recognize that men also struggle with these decisions, as can be seen in this book, their gendered paths are quite different from those of most female academics.

I also recognize the value of using the life course perspective and its emphasis on timing, age-related transitions and trajectories, and life course events (Bengtson, Burgess, & Parrott, 1997) to understand the career trajectory of a female academic. Each life stage needs to be considered in relation to others leading up to it. Thus, I realize how decisions I made early in my career will affect me in later life, financially and otherwise (see for example Berger & Denton, 2004). The gendered nature of the life course and the importance of timing are felt quite strongly by many women due to the ticking of their biological clocks; however, this pressure is intensified in the academic world since completing graduate school and landing an academic job happen at precisely the time when many choose to have children.

Compounding this in my story and others interwoven in this book are issues around fertility, miscarriages, pregnancy complications, and resulting health issues. Further, the largest challenge that I continue to face involves

commuting over three and a half hours each way to work and regularly spending part of the week away from my family. I have been fortunate that my
schedule has allowed me to be away from my children only one or two nights
a week in recent years, but I continuously have to overcome various administrative hurdles to achieve this—and there are no guarantees that this will be
the case in the future.

Identity negotiation continues to be a constant struggle, reflecting my
desire to be both a productive academic and a good mother. I am struck by
how much I am affected by Cooley's (1902) notion of the looking-glass self
and the realization that our identity is largely shaped by our interactions with
others and their perceptions or perceived perceptions of us. I have spent
way too much mental energy worrying what other people think of my decisions—to be an academic, to take on a tenure-track position in a different
city (and commute), to get pregnant before being tenured, and to continue in
this position once I had children (most thought I would have quit by now).
While I recognize that I put too much stock into others' opinions, many of
these thoughts have been put into my head by "innocent" comments from
colleagues, family, or friends during my journey as an academic. For example,
I attended a workshop on going into academia while in graduate school and
the group was advised by one of the female academics leading the discussion,
"Wait until after you have tenure to have children or it will be career suicide."
Similarly, after completing my PhD, one of my mentors said to me, "Don't have
kids. It will ruin your career."

If you can find some way to develop a thicker skin and let negative comments slide off you or, more importantly, find a way to avoid internalizing
them, you will have won half the battle. I realize that I am overly sensitive to
these comments and admit that they may have caused me to delay having children or may have made my journey a more difficult one. When I was deciding
when the right time was to have children, I was worried that I should first
complete my PhD, I should first work at my new job for x number of years, I
should first devote time to the new certificate program I had created, I should
first wait until I have tenure.... I know better than to be guided by "shoulds"
and I have now come to the realization that there is never a right time. So
what advice would I give to young female academics? I would tell them that
they need to do what is right for them and not listen to comments from others
about waiting until a certain point in their academic journey to have children.
Even after getting pregnant (after years of trying and a miscarriage), I worried about telling members of my department this news and I still felt guilty
about taking a leave. I quickly learned that everyone is replaceable. Not to say
that I was not valued or appreciated in the department, but I now know that

if someone came in to teach one of my courses or if the department held off offering one of these courses for a year, the world did go on. Coming to this realization actually lessened my guilt and thus I state this here only for others to ease their conscience as well.

When I went on my second maternity leave, I was eligible for sabbatical but was able to delay it for a year so that I could take it after my maternity leave. I realize that I was very fortunate to be in this position, yet I still managed to feel guilty about taking my sabbatical after being on leave. After feeling a great deal of angst throughout those two years and feeling somewhat disconnected to my department since I did not go into the office regularly, being in another city, the first comment I remember from a (male) colleague when I returned to work was "How was your two-year vacation?" This is appalling on so many levels—as women, we continue to struggle to be equal if we choose to stay at home with our children, even for one year, and those who have stayed home know that being with a newborn is vastly different from being on vacation. As academics, we struggle to justify to others that a sabbatical does not mean a break from work. Yet here I was baffled by this comment. And this was not the only one. Another (female) colleague when introducing me to someone said, "I can't keep track—are you on sabbatical or mat leave again?" While these passive-aggressive comments may or may not have been intentionally hurtful, they always managed to inflict negative emotions on me.

I also should point out that while academic life does have its advantages for parenting, its very nature is counterintuitive to taking maternity leave. While I was able to take one year off teaching, my research projects with co-investi-gators were not put on hold, and so I was working on a literature review when my son was five weeks old (and resenting this work immensely). This made me even more frustrated when I would get the feedback that many new mothers encounter: "Are you enjoying your time off?" or "It must be nice to be able to take a year off!" I admit that I am fortunate to live in Canada, where I can take a year of maternity leave, and to work at an institution that tops up my benefits for part of this time. But, not only was I busy taking care of my newborn child, I was also busy working on research projects most of the time, making these comments even more inaccurate and disconcerting. In fact, I think I spent most of my maternity leaves feeling conflicted between spending time with my new baby and working on research projects.

One of the advantages that I believed academia held was flexibility, which I thought would lend itself well to having children. In fact, one early mentor shared with me her experiences in the academic world and described how flexible it was for women with children. I was inspired by this comment early on in my career. Was I wrong? I quickly discovered that while this was partly true, there was much more to the story, and there were many, many sacrifices and challenges to be overcome along the way. I am very fortunate that I can mark papers at home, do research in my home office, stay home with a sick child if I need to (on a non-teaching day), and finish my work once my kids are in bed. Most workplaces do not allow for this flexibility. I have friends who struggle to leave the office at five or six and rush home in traffic to see their kids for only an hour or two before bedtime. So no, academia is not a nine-to-five job, but most of the time I think that is actually a good thing.

With respect to commuting, I have heard countless comments along the lines of "How can you leave your kids at home every week to come here to teach?" Similar questions were not being asked of my male commuter colleagues also "leaving" their children at home. Similarly, when discussing how happy I was that thanks to technological advances in recent years, I could now use Skype or FaceTime to talk to and see my children at home on the days I was out of town, one colleague said, "You are like an abstract mother. It is like the kids can see you but you are not really there." This one comment struck a chord in particular—here I am thinking how great it is that these advances in technology allow me to see my children when I am not at home, yet that comment quickly turns my attention back to the continuous guilt I feel being away from them on a regular basis. It did not help that my five-year-old daughter often cried to me, "Don't sleep at your work again, Mommy." Interestingly, when discussing this guilt while being away at a conference, one female colleague mentioned that "bribes" (gifts) work well to ease this guilt and the child's despair, and many agreed that they did this on countless occasions. In fact, not too long after I gave gifts to my children after that conference, my daughter asked me, "When are you sleeping at your work again, Mommy?"

Of course all of this would not be possible without the continued support of my husband. He is a great father, and not having him as my partner during this whole process would likely have made this journey impossible. We are also fortunate to have support and caregiving help from our parents—part of the reason why I am not able/willing to move when my children are young. When contemplating whether all these struggles (getting tenure and promotion, commuting, guilt over leaving them part of the week, etc.) are worth it, I will not forget one comment made in passing to me by someone at my daughter's school: "Think about how proud your daughter (and son) will be of you and the role model that you are for them." To be honest, I do not think that I ever actually looked at it that way. I was so worried about the guilt I felt on a daily basis that I had overlooked this key element. I could now see that I was continuing to choose this career path not only for me, but also to show my daughter and son that women can and do successfully negotiate a career and a family. They might not appreciate this now, but I hope that many years down the road this will help them with their own career ambitions and their understanding and appreciation of gender roles in general.

Even now as I look back on my journey and the ups and downs of negotiating pregnancy, health issues, and career progression, it is still very hard for me to actually take a step back and realize that I am now in a relatively good place. By putting my struggles with fertility, miscarriages, and pregnancies behind me (and by writing this narrative), I feel like I can actually gain closure on that part of my life. This helps me to move on psychologically from these challenges and sit back and reflect on my current position. So yes, I am now an associate professor and have successfully started a family, but this puts me in a situation where I must continue to negotiate an academic career in a different city with two young children at home. I have learned that there is never a perfect or even a right time to have children. Achieving a comfortable balance between work and family continues to challenge me, and I only hope that choosing to have fewer publications, grants, service, and so forth, than others in my cohort in exchange for having more time with my family will ultimately be the right choice for me. So one goal that I hope this book accomplishes is to reach out to other women who feel alone in this process and let them know that it is possible to have a family and have a successful career. Yes, there may be challenges and gaps in your career path along the way, but looking back now, I would not change much about my experience, since I would not be where I am today without these challenges.

References

Bengtson, V. L., Burgess, E. O., & Parrott, T. M. (1997). Theory, explanation and a third generation of theoretical development in social gerontology. *Journal of Gerontology: Social Sciences, 52B*(2), S72–S88.

Berger, E. D., & Denton, M. A. (2004). The interplay between women's life course work patterns and financial planning for later life. *Canadian Journal on Aging, 23*(suppl. 1), S99–S113.

Cooley, C. H. (1902). *Human nature and the social order.* New York, NY: Scribner's.

McMullin, J. A., & Berger, E. D. (2006). Gendered ageism / age(ed) sexism: The case of unemployed older workers. In T. M. Calasanti & K. F. Slevin (Eds.), *Age matters: Realigning feminist thinking* (pp. 201–223). New York, NY: Routledge.

PART TWO
Making the Big Decision

Conversations with Women
Mothers and Academics

Erin J. Careless

I am a woman with three university degrees and in the process of obtaining my fourth—a doctorate. I have completed a master of education degree and teach at the graduate level while working as a research assistant. I am a daughter, sister, wife, stepmother, and friend. I hope to spend my career teaching and learning with others, promoting a just society both globally and locally, and developing social science research that is relevant to my community, but I also want to have children of my own. I believe that motherhood and academe are not and should not be mutually exclusive life choices; however, through conversations with five women who are both mothers and academics, the decision appears more complex and multilayered than I had initially imagined.

At the start of my master's degree I was twenty-nine years of age, and at the end I was defending my thesis the day before my thirty-second birthday. During that two-and-a-half-year whirlwind, several of my close friends gave birth to beautiful baby girls and boys. None of my "mommy" friends worked in academe, but several held positions as educators in the public school system. I watched as without hesitation or concern for their employment status, they packed up their materials for the standard one-year maternity leave. They were then able to dive headfirst into motherhood—the late nights, schedules, crying, eating, dirty diapers—certain that their positions would be there for them when they returned in twelve months' time, without penalty.

As I became increasingly aware of the demands involved in obtaining academic tenure, I furthered my reading of critical feminist literature (Acker, 1997; Alcoff & Potter, 1993; Ng, 1993; Stalker & Prentice, 1998; Taber, 2005). In placing gender and the experiences of women at the forefront of my inquiry, with the goal of influencing academic policy for academic mothers, I found this literature instrumental in framing my query: What are the experiences

n who pursue academic careers while raising young children? As a
my graduate courses were scheduled in the evenings to accommo-
e working full-time, and many professors (men and women) were
available via office hours during the day. The work hours of a university professor are irregular, and I would often receive instructor feedback via email
during the wee hours of the night. Do the demands of the institution lead to
women working through the night? With such irregular hours, how is childcare arranged if needed? Does the intensity of the tenure track support women
who take maternity leave? I began developing the research framework for my
thesis, and the journey began.

The final research contribution, in the form of my master's thesis, *Dueling
Clocks: How Women Academics Balance Childcare with the Road to Tenure*,
speaks to the challenges of role-balancing for a few women employed in east-
ern Canadian academic institutions. Writing from a critical lens and feminist
perspective, my goal was to bring light to issues of inequity in academe and
to challenge the pervasive neo-liberal influences in society that have invaded
the public and private spheres. Competition, productivity, and individuality
have replaced cooperation, contributions in multiple areas (teaching, research,
and student support), and unity in the workplace (Saunders, 2010). In a way,
the research was self-serving—I wanted to improve a situation and challenge
barriers that I may also face one day. However, I also see the research as a
way to challenge the neo-liberal focus on individuality and, I hope, contribute to supports for academic women and men across Canada. What follows
are explorations of the literature and lessons from fellow women in academe
through their lives as mothers and educators.

You Can Climb the Ladder Only So High

Despite the decades that have passed since the first and second waves of feminism, there is a great deal of research across academic disciplines identifying a
gender imbalance among high-ranking faculty members (Laster, 2010; Perna,
2005; Stalker & Prentice, 1998; Wolfinger, Mason, & Goulden, 2009), with
men consistently outnumbering their female colleagues. While researchers
propose several reasons for this continued inequity, my research and that of
others (Acker & Armenti, 2004; Ward & Wolf-Wendel, 2004) focus more on
the lack of supports for academic mothers in combination with a pervasive
neo-liberal influence over academic and tenure policies. More specifically, current literature and the information obtained through interviews I conducted
with five academic mothers revealed five themes that became key points in
my research: the gendered division of childcare and housework, unequal
treatment of women in academe, lack of sources of support for women, the

influence of neo-liberalism in academic institutions, and varying tenure and family-friendly policies.

As a caveat to the following discussion, it should be noted that while in-depth, the interviews are representative of a small, homogeneous sample of academic mothers. The five women are all white, heterosexual, and middle class; however, they were the only participants to respond to my widespread request. I believe this may be indicative of two ideas: first, that the academic sector is not representative of a truly diverse population (Dedoussis, 2007; Garrison-Wade, Diggs, Estrada, & Galindo, 2012; Gay, 2004), and second, that the intersecting factors of gender, race, and ethnicity may lead to further inequity and a hesitation to speak with others about personal experiences. This is purely conjecture on my part, but diversity among women in academe is a necessary discussion (Alcoff & Potter, 1993; Guo, 2010; Ng, 1993), as it is important to challenge the traditional representation of white, middle-class individuals as the majority in academic institutions. Likewise, critical feminism requires us to challenge the traditional gender representation and roles in the home.

"It's not on their brain, but it's on yours ...": Gendered Division of Childcare and Housework

A snippet from one of my semi-structured interviews, the above quote describes how one academic mother felt about the division of childcare between her and her husband. She felt that she considered her child's needs before her husband did, so it was easier to "just do it" herself (Careless, 2011). While women's presence in the workforce continues to grow, they often remain primarily responsible for childcare and household duties (Correll, Benard, & Paik, 2007; Jacobs & Winslow, 2004). Participants in Acker's (1997) research had busy academic careers intertwined with time spent caring for others: "The careers sound less like linear progressions than like complicated puzzles representing marriages, divorces, children, teaching work, higher degrees, sessional university teaching and perhaps a few other odd-shaped segments" (p. 72). My research looks primarily at childcare as a caring responsibility, but the past decade or so has seen a dramatic increase in the number of women who also care for elderly family members (Singleton, 2000).

The women I spoke with (who were in relationships) all identified a gendered imbalance in the childcare and household duties in their own homes, albeit to varying degrees. Single mothers working in academe particularly talked about the strain of being sole provider and carer for their families: "A lot of my fellow colleagues work around ninety hours per week; I can't do that. I do work a lot of hours, but a lot of my hours are spent with my kid as well.

There is some anxiety for me around that" (Careless, 2011, p. 63). The demanding hours required in some academic institutions can make it challenging for women to achieve a sense of balance between work and family: "I had to drive [my child] to and from school every day … that really cut into my work time, and I felt like I had to hide that from people at work. I do feel sometimes that I'm seen more as 'the mother' at work rather than as 'the academic.' I don't think that helps me long-term in my career" (Careless, 2011, p. 59). Academic institutions can no longer reflect economic marketplace values to produce and compete with others if women are to achieve balance in their lives. These competitive values currently present in many academic institutions can lead working women to refrain from speaking out against unfair treatment or a lack of support that they may experience.

"I worked up until the week I was due and was back in six months …": Unequal Treatment of Women in Academe

Academic life can both encourage and inhibit mothers from obtaining a tenured position (Gouthro, 2002; Heller, Puff, & Mills, 1985; Suitor, Mecom, & Feld, 2001; Toren & Moore, 1998; van Anders, 2004). Irregular teaching schedules, publication demands, and required committee and student support make for a heavy workload (Comer & Stites-Doe, 2006). Although there can be some reprise in terms of flexible schedules, for many academic mothers this simply results in "making up time" at home (Careless, 2011). One woman said during our interview that "bedtime is at eight o'clock.… On average throughout the year I work from eight to ten or ten-thirty on four or five nights a week" (Careless, 2011, p. 62). This demanding schedule does not seem to have changed much over the past few decades: "Making an impact on the field involves, for all but the most talented, considerable time and effort" (Acker, 1997, p. 82). Time and timing are critical for academic mothers.

In some cases, outright discrimination was experienced by the women I spoke with: "The Equity Officer said he was going to the washroom and would meet us downstairs [to go to lunch]. He left the room, and this old professor … said, Oh good, now we can ask you the real questions.… The others listened while he interrogated me [about having a husband and children]" (Careless, 2011, p. 60). The assumption appeared to be that her family responsibilities would in some way have an impact upon her productivity level, and one wonders how many male candidates were asked the same questions. These experiences led me to believe that as a woman pursuing a career in academe, I would have a steep climb ahead of me. Neo-liberal, capitalist influences have invaded this sector and shifted the way many academics view their work (Saunders, 2010).

"We have this idealized view of motherhood ... it just doesn't happen ...": Sources of Support

Throughout my interviews with academic mothers, I asked about two sources of support: spousal and institutional. Although their responses and experiences varied, the underlying theme was that the women felt a lack of support, particularly at the institutional level. Whether women chose to start their families during postdoctoral appointments, tenure-track positions, or as a secure, tenured professor, they all spoke of the issue of timing. One participant talked about the struggle of time: "And it's hard to know—when is the perfect time? When you're writing a thesis? Or after that when you're ... going to interviews pregnant? That doesn't work either. And then when you start a job ... you're going for tenure, so how is that going to look?" (Careless, 2011, p. 65). I could not conceive of the time, work, and dedication that these women (and many others) had put into their academic careers, only to be left insecure and intimidated at the idea of combining work with family.

I do not mean to suggest that all women feel this way, and that was not the basis of any claims made in my research. It is, however, vital that we bring these conversations out into the open so that we can critically reflect on the supports and barriers experienced by women in all employment sectors. Only then can we strive for equity and equality in society. This need for critical reflection was clear to me from my conversations with academic women, and also through an analysis of the available literature: "The expectation that assistant professors will teach evening classes, attend meetings held after 5pm, and attend other evening or weekend activities was perceived as wise to comply with in light of tenure; on the other hand, these kinds of commitments were described as difficult for many mothers given their family responsibilities" (Young & Wright, 2001, p. 563). For some, tenure signifies a choice between *publishing* or *perishing*, an all-or-nothing attitude shaped by the values of neo-liberalism.

"It's all about time, and you have to produce ...": Neo-liberalism in Academe

Neo-liberal ideals remove the distance between the market and the state, imparting economic rationality onto the social sphere. Within this context, greater emphasis is placed on individual responsibility for making "wise choices" in society and the ability to compete effectively in the workplace (Careless, 2011). Many critical and feminist theorists write about the dangers of neo-liberal influence in education, instead focusing on emancipatory learning and social justice—the original goals of lifelong learning (Fenwick, 2004; Gouthro, 2009; Plumb, Leverman, & McGray, 2007). The idea of education as a commodity, of students as consumers and educators as producers of knowledge, is not new, but it is a frightening concept that has continued to gain speed over the past few decades. Lifelong learning and education have become increasingly professionalized, moving away from their roots in community (Murphy, 2000).

The five women who spoke with me, as well as some women represented in the literature, are confronted with patriarchal ideals and values throughout their careers. The traditional employment trajectory for academics is a linear progression from graduate studies through tenure track to an appointment as full professor, a trajectory that discounts the importance and needs of one's family and instead focuses on profit and production. One participant succinctly said, "We're letting a scientific business model run the world and that's the problem. It's completely inhumane and everything is reduced down to dollars, dollars, dollars" (Careless, 2011, p. 70). These values reflect our lives in a neo-liberal society: "The values of the marketplace in educational contexts are also associated with masculine behaviour, in that a linear focus on schooling/career and more assertive behaviour are viewed as positive attributes" (Gouthro, 2005, p. 13).

An environment of competition has replaced a sense of camaraderie in academe, seen in the push for grant money, recognition, tenure, and salary increase. More and more academics are publishing on their own (rather than with colleagues) and even undermining the work of others: "People walk up to me and say, 'I could have done that' … And this is women doing this to other women" (Careless, 2011, p. 69). This research participant felt that others (men and women) were consistently challenging her research position and the work that she produced.

"There are no set rules so that you can be assured there is a process in place and you will not be negatively impacted ...": Ambiguous Policies

Across academic institutions, and departments in some cases, policies around tenure and maternity leave can vary. It would be comforting to know that, as in many other employment sectors, women were entitled to a maternity leave period of one year. However, it seems that this is not always the case. According to Perna (2005), "Individual campuses and departments should examine the extent to which existing policies, practices, and cultural norms support the ability of women and men faculty to assume and manage family ties" (p. 302); policies should be re-examined regularly, and there should be room for case-by-case modifications.

From a societal perspective, effective family-friendly policies can have a positive influence not only on working parents, but on society as a whole: "Good parenting, for example, increases the likelihood that a child will grow up to be a caring, well-behaved, and productive adult. This lowers crime rates, increases the level of care for the next generation, and contributes to economic productivity" (Budig & England, 2001, p. 205). To me, it seems only logical that employers would want to support the growth and success of individuals who will maintain the functioning of society. In an academic sense, many children born to academic parents will one day be paying tuition as a student.

With resounding agreement, the single most important policy for the women interviewed for my research study was on-site, reliable childcare: "Daycare should be subsidised and arranged much better in this province for everyone, but at the university level I think that that is something they could do" (Careless, 2011, p. 71). Also of great importance, particularly from the perspective of someone who has yet to have children, are clear policies that outline the process of taking leave and resuming one's career. One participant voiced this concern by saying, "There is nothing in the collective agreement that says, when you do this, time [on tenure track] will stop. When you come back, the [tenure] clock will start ticking again" (Careless, 2011, p. 72). It seems to me that some women find themselves in a somewhat perilous state while employed in tenure-track positions.

Reflections

My research on the experiences of women who attempt to balance child-care with tenure and tenure-track positions has been rich, rewarding, and eye-opening. As a woman at the start of an academic career path, I want to challenge the barriers along this path for myself and for others. I have presented variations of these research data at several academic conferences, and each time I am amazed at how many women approach me afterwards to share their story and comment on the participants' experiences. Perhaps most powerful is the realization that I spent two years researching and writing this study, in an attempt to bring awareness to the struggle of work–family balance for some academic mothers. However, despite this goal and the passion I feel regarding this research, I still find myself questioning the "best" time to have children that will not "interfere" with my career plans. How deeply ingrained it is to keep our struggles silent. This is not an isolated incident or the misstep of one institution. This is a systemic problem with wide-reaching implications for women, men, students, and children.

If women continue to take on primary responsibility for childcare, there must be policies and supports in place that will enable them to successfully combine this role with a career, if they should choose to do so (Careless, 2011). After all, feminism is not about duplicating male support structures for women; it is about supporting women in ways that are necessary for them to be able to rise to their full potential, because "unless you support women in their role as mother, you will never get equality of opportunity" (Hornosty, 1998, p. 180). As a woman, daughter, sister, wife, stepmother, friend, and academic, this will be my cause to champion.

References

Acker, S. (1997). Becoming a teacher educator: Voices of women academics in Canadian faculties of education. *Teaching and Teacher Education, 13*(1), 65–74.

Acker, S., & Armenti, C. (2004). Sleepless in academia. *Gender and Education, 16*(1), 3–24.

Alcoff, L., & Potter, E. (Eds.). (1993). *Feminist epistemologies: Thinking gender.* New York, NY: Routledge.

Budig, M., & England, P. (2001). The wage penalty for motherhood. *American Sociological Review, 66,* 204–225.

Careless, E. (2011). *Dueling clocks: How women academics balance childcare with the road to tenure* (Master's thesis). Mount Saint Vincent University, Halifax, NS.

Comer, D., & Stites-Doe, S. (2006). Antecedents and consequences of faculty women's academic–parental role balancing. *Journal of Family and Economic Issues, 27*(3), 495–512. doi:10.1007/s10834-006-9021-z

Correll, S., Benard, S., & Paik, I. (2007). Getting a job: Is there a motherhood penalty? *American Journal of Sociology, 112*(5), 1297–1339.

Dedoussis, E. (2007). Issues of diversity in academia: Through the eyes of "Third-Country" faculty. *International Journal of Higher Education and Educational Planning, 54*(1), 135–156.

Fenwick, T. (2004). What happens to the girls? Gender, work and learning in Canada's "new economy." *Gender and Education, 16*(2), 169–185.

Garrison-Wade, D., Diggs, G., Estrada, D., & Galindo, R. (2012). Lift every voice and sing: Faculty of colour face the challenges of the tenure track. *Urban Review: Issues and Ideas in Public Education, 44*(1), 90–112.

Gay, G. (2004). Navigating marginality en route to the professoriate: Graduate students of colour learning and living in academia. *International Journal of Qualitative Studies in Education, 17*(2), 265–288.

Gouthro, P. (2002). Education for sale: At what cost? Lifelong learning and the marketplace. *International Journal of Lifelong Education, 21*(4), 334–346.

Gouthro, P. (2005). A critical feminist analysis of the homeplace as learning site: Expanding the discourse of lifelong learning to consider adult women learners. *International Journal of Lifelong Education, 24*(1), 5–19.

Gouthro, P. (2009). Neoliberalism, lifelong learning, and the homeplace: Problematizing the boundaries of "public" and "private" to explore women's learning experiences. *Studies in Continuing Education, 31*(2), 157–172.

Guo, S. (2010). Migration and communities: Challenges and opportunities for lifelong learning. *International Journal of Lifelong Education, 29*(4), 437–447.

Heller, J., Puff, C., & Mills, C. (1985). Assessment of the chilly college climate for women. *Journal of Higher Education, 56*(4), 446–461.

Hornosty, J. (1998). Balancing child care and work: The need for a "woman-friendly" university. In J. Stalker & S. Prentice (Eds.), *The illusion of inclusion: Women in post-secondary education* (pp. 180–193). Halifax, NS: Fernwood.

Jacobs, J., & Winslow, S. (2004). The academic life course, time pressures and gender inequality. *Community, Work and Family, 7*(2), 143–161.

Laster, J. (2010). Unlike men, women scientists have a second shift: Housework. *Chronicle of Higher Education, 56*(20), 10–10.

Murphy, M. (2000). Adult education, lifelong learning and the end of political economy. *Studies in the Education of Adults, 32*(2), 166–180.

Ng, R. (1993). "A woman out of control": Deconstructing sexism and racism in the university. *Canadian Journal of Education, 18*(3), 189–205.

Perna, L. (2005). Sex differences in faculty tenure and promotion: The contribution of family ties. *Research in Higher Education, 46*(3), 277–307.

Plumb, D., Leverman, A., & McGray, R. (2007). The learning city in a "planet of slums." *Studies in Continuing Education, 29*(1), 37–50.

Saunders, D. (2010). Neoliberal ideology and public higher education in the United States. *Journal for Critical Education Policy Studies, 8*(1), 41–76.

Singleton, J. (2000). Women caring for elderly family members: Shaping non-traditional work and family initiatives. *Journal of Comparative Family Studies, 31*(3), 367–375.

Stalker, J., & Prentice, S. (Eds.). (1998). *The illusion of inclusion: Women in postsecondary education.* Halifax, NS: Fernwood.

Suitor, J., Mecom, D., & Feld, I. (2001, Fall). Gender, household labor, and scholarly productivity among university professors. *Gender Issues,* 50–67.

Taber, N. (2005). Learning how to be a woman in the Canadian forces/unlearning it through feminism: An autoethnography of my learning journey. *Studies in Continuing Education, 27*(3), 289–301.

Toren, N., & Moore D. (1998). The academic "hurdle race": A case study. *Higher Education, 35,* 267–283.

van Anders, S. (2004). Why the academic pipeline leaks: Fewer men than women perceive barriers to becoming professors. *Sex Roles, 51*(9/10), 511–521.

Ward, K., & Wolf-Wendel, L. (2004). Academic motherhood: Managing complex roles in research universities. *Review of Higher Education, 27*(2), 233–257.

Wolfinger, N., Mason, M., & Goulden, M. (2009). Stay in the game: Gender, family formation and alternative trajectories in the academic life course. *Social Forces, 87*(3), 1591–1621.

Young, D., & Wright, E. (2001). Mothers making tenure. *Journal of Social Work Education, 37*(3), 555–568.

Academia, My Mother, and Me
Reflections on Intergenerational Emotional Geographies of Academic Parenting

Sara L. Jackson

My first experiences in graduate school were in utero. In 1980, my mother was pregnant for the third time (this time unexpectedly), when she was about a year into her PhD program. Since then, I have observed her struggles and successes in and out of academia. I have also listened to her laments about her PhD process and my early childhood. In this narrative, I want to explore the emotional geographies that are a part of academic parenting, including feelings of distraction, displacement, guilt, and shame, as well as pride and unqualified love for her children. To get to the heart of these issues that have affected us both throughout my life, I interviewed my mother about her choices and non-choices as a parent, a wife, a divorcee, and an off/on academic. Although this narrative centres on my mother's experiences, I must admit that what I write is almost as much about me as it is about her. I was a PhD candidate when I interviewed her and wrote this piece, and I am still a young woman progressing deeper into a currently childless but happily partnered thirties. The experiences of my mother, and her (un)wanted advice, profoundly shape how I approach my life cycle and career anxieties. Intuitively, I know that my feelings toward a career and a possible future family are deeply tied to her experiences, suggestions, and silences in the emotional spaces she occupied and where I am as an academic and (potential) mother.

To frame our experiences, I want to draw on geographic literatures that explore emotions, motherhood, and academics. My mother describes conflicting emotions of shame, guilt, and pride, which geographers Longhurst, Hodgetts, and Stolte (2012) argue are integral to (single) mothers' experiences of higher education. These feelings relate to the literature on emotional geographies (see Davidson & Milligan, 2004; Davidson, Smith, Bondi, & Probyn, 2008), which in the feminist tradition (Davidson & Bondi, 2004) elucidate feelings about the spaces of home, work, parks, and hospitals, among many others that intersect with motherhood. The challenges my mother faced illustrate not only how education, work, family, and research become both segmented and intertwined, but also how academia as a kind of work is a site of distress, compromise, and creativity by making do with what one has where one is (Gibson-Graham, 2006; Pratt 2004). Furthermore, this narrative illustrates how academic parenting goes beyond family-planning stages and stretches into the adult lives of children.

My mother's reflections are also part of a larger story of women and men who continually renegotiate family commitments, work, and self-fulfillment to reveal some of the complex and contradictory emotional geographies of parenting as a form of caregiving. Academic parenting is part of trends that "suggest women's roles as unpaid informal family caregivers are becoming increasingly complicated" (Williams & Crooks, 2008, p. 224), particularly within the context of government retrenchment, unpaid care work, and flexible employment. However, academic parenting is also *particular* as hiring and tenure committees (un)consciously ask how many papers a baby is worth (see Klocker & Drozdzewski, 2012) when comparing candidates for placement and advancement and because "academia seems to operate according to its own principles of labour regulation" (Bauder, 2005, p. 232). It is within these universal and particular spaces of parenting where my mother found herself, where I grew up, and where I now encounter my own emotional geographies (read: anxieties) of academia and thoughts of child-rearing.

My mother's career spans over forty years. She earned a BA in psychology (1969), an MA in counselling (1978), and a PhD in communication (1984). I was born in 1980 and I have two older brothers, born in 1974 and 1978. As a small child, my middle brother was in and out of the hospital with severe asthma. My parents were married in 1969 and divorced by 2000. During their marriage, my mother taught at community colleges and consulted with several major corporations and the US Air Force (until she resigned in protest over the first Gulf War). After the divorce, my mother became a professor at a university in South Carolina. At the time, my middle brother was living alone as the sole caretaker of the house where we grew up. Five years later, my mother returned to Colorado and eventually became a department chair at a local community college. In 2010, she ran for and was elected to a position in local government. She also frequently babysits for my middle brother's two children.

During our interview, perhaps because I was in graduate school, we talked a lot about her experiences in the PhD program. I began by asking why she pursued her PhD. As she expressed throughout the interview (and in other conversations with me), her relationship to academia was always ambivalent and connected to a sense of who she wanted to be and a desire to learn rather than a specific career goal.

> I think it was after I finished my master's and I felt really unprepared. I was taking psychodrama training and I really felt that I didn't know enough. A lot of the people in the training had PhDs. I didn't really know what one was for, but I knew that they had them and that they knew more, and so I thought that maybe that was a way for me to gain some confidence and to also learn more so that I could do more.

When I asked what my father and her parents thought, she said he "didn't care" and they "thought it was nice." When I asked what my oldest brother thought, she said he didn't say anything, but she replied, "I probably ... started to neglect him because I was so busy." Here, my mother's discourse of "neglect" begins and continues to shape how she talks about being a mother. Motherhood was one of her greatest joys, but it was also home to some of her deepest regrets.

She then described being a parent in graduate school as "impossible." When I asked why, she replied,

> Because it was just too much. I lost focus on both. It's not necessarily true of everybody who is a parent and in graduate school, but I didn't know what I was doing in either arena. I'm being really honest with you. I think I lost my way in both. So, while I loved you guys unqualifiedly and tried to do my best for you, I wasn't totally focused on you. Nor was I totally focused on my graduate work. I think both suffered for that. If you know what you're doing and have a better sense of self and if you have a real purpose in your graduate work, other than "to learn"—that's sort of been my thing. I just love learning.... But as an overall practical matter, sometimes I feel I could have done better. I think it's because your attention is divided and both of those things require so much of a person. They're both really, really overarching life things.

Here she shows guilt and to some extent shame or a sense of failure, both as a mother and as an academic. There was not enough space for both motherhood and graduate work, at least in her case because she "lost focus" on both.

She often describes her headspace at the time as "distracted" or in a state where she was neglecting both her studies and me and my brothers. Being at the park with us was a space that highlighted the juxtaposition of her mother/student paradox.

We have a photo of you guys at the park and me reading. So you want me to push you on the slide. I have to put down my book and go push you on the slide or just say, "No, I'm too busy." Either way there's this "where do I put my time and attention?" That's just a simple example, but multiplied by hundreds.

The example of the park illustrates a space where she was not mentally and physically "there" to care for my brothers and me. We were a distraction from her studies and her studies were a distraction from us. This sense of "here" and "there" through the memory of the photo evokes the spaces of "togetherness" that Rose (2004) identifies in mothers' emotional geographies of family photos. Simultaneously banal and emotionally charged, the park photo is a stark reminder of the dilemma my mother felt as a parent and student.

She further elaborated on these constraints of being "here" and "there" in relation to caregiving and hired babysitters.

We had this series of babysitters. Well, we had to have babysitters so I could go to class. So were they always the best babysitters and did you always get the best care? Probably not. And because, and I'm not trying to be nasty, but because your dad was not real involved, it was hard. It was really hard because it was all up to me to find all those babysitters. So, we messed up. We neglected you guys and I feel really, really bad about it. You turned out wonderful. I love you all and I always have and will and all that, but I feel that even though we did a lot of things together. I tried to make sure that we had family adventures and did things on weekends and we had trips. So I don't think it was horrendous, but it wasn't as focused as I see now it should have been.

To make up for not being "there" for us, she tried to find someone else to care for us and to organize "family adventures." And again, she repeats how much she loves us and that we did turn out okay, re-emphasizing the guilt she continues to feel for not being "there," which for my brothers and me was "here." Furthermore, she views my father's level of involvement and his own "here and there" as an added source of stress to the situation.

As previously mentioned, my middle brother was seriously ill as a small child and was frequently hospitalized with severe asthma. Today when she talks about his illness, she frequently chokes up because it took such an emotional toll and because it was such a scary time for her. I asked her how his illness affected her experiences as a graduate student.

Well, oh, it was so hard. I remember going to statistics class thinking, "Thank God this has nothing to do with feelings or anything else" because I was just overwhelmed. I was just totally overwhelmed. And it was scary and it felt out of control and I really didn't have a support system, or not much of one. But people would come and babysit for you. Uncle Dave came. Cousin Sharon would come. I had another cousin that would come when we had to take him to the hospital. It was a really hard time.

For my mother, the hospital was an ongoing space of motherhood after childbirth. It was where my parents had to take my brother when he could not breathe. The statistics classroom became a place where my mother could be in a space of abstraction away from worrying about my brother. In addition, because these were emergency hospital visits, extended family members would care for my oldest brother and me while my parents were away. This illustrates both the difficulty of hiring babysitters on short notice and the need for intimacy of care at home when my brother was ill. It was important for family members to be "there" for my oldest brother and me during such times.

Compounding her daily struggles as a studying mom, my mother's feelings of displacement were also related to where we lived in relation to her university. Although she said having children was more or less a non-issue for her professors and classmates, living in our particular suburb was symbolic of not-quite-belonging in her PhD program, as she explains in the following exchange.

DAUGHTER: I remember you saying that people would say, "Oh, you're the mom from Aurora."

MOTHER: That was in Boulder, yes. I was very much disparaged in Boulder. That was in my PhD program, because I had no perceived status.

D: Because you lived in Aurora?[1]

M: It was a very snobby situation, and of course, I didn't know what I was doing anyways. So it was maybe well founded. But my one philosophy teacher loved me, because I have an "inquiring mind." But by and large, it wasn't discussed. I wasn't part of the scene.

D: Was that because you had kids or was that because you were in Aurora?

M: Probably all of the above. I wasn't a Boulderite. I'm not cool. I'm a mom. I'm not hot stuff. You're in graduate school, you

> know about the snobbery. I wasn't a hot stuff publisher. I
> was basically stereotyped as the mom from Aurora. But a
> lot of them were younger, too.

Her "suburban mom" example illustrates a space where her identity was caught between study and motherhood. Her identity as a suburban mom, coupled with her own ambivalence about being in graduate school, made her feel like an outsider. Not only could she not fully participate in graduate school because of her family commitments, but also the actual location of her family prohibited full acceptance and, therefore, participation in her graduate program.

Despite my brother's illnesses, problems picking a topic and punch-card computers, feeling a lack of direction and lack of support from her advisor, my mother finally finished her degree. Regarding the difficulty of finishing, she said, "It was a very lonely time, not unlike some other parts of my life. And I was convinced to do it." My father gave her support when she was discouraged. He would say, "If you're swimming in the middle of the Atlantic Ocean, it doesn't make any sense to stop." She recalls this as "a really good piece of advice. So I kept going and finished the whole thing. And then at graduation you were *really* sick. It was out in Boulder on the lawn." Finishing the PhD no matter her ambivalence and feelings of displacement was a goal that she was determined to accomplish. But motherhood is again at the forefront of her memories of graduation. Furthermore, I remember her graduation. I remember being on the lawn, but unlike my mother, I do not remember being sick. I do not know why I remember her graduation—perhaps because of the photographs displayed in our house. Regardless, my illness is intertwined with her memories of graduation.

Being a graduate student set patterns not only for how she would care for my brothers and me throughout her career, but also for her marriage. When I was growing up, my parents always had different schedules. My dad ran his engineering business during the day and my mother often taught night classes. Although I remember spending plenty of time together as a family, she sees distance setting in early on between her and my dad.

> Anyway, I got through [the PhD]. But you have to have a certain
> single-mindedness to do a project that big. And so, something's
> got to give. So I don't know if that's when your dad and I, well,
> it wasn't that your dad and I didn't get along—because we did.
> But we established kind of a pattern of incredible amounts of
> self-time. He went his way and I went mine—most of our mar-
> riage. So, that was just a piece of that, but I didn't recognize it
> because I was so busy trying to balance schoolwork. I don't think

I did all the reading I could have done. You know the depth that you really can get to, right? You're travelling all over the world. You're doing everything you can for your research. I had to stay in Aurora, basically, and the things that I did had to centre around that. Had I been more mindful and thoughtful and understood more, I might have chosen something closer to home that's actually interesting as a topic and not so abstract. But in hindsight, I've done a lot of things since then.

My mother and father do both like a lot of self-time, something that we all share in my family. She sees that her marriage suffered because of her school-work, but as she goes on, she expresses more guilt about the schoolwork than about the distances created in her relationship with my father. Perhaps doing their own things was what helped them get along, or at least that is how I have often interpreted their relationship lasting as long as it did. She expresses guilt even more strongly when she compares my relative freedom to read and travel to the limits imposed on her when she was doing her PhD as a mother in Aurora. I feel that the choices I make to travel and to be relatively independent during graduate school were a result of my interpretations of her PhD experiences. I do not read everything that I can, but I have tried to avoid the guilt and disappointment she has often expressed.

My mother's career as a part-time, flexible worker who often taught at night and on weekends as an adjunct at the local community college continued patterns of babysitting and detachment from my father that shaped her experiences in graduate school.

> D: I remember you teaching classes at night.
>
> M: Right. And weekends. Which is terrible when you have a family. I don't know what I was thinking. Quite frankly, some of it had to do with my relationship with your dad and feeling constrained and wanting to get out a little bit more. He always just wanted to stay home. It was a lot more interesting and a lot more fun to go teach and get paid for it. So again, I think I put that before you and that was probably not a good thing for you.
>
> D: So it wasn't like they said, "The only class we have for you is at night."
>
> M: Oh yes, oh definitely.
>
> D: That was true?

> M: It was true. I would teach during the day if they had day-
> time classes. I took what they gave me. But what I didn't do
> is say, "I will not teach at nighttime or on the weekends."
> But, I mean, it's hard. It's hard. For a woman, what's the bal-
> ance? It doesn't matter whether it's academia or anything
> else. Even if you're at the grocery store, your attention is
> split. Think about being a doctor or a nurse or a lawyer,
> a politician. I know people who are politicians who have
> families. I'm never home. I don't know how they do it. So
> it's not just academics who have this issue and that's real
> clear.

My mother's curiosity led her again out of the house and into the classroom
as a student and then lecturer. But she does not see her flexibility and desire
to work as something isolated to academia. Rather, any working parent shares
her experiences. This is a connection that must be made between academia
(where we often see ourselves as "outside of society" in an isolated field) and
the rest of the working world. Academia is a job even if we treat it as a lifestyle.

For many years, until I left for university, my mother continued to work
for community colleges and to work as a consultant. However, after I left for
university and after my parents' separation, my mother began looking for
university positions. She found a position in South Carolina, which she often
describes as her second chance at being a graduate student.

> It was a lot different because I had this incredible … it was like I
> felt that I was finally going to graduate school and I could read. I
> could travel. I helped start the Russian Communication Associ-
> ation. I gave papers at conferences. I wrote papers. I was part of
> the scene. It was really fun because I wasn't divided, except for
> taking care of my lawn and whatever else. But it was a lot easier
> and I felt that I could do the background reading and do the stuff
> that I needed to do.

Without the constraints of family obligations, she finally felt free to follow her
intellectual pursuits without guilt or shame. She was finally in a space unen-
cumbered from the daily needs of children or even a husband. But that lasted
for only about five years when family obligations and a job prospect lured her
back to Colorado.

> D: You said you left South Carolina for many reasons, but one
> was because of my brother?
>
> M: Yeah, because of your brother and my mother. Because
> the college called me and said, "Come back. We'll pay you

to come back and redo this department." It was a job I had wanted, that I had been turned down for ten years before. So I was to run the customized training office. So I thought, well, okay. My mom is dying. My son needs me. It's hard for you to get out here. I'm fighting with the chair of the department. Maybe I'll leave. But it was partly family, I would say.

Her decision to leave her tenure-track position was based on obligations to and distances from family and a return to the community college.

Everyone suffered from my parents' divorce, but it often seemed as if my middle brother suffered the most. He stayed in Colorado after my mother, my oldest brother, and I left for various university opportunities. He also remained alone for a year in the house where I was raised until my mother sold it. I asked her to explain why she still feels so much guilt about leaving my brother.

He really was [suffering] and had I known, because I remember having a conversation with him when I had just got [to South Carolina]. He was so upset. I was sitting in this motel, because I didn't even have a place to live, and said, "Should I come home?" Of course he said no. But I should have known better. I should have known. You will have this in your life and maybe you do now, but I've got like six huge guilt points in my life of things I really blew. And that's one of them. I should have gone. Although I really loved being at the university and it was an unforgettable experience, he really needed me and I let him down, again. Is he happy now? Just one of the things that makes me sad is that I really let him down. I should have got back in that car or got on an airplane and just gone home and taken care of him. I remember talking to him on the phone a couple times, but I should have got on a plane. Five years later I did.

After my mother moved to South Carolina I remember that she would call us and ask us if she made the wrong decision, but we always told her it was time for her to do something for herself. We were proud to be able to finally say that our mother was a professor. We also told her that we were adults and that we could take care of ourselves. Nonetheless, my brother was suffering and she sees her failure to take care of him, a man in his early twenties, as a missed opportunity to make up for neglect from our early childhood.

After South Carolina and her return to the community college, for me her role as an academic parent was as an academic mentor. She often tried to give me advice as I struggled through my master's degree. Once I finished the degree and began teaching, she helped me find work at the college and gave me lots of teaching advice. I also began teaching on another campus where I remember going as a child. These same academic spaces were part of my childhood and I remember them as my mother's spaces of work and study. Her spaces of work became my spaces of work. But when I asked her if she thinks she influenced my decision to become an academic, she said,

> No, I don't. I think you would have been probably less likely to think of doing [a PhD] had I not done one. And I think it would be less likely for you to have travelled as much had I not wanted to travel and pushed the family to do a little more travelling than your dad, specifically, was comfortable with. So I think that in some ways I did provide a little bit of role modelling for you. But I would not ever take credit for it, because if we know anything about [my daughter], we know that she has her own mind. So, it became an option in your menu of options of what to do with your life. It was there. It was like, "Oh, I could do this."

As I mentioned above, academic spaces are the spaces of my childhood and working adult life as an adjunct and graduate student. Even though she does not attribute herself as a direct role model, my relationship to academia is different from that of many of my colleagues who are from non-academic families. Because my mother has worked successfully in and out of academia, I see the institution as fluid and not the only option for me. In the context of the movement in higher education to fewer and fewer tenure-track positions following the corporatization of universities (see Bauder, 2005; Meyerhoff, Johnson, & Braun, 2011; Smith, 2000), I at least feel more prepared for the reality of life with a PhD. Because of my mother, I know that I too can "make it work" without a tenure-track position even though we are still being trained for such (unrealistic) expectations in my discipline and department. On the other hand, although my mother and other part-time academic parents I know appreciate the flexibility that comes with part-time teaching appointments, the uncertainty and insecurity of those positions creates anxiety and stress.

To try to understand how she feels about my decision to "follow in her footsteps" at least within the realm of social sciences, I asked her what she thought when I decided to pursue a PhD.

> I just wanted to make sure that you knew why you were doing it, because of my own experience with not exactly knowing what I was doing or why and then feeling lost in the process. The older I get, the more important I see it is to have a purpose and that

> really helps you when things get tough. I remember waking up
> in Russia one morning and saying, "Why the heck am I here?"
> and you have to have an answer to that. And now here you are
> in the middle of Mongolia, and if you didn't have a purpose for
> starting that PhD, the answer to the question of why you're in
> Mongolia is harder.

Her wanting me to know why I am doing what I am doing has, opposed to the reflections I made above about being at home on campuses, made me feel as if she does not *like* what I am doing. I remember asking my undergraduate professors about pursuing a PhD and having conversations about the pros and cons. When they started to list off the negatives, I would tell them, "You do not have to do that. My mother is a professor and she tells me all the time why I should not go into academia." My mother frequently tells me that she is proud of me because I am doing "all that I can" to do my PhD the way I want to do it. However, she still asks, "If all you want to do is teach at a college, why are you writing about Mongolia?" And, "Why do you have to go so far away for your studies?" I guess I do not have a very good answer for either of those questions other than that they are the things I want to do and I am lucky to have a flexible partner.

Speaking of boyfriends, partners, and husbands and heteronormativity, I asked my mother about generational changes, in part, because so many women in my department have been having children, both students and faculty. She said that for working women, having children now is "easier for women in general. Easier. But not easy." This she attributes to changing gender norms and parenting.

> I think [having children is easier now] because both the woman
> and the husband are involved, or both partners are involved,
> and the systems understand better what the conflicts are. I think
> that because it's more talked about, there is more support for
> the difficulties. Back in my day, you were a hotshot or you were
> nothing. Like I said, you got minus points for being a mom back
> in my day. Whereas now, it's like you say, whatever.

Since she had small children, there has been a significant generational shift, both culturally and institutionally. This has made it more okay to take maternity/paternity leave, to adjust schedules for childcare needs and daycare at the university. Nonetheless, as Klocker and Drozdzewski (2012) argue, having children continues to impose emotional and material barriers to academic advancement.

This generational shift is in stark contrast to her undergraduate days in the 1960s. Several times she has told me the story about her senior psychology seminar and the reaction of the professor to several female students taking the course.

> Did I ever tell you about when I was an undergraduate? I was majoring in psychology and I was in the senior seminar and the professor was saying something about graduate school— which I had no idea what it was, by the way. Remember, I had no background in higher education. I mean, my father didn't even graduate high school. My mother, I think had one year of college, somewhere. She never talked about it. So, he said to the class, "Well, I'm not sure why you girls are taking this class because none of you are going to graduate school." Again, it was a memorable phrase because it was like, "Well, what is graduate school? And how does he know I'm not going do it?" I didn't go to graduate school until ten years later, but it stuck in my mind. That was the tenor of the times. It's interesting that academia is in some ways a very conservative culture. In some areas because it's the preservation of knowledge and tradition. I mean, the social sciences are often progressive and the arts are often progressive, but there's a lot of academia that's dedicated to the preservation of knowledge and tradition, which should not be thrown out.

Although some things have changed, she argues that academia as an institution continues to be conservative. Challenging elements of the institution that continue to make parenting difficult is, as I see it, the purpose of this collection of narratives—to get beyond the current problems parents face on the academic track.

Finally, I also wanted to know what my mother feels about my own plan of hoping to have children and working on an academic career. Of having a family, she said she hopes "that you enjoy it and the career thing is just a career. Life is a long time. So … enjoy your family and treasure your partner and don't move too far away from your mom." She does not want me to feel torn, but to keep distance in mind to ensure her plenty of grandparenting time.

She does, however, argue that work was important to her and that being just a mom couldn't work for her because being just at home was boring.

> To not work and have a baby, I tried that for a couple of years and it drove me crazy because I didn't have anything to do with my mind. Even though I read books and I remember washing ceilings and making everything from bread to clothes to keep

> myself busy, it was really hard. You've got to have something, which is why part-time teaching I felt was a good solution to that. But even so, I think you still need to balance because you want to be there for the kids' plays and all that stuff. You want to be there. You want to be there for your kid's first step. But you're a very different person than I am or was. And so I'm fully confident that you and Noah will work this out really beautifully.

The space of the home was not enough for my mother. So despite the incredible guilt that she expresses throughout the interview for not being "there" for my brothers and me, in many ways being "there" all the time was not an option for her. I do not think this was her attempt to have it all. When I was growing up, her teaching wasn't about ambition; it was about finding something interesting to do with her time. Family wasn't enough for her, but she also never felt as though she had enough to give to academia until her family obligations receded.

Throughout this discussion with my mother, themes of neglect, ambivalence, distraction, displacement, and paradoxes emerged to articulate her struggles, regrets, and triumphs as an academic parent. For over thirty years she never really felt satisfied with being "here" or "there" for her studies, career, and family. Even in more casual conversation, when we discuss my childhood, my mother often expresses disappointment in her attempts to balance her intellectual curiosity and responsibilities to her family. Although intellectual work is something that she has always loved and pursued, she continues to feel guilty about the choices she made as parent far beyond our childhoods and into our adult lives. For both my mother and me, academic spaces became spaces of family and family spaces became academic spaces. Furthermore, academia also became a space of escape from the stresses and boredom of family life when we were small children and after the pain of my parents' divorce. All of these small examples build a sense of internal conflict that will always be with my mother and that consciously or not shapes how I view and lead my life in academia with or without a family.

As I pursue an academic career, I know that my feelings as a child and my mother's advice shape the decisions I make. But my emotional relationships to the spaces of academia also shape my decision-making process. To me, being a child or even having a child in academia is less uncertain because I have been there for over thirty years. Nonetheless, I still worry about what will happen if I am pregnant during job interviews or while teaching on a contract. I have to explain to people I work with in Mongolia that I might not be able to come back as often in the future if/when I have children. I do feel that my "commitment" to my job could be questioned if I have a family. But at least I know I can do it, because even though my mother still feels guilty, we always knew that she loved us. After all, my brothers and I did turn out okay.

Emailed Postscript from My Mother

By the way, I thought of a few things I neglected to tell you this morning. Do you remember me telling you that when I found out that I was pregnant with you I had a series of "in vitro" conversations with you, asking for your forgiveness that I was in school and perhaps neglectful? But you were such a sweetie, and smiled when you slept. So beautiful and peaceful.

Note

1 Boulder is often considered one of the "hippest" places to live in Colorado. My suburb, Aurora, is often derided as one of the "least cool" places to live in the Denver metro area.

References

Bauder, H. (2005). The segmentation of academic labour: A Canadian example. *ACME, 4*(2), 228–239.

Davidson, J., & Bondi, L. (2004). Spatialising affect; affecting space: An introduction. *Gender, Place and Culture, 11*(3), 373–374.

Davidson, J., & Milligan, C. (2004). Embodying emotion sensing space: Introducing emotional geographies. *Social and Cultural Geography, 5*(4), 523–532.

Davidson, J., Smith, M., Bondi, L., & Probyn, E. (2008). Emotion, space and society: Editorial introduction. *Emotion, Space, and Society, 1*, 1–3.

Gibson-Graham, J. K. (2006). *A postcapitalist politics.* Minneapolis: University of Minnesota Press.

Klocker, N., & Drozdzewski, D. (2012). Commentary. *Environment and Planning A, 44*, 1271–1277.

Longhurst, R., Hodgetts, D., & Stolte, O. (2012). Placing guilt and shame: Lone mothers' experiences of higher education in Aotearoa New Zealand. *Social and Cultural Geography, 13*(3), 295–312.

Meyerhoff, E., Johnson, E., & Braun, B. (2011). Time and the university. *ACME, 10*(3), 483–507.

Pratt, G. (2004). *Working feminism.* Philadelphia, PA: Temple University Press.

Rose, G. (2004). "Everyone's cuddled up and it just looks really nice": An emotional geography of some mums and their family photos. *Social and Cultural Geography, 5*(4), 549–564.

Smith, N. (2000). Who rules this sausage factory? *Antipode, 32*(3), 330–339.

Williams, A., & Crooks, V. A. (2008). Introduction: Space, place and the geographies of caregiving work. *Gender, Place and Culture, 15*(3), 243–247.

Patchwork Academia

Sarah Milmine

Writing about myself and my journey is not something new for me. I have spent a number of years in both the academic and clinical world of social work, and two of the key tools are self-reflection and analysis. The majority of my education was in a school that took a generalized approach to clinical practice with an anti-oppressive theoretical framework. Some may argue that "anti-oppressive social work is best understood as a perspective or stance in how you approach practice or clinical issues" (Anti-Oppressive Social Work [AOSW], 2012). I was taught that anti-oppressive practice was an approach that sought to eradicate social injustices that were rooted in societal social inequalities. Anti-oppressive practice encompasses a number of approaches, including but not limited to radical, structural, feminist, anti-racist, critical, and liberatory frameworks (AOSW, 2012). Anti-oppressive practice and ideas frame how I present my story to you the reader and, I hope, will provide some useful context for my experience.

In the process of writing about my life and journey, I experienced a myriad of emotions, from anger to sadness and frustration with a system and, at times, frustration with myself. The process of writing this chapter was difficult. Although it can be very liberating to tell one's story, it can also be terrifying. The reality for women in the workforce is that we continue to make less than our male counterparts (Statsna, 2012), and women in academia face unique challenges related to balancing their formative careers with their ticking biological clocks (Gulli, 2012; van Anders, 2004, p. 519). As a woman who is still living and experiencing the frustration associated with navigating a family and career, I found that I was concerned that telling my story may continue to affect the path I am on. At the same time, I also understand that social action and change do not occur without examining the situation and finding points for potential change. I strive to be honest and genuine about my feelings and hope my experience validates that of others and is one that resonates with countless other parents or parents to be.

I grew up in central Hamilton, Ontario, a port city southwest of Toronto and steps away from a large CFL football stadium. Hamilton is known as a steel town, and until recently the steel mills in the north end of town employed the majority of the city's population. Although my neighbourhood was diverse and welcoming, it has become very run down over time. Each school that I went to growing up was within one block of my home, and I was lucky to have a number of close friends whose parents had similar professions around the city. I am not sure when I realized that my family did not live in an affluent portion of town, and I never really had any concept of class growing up. However, when I was in high school I can remember an English teacher very clearly correcting me that I was from a "working-class," not "middle-class," family as I had identified for some sort of class project. I remember in that moment feeling defensive and embarrassed but not really understanding why—just never realizing that I was ever anything less than anyone else.

I grew up in a family that took on traditional gender roles within the home. My father was employed at the local steel mill, working his way up from collecting time cards in the plants to retiring from a sales position over thirty years later. My mother went to a local college for nursing, retired once I was born, and elected to stay at home to raise my brother and me. I never asked her if she had wanted to continue working after my brother and I were born; however, she did engage in part-time work as we entered our teenage years. Interestingly, she worked in bookstores and restaurants and volunteered; she did not take on "caretaking/nursing" roles again until her late forties and fifties. My brother and I were very well taken care of, and although we may not have had all the latest things, we were happy. We had a close extended family, and I was in many ways co-parented by my grandparents (maternal and paternal). My maternal grandmother has always been one of my biggest supporters. From a young age, Grandma Kay taught me everything from sewing to money management and dog grooming, and how to play every game known to man. She was a librarian before she got married, and she always told me, "When you get older you will be a teacher … it's a good job and you will be very good at it." Even to this day she tells me that I should teach. Other than my grandmother, I really do not remember many conversations about "what you want to be when you grow up," as the majority of the females in my life were full-time homemakers.

I was the first person on my father's side of the family to go to university. My parents encouraged me to go to school, but they did not save or have the ability to finance my academic journey. I never thought twice about applying for Ontario Student Assistance and later in my academic journey taking on thousands of dollars in academic debt. I truly do not remember conversations with my parents about post-secondary education. Any conversation I had about careers took place at school with the guidance counsellor or in sessions with university recruiters. I initially applied to university with the hopes of becoming a midwife. There was a three-part admission process and I had positive feedback about my application, but they felt I was too young and I needed more life experience before entering the program. I entered a general arts program with the hopes I would figure out what I wanted to do.

University was a learning curve for me. My parents were very religious and I spent a large portion of my life deeply involved in church life and activities. It would not be uncommon for me to spend upwards of four nights a week at church. My parents were guarded about content that I was exposed to growing up as well. I can remember my father reading each book I had before I did and blacking out portions he felt were inappropriate; as a result, I used to carefully examine every portion of blackened text trying to figure out what I was missing and why it was so inappropriate. I grew up surrounded by heterosexual families, where you waited to have sex, got married, had children, and the woman often stayed home to take care of the children. University for me was the first time that I was open to exploring what role religion had in my life. It was also the first real exposure I had to any idea of "difference," be that sexual identifications, religion, or race/ethnicity. I took women's studies courses and learned about different religions, and my parents were told by others in my family that they should not have let me attend these types of classes. I laugh about this now, but these classes provoked a great sense of responsibility to critically examine difference/injustices in life, and how some of the religious institutions I had been raised within often were a great source of oppression for others. I learned to be critical and to think critically about everything that I came across in life. I loved learning, debating, and writing, and found my niche in the social work world. In hindsight, my academic selection was largely influenced by both my religious upbringing and my strong desire to help correct some of the privilege I had benefited from.

I entered the social work program two years after I started school, and after a brief break from academia I felt refocused on a path that seemed right for me. Throughout my undergrad education, I worked two part-time jobs at non-profit programs for at-risk populations, and faithfully volunteered on the sexual assault crisis line while I completed my undergrad degree in social work and religious studies. My social work classes helped me understand and examine more fully the identity and privilege I had. I became aware of this "invisible backpack" of privilege I carried as a white, educated, English-speaking, heterosexual woman, and from a Christian background (McIntosh, 1989). I threw myself into my studies and was secretly disappointed that school was over at the end of my degree. I was hired by the Children's Aid Society (CAS) before I graduated school and jumped into the world of child welfare days after I finished classes.

About two years into my work in child welfare I met my husband. We got engaged two years after we started dating and began what our family referred to as our "marathon engagement." As we discussed our own goals and hopes for our lives together, I expressed a desire to advance in my career. I quickly recognized the need to return to school to advance my skill set and ensure that I would not be stuck in one level of social work for the duration of my profession. My husband was my biggest cheerleader, and we placed everything on hold—the wedding, a family—as I knew that school would become only more difficult to fit into our personal lives as we took on more personal responsibility (a mortgage, family, etc.). I felt that school needed to happen now, or I would not have the opportunity to return to academia until well after any children we might have were in grade school.

I took a year off work to complete my master's in social work. I was in my late twenties and felt that I still had time to have a baby. Although not a pressing thought, my reproductive health was always in the back of my mind with any planning for my life and career. The majority of my friends from work had children; some women the same age as me or younger had quickly had children after marriage and would often make comments to me that they didn't have time to do anything "academic." Some of my friends would talk about how their lives had changed significantly with children and would report little time for themselves, and although some may have wanted to change things with their career, they didn't feel they had the time or the ability to do so. I did not have a lot of pressure from anyone to have children, but there were many comments about how children did interfere with potential promotions in our workplace and that timing was everything.

Returning to school only helped to reignite my love for academia, and a year away from the busyness of child welfare was a happy alternative. So rarely do we have the option to reflect on our practice when out in the field that research and learning were welcome. My master's was very different from my undergrad—everyone was older, there were few students who had just come out of undergrad, and most people were returning from time in the field. I was a teaching assistant for the year I was in school and loved every minute of the teaching experience, and the times I had to guest lecture. When I finished my degree, I could not help but contemplate going on to do my PhD. My thesis supervisor strongly encouraged it and thought I could take my thesis a great deal further.

The thought of a PhD had never crossed my mind before, and I certainly never had family members who made a career of academia. My parents, although supportive of my university experience, were not overly invested in my progress and were most concerned with making sure I had a job at the end of it. Academic careers were completely foreign to me, but not foreign to my husband. He had a family filled with doctors, lawyers, and academics, and he was nothing but supportive; however, my complication was my employer. My husband was and is self-employed, running a studio out of our home. Unfortunately, there are no benefits, and work remains completely dependent on the market demand. At the point I returned to school I had been in my position at the Children's Aid Society for close to five years. This position had exceptional benefits, a pension, and significant time off and flexibility with time. It was an excellent job, but there was a ceiling to achievement levels and the work could be incredibly depleting. Although I have never found research to support this statement, it is a common discussion among child welfare workers that work burnout is eighteen months in the field of social work. Workload is an ongoing issue; you work a great deal of overtime while experiencing trauma, which is a reality for many social workers. I had been offered only one year of leave from my position for my education. I had avoided signing the education commitment my employer requires when workers participate in an education leave. This "commitment" ensures that employees return to their positions at the agency for at least one year prior to completing their education; it also provides 20 percent financial reimbursement for tuition. I received a full working scholarship from my university and did not require financial assistance from my employer; at the same time, I wanted the freedom to leave the employ of my workplace at the end of my master's if I was able to obtain a position elsewhere. However, education leave for a PhD had not been granted to workers at my agency in the past, as it was deemed that a PhD was not required/relevant for our work. I was concerned I would not be able to negotiate a leave from my agency to support doctoral studies in university.

Around this same time an interesting sequence of opportunities presented themselves. My wonderfully supportive thesis supervisor offered me a research assistant position. The hours were very few, but it was an excellent opportunity to advance my interest in research and obtain more experience in this field. In addition to this position, I was offered a teaching assistant contract in a child welfare class at my alma mater, and I was approached by a local community college to take over two days of teaching in their social service worker program.

I was excited and trying to see what I could do to piece together enough work to make it all happen. My husband and I discussed our options; each of these positions was part-time and did not offer nearly the same amount of money that my position at CAS did. The teaching position paid by the hour and there was no preparation time built into the contract. I had worked so hard to get a position with stability, but if I was going to take the leap into a more academic life, this seemed like a good opportunity, and I was willing to overlook some of the downfalls. I approached CAS to see if there could be any flexibility with my position to allow me to work all these positions into my schedule through job sharing, creative vacation planning, and so forth. After weeks of waiting for an answer, they responded that it was just not possible; I was devastated and felt trapped. After a year of dreaming, thinking, and feeling invigorated about practice and research, I felt as if I was losing my options. In hindsight, I could have just taken the leap and we could have found a way to figure out our finances. However, I feel that decision would have been irresponsible for me, a woman in my late twenties, with a mortgage and other life responsibilities. Perhaps if I were in my early twenties the situation would have been different, but I needed to return to my job and think about my options a bit further.

I returned to work and started to prepare for our wedding. Although I was hugely disappointed and frustrated with my employer about the lack of flexibility, I had a great response from my executive director about my research. She offered me a number of opportunities to speak about my thesis and work at both our agency and with a number of other key stakeholders in Children's Aid Societies throughout Ontario. I was sucked back into work and the busyness of the job, but continued to try to find opportunities to advance my career. I continued to fulfill my teaching assistant duties and remain connected with the school community; I said yes to every opportunity presented to me in hopes of building my resumé. I began feverishly looking for jobs outside of my agency, anything that would provide me a chance to advance or to utilize my skills in research and my passion for program development. I had a couple of positive interviews, but it became apparent again that my master's was not going to be enough to move me forward to the positions I was interested in.

When my husband and I sat down to regroup and discuss our options, the discussion of doing a PhD re-emerged. We talked about the pros and cons of returning to school. It became clear that the list of cons was far bigger than the benefits. I was worried about time away from my job, of losing seniority, stability, pension, and all the rest. I knew that although time in school and working on research would be amazing, it would be difficult. We were at the point in our lives where we were ready to start a family, and I was worried about my age and what that meant for my own reproductive health. Then we thought about how it would work to have a family and be in school, and it just did not seem possible. Even if I could find a job teaching one or two classes, there would be no benefits. The outcome of a PhD could do good things for me, but I was not sure the outcome would outweigh the downfalls. Acquiring a tenured teaching position at a university would be an amazing outcome, but it was a long road to such a lofty goal. I had heard friends and colleagues talk about how much work it was to obtain research grants, with pressure on publishing and creating a professional presence in the academic world, never mind trying to balance that with the responsibilities of being a part of a family (potentially with children). I knew that the pressures of being a woman in the workforce and a mother would become increasingly demanding, and I knew the statistics related to work–life balance, the reality related to shared household responsibilities, and, despite having a fairly forward-thinking partner and an awareness of these issues, also my own personal limits.

I decided that I needed to find a way to make my degree and education work for me. I started to really examine the job descriptions of the positions I was interested in, and they largely required a combination of both clinical and business/administrative knowledge. I wanted to work in a position that had more influence on the bigger scope of social work practice and that would potentially provide avenues for change in vulnerable sectors. I felt that I needed to rethink the assets I had in my history and experience and make them work to my advantage. I went to interview for a prestigious position as the director of social workers for a government organization, and realized quickly that my gaps in knowledge of the business side of organizations was a priority for improvement. I decided to return to school again, but this time for business administration. I would engage in long conversations with myself about how this was not settling—it was creating success for me in a different way. I still struggled and was incredibly frustrated that I was giving in and not challenging systemic norms; however, I pushed myself to attempt to obtain a similar outcome of a PhD by working hard at building other parts of my academic life. I continued to guest lecture, sit on committees, and find options to write whenever I could, while keeping the stability of my job.

This brings me to my present circumstances where I continue to work at my agency, volunteer on the union executive, attend training any chance I get, guest lecture, and TA. I like the busyness and mix of things in my life, and I find myself trying to concoct ways to have a multiple birth to keep myself from having too much time away from my career. I feel that I am at a moment in time where I have momentum, and at any moment something could come my way that could be great for me and my family. However, I have to fit children in there somewhere, and I know that inevitably all the things I am doing will slow down when children enter into my life. I struggle because I feel that things should not slow down and opportunities should continue to present themselves. I want to remain positive, but I am very aware of the reality of women in the workforce.

In addition to the obvious discussion related to gendered work and women's roles in the workforce, I thought it was interesting when I reviewed my narrative that reproductive health (timing, parental leave, etc.) was/is an active thought in my decision-making process. Van Anders (2004) discussed in her article "Why the Academic Pipeline Leaks: Fewer Men Than Women Perceive Barriers to Becoming Professors" how women were more likely to "self-select away from academia in response to specific systemic barriers" (p. 518). Although men and women often shared the same values and goals related to teaching and research, women ranked mobility and plans for parenthood higher than men did. In addition, the realities of having children concern women more than men, women are more certain when they want to have children, and her research strongly suggests that women are well aware of the need to plan child-bearing in accordance with fertility and their career stage (p. 519). When my husband and I would engage in conversations about career and school, I was often the person raising the issue of children and timing. This is likely because women carry the responsibility of having to balance both the needs of their careers, and the reality of their reproductive health during the developmental portion of their careers. We are reminded that the longer we wait to have children, the greater risk we pose to any future children, to our own health, and to our fertility (Gulli, 2012). I did not realize how much these conversations had weighed on me until writing this response. When I reflected on how often I had thought about maternity leaves, benefits, schooling, timing of who was retiring, and when the most strategic time to leave a position might be, I was incredibly conflicted. I felt frustration for having to think about these things, yet at the same time guilt for waiting and gambling with my age and health.

Perhaps this is a simple dilemma and others would say it is not as difficult as it seems. I believe there are obvious observations that I can articulate about my experience that show how it has been socially organized. I can see how being female and raised in a predominantly Christian family with values related to helping others has led me to the world of social work. Social work, in turn, is a largely female-dominated profession, and although I would say I had ample examples of both female and male teachers in university, the majority of the higher-paid, tenured staff were male or childless. Social work tends to be a profession that challenges societal norms and works to address areas of injustice and imbalance; however, social workers are still bound by an academic model and a system that is largely male driven. Quite simply, academia is not built for families and does not reward those who have families (Kuther, n.d.). If you look at professions that are more accommodating and touted for their family-friendly approach for their workers, they are not necessarily academic. Canada's Top 100 Employers lists numerous family-friendly employers, from Johnson Inc. to HP and various hydro and banking institutions (Canada's Top 100 Employers, 2012). These employers offer things like on-site daycare with flexible hours, health benefits for family leave (be that maternal or paternal), and flexible work hours to accommodate parents who want to be home for sick children or PA days (Canada's Top 100 Employers, 2012). Few academic institutions are on this list, and the academic employers that are listed seem to have benefits connected to the number of hours worked, contracts, and so on (Canada's Top 100 Employers, 2012).

I question how employer benefits in academic institutions affect parents in teaching or tenured positions. Are the universal benefits offered at an academic institution relevant and helpful to all employees? My understanding of academic pursuits means long hours, travel, time to commit to teaching, research—in short, sacrifice. How employee benefits are organized and dispensed may need to be different to accommodate the demands placed on those in research/teaching positions. Although this approach may require more work on behalf of the employer to develop supportive parenting plans with employees, it also means changing the core values and philosophy of how they operate as an organization. But the onus should not be placed solely on the employer. Societal attitudes and gendered approaches to parenting, what families look like, and how they are defined need to be addressed by government policies and programs. Cheryl Sandberg, the chief operating officer of Facebook, recently spoke about the Canadian government's responsibility to address policy around parenting. She argued that the workforce and public policy are organized as though everyone were working full-time, full year, and did not have children (Statsna, 2012). This situation does not even begin to address issues faced by families from the GLBTQQ communities, single parents, or parents with fertility issues. Public policy needs to address the needs of parents while understanding that each situation is unique and find a way to marry ideas related to work and family responsibilities that continues to create equal opportunity.

When I felt that I was close to finishing this narrative, I sent it out to a number of my colleagues to read and provide feedback. I had some interesting reactions. One friend, who is also childless, felt overwhelmed after reading and identified a number of similarities and could not provide feedback initially. Another friend, who is a mother and currently out of work, sent me portions of my narrative with quotes talking about how she could not express how much she connected with some of my feelings. However, when we talked about what we could do to make things better, we were perplexed. It is easy to argue that on-site daycare, flexible hours, and working to address parents' needs in a unique and supportive manner is a good start. Nevertheless, it is not something that will change while I am in the thick of my journey. Discussion begins to create awareness; we can find comfort in shared experiences and learn how to problem solve together through tougher times. For me, it has also meant that I have had to redefine what success means to me. I feel as if I am making some sort of academic quilt with patches of experiences, training, and education that will help me create the success I am hoping for. Although there is part of me that feels this approach means I'm settling, I need to be aware that the system itself is flawed in such a grand way. Perhaps my story would be different if these barriers were not present from my inception, and there is hope for future generations that this gap will disappear as increased awareness, discussion, and change occur.

References

Anti-Oppressive Social Work. (n.d.). *What is anti-oppressive social work?* Retrieved from http://aosw.socialwork.dal.ca/whatisaosw.html

Baker, M. (2012). Gendered families, academic work and the "motherhood penalty." *Women's Studies Journal, 26*(1),11–24.

Canada's Top 100 Employers. (2012). *Canada's Top Family-Friendly Employers.* Retrieved from http://www.canadastop100.com/family/

Canada's Top 100 Employers. (n.d.). *Canada's Top 100 Employers 2013.* Retrieved from http://www.canadastop100.com/national/

Gulli, C. (2012, March 14). A new fertility test is changing women's lives. *Maclean's.* Retrieved from http://www2.macleans.ca/2012/03/14/time-is-not-on-your-side/

Kuther, A. (n.d.). Gender, stress, and health in academia. Retrieved from About Education: http://gradschool.about.com/od/forwomen/a/genderstresshealth.htm

McIntosh, P. (1989). White privilege: Unpacking the invisible knapsack. Retrieved from http://nationalseedproject.org/white-privilege-unpacking-the-invisible-knapsack

Statsna, K. (2012). Canada's working moms still earning less, doing more than dads. *CBC News.* Retrieved from http://www.cbc.ca/news/canada/canada-s-working-moms-still-earning-less-doing-more-than-dads-1.1184685

van Anders, S. M. (2004). Why the academic pipeline leaks: Fewer men than women perceive barriers to becoming professors. *Sex Roles, 51*(9/10), 511–521.

Motherhood and Graduate Studies

The Untold Stories of Summer Residency

Melissa Corrente

July 2013 marked the beginning of my PhD journey. I remember spending countless hours in the library reading, writing, attending classes, researching, and presenting. The workload was overwhelming, and my twenty-eighth birthday came and went in the blink of an eye because I had a major paper due. One of the highlights for me was facilitating a yoga class for my small PhD cohort in the library. I wanted to help everyone relax and de-stress, and what better way than to focus on deep breathing and being in the moment. The bond I formed with the nine individuals in my PhD cohort was strong because we could all relate to one another in what we were experiencing academically. I appreciated the relationships and friendships I formed that month; each person brought something unique to the table.

To provide some context, the PhD program I am currently enrolled in is four years in length, with two summer residencies built into the first two years. For the month of July my doctoral colleagues and I are expected to be on campus completing all our mandatory coursework. Throughout the academic year, most PhD students complete their three elective courses online. Once both summer residencies and three elective courses have been completed, students can apply to write a comprehensive exam.

At the end of my first PhD summer residency, I remember feeling drained, exhausted, and proud of my progress. A few weeks later I started noticing changes in my body and found out that I was pregnant! The exhaustion finally made sense and I was thrilled to start the journey of motherhood. After the initial joy, nervousness, and excitement set in, I started to think practically about what this was going to mean for my life. Would I take a year off once the baby arrived? Could I swing next summer's residency with a three-month-old baby? Would I finish teaching my university course in April after the baby arrived? It is amazing what questions pop into your head when you're trying to sleep at night.

Based upon my experiences as a newly pregnant woman, I began to ask friends and colleagues about my hesitations. I quickly learned first-hand that feelings of guilt and judgment surround motherhood, and thus I developed a curiosity about the literature on this topic. The purpose of this chapter is to inquire into my experience as a married heterosexual graduate student mother. I hope that others considering combining school and family feel supported and encouraged upon reading my story. I have employed the structures of narrative inquiry as a suitable methodology through which to explore and understand my lived experience. First, I review relevant literature surrounding graduate student parents. Second, I share my personal journal entries and reflections from the summer residency. Third, I discuss themes and lessons learned about the topic through considering my own journey of parenting and working toward a PhD simultaneously.

Since my son was born, I have read many books talking about women in academia, including *Mama PhD: Women Write about Motherhood and Academic Life* (Evans & Grant, 2008); *Do Babies Matter? Gender and Family in the Ivory Tower* (Mason, Wolfinger, & Goulden, 2013); *Academic Motherhood: How Faculty Manage Work and Family* (Ward & Wolf-Wendel, 2012); *Mothers in Academia* (Castaneda & Isgro, 2013); *Professor Mommy: Finding Work–Family Balance in Academia* (Connelly & Ghodsee, 2014); and *Mothers on the Fast Track: How a Generation Can Balance Family and Careers* (Mason & Ekman, 2008). Although these books include inspirational stories and many experiences I could relate to as a new mother, I felt the overall tone was negative—it seemed to me that the hardships and challenges of being a working mother in academia outweighed the positive aspects of fulfilling both roles simultaneously. As I dug deeper for stories pertaining to graduate student parents, I found three articles in total (Brooks, 2012; Moreau & Kerner, 2015; Springer, Parker, & Leviten-Reid, 2009).

The general theme that exists in the literature surrounding women in doctoral studies is the impact of gender on doctoral experiences. The research focuses on the conflicts and challenges for women in doctoral programs, including timing, tension between work and home responsibilities, and the logistical challenges of attending conferences (Brown & Watson, 2010; Carter, Blumenstein, & Cook, 2013; Moreau & Kerner, 2015). Lynch (2008) discusses the strategic practices that graduate student mothers use to deal with their dilemma, such as "maternal invisibility" and "academic invisibility." Maternal invisibility refers to downplaying the role of mother in the academic setting, while academic invisibility is downplaying the role of student outside the university.

Using McCluksy's (1963) Theory of Margin, which describes the impact of increasing demands and pressures on adult learning over time, Grenier and Burke (2008) investigate the sources of power and load that graduate student mothers encounter during doctoral studies. They discuss the support of faculty, spouses, and friends as sources of power while naming stress and time as sources of load. The authors state, "The increasing number of women in graduate school choosing to have children calls for deeper understanding of the unique experience and needs of this population" (p. 599). This reminds us that more support is needed for graduate student parents, and it compels us to consider how many bright and enthusiastic parents are being lost along the way.

Few Canadian research articles exist that focus on parents in doctoral programs. Eisenbach (2013) wrote a narrative account of her struggle to balance motherhood and the doctoral process. Throughout her autoethnography, she is open and honest as her goal is to create a dialogue for other mothers to share their experiences. She indicates, "Few studies seek to reveal the areas of tension that exist for mothers within doctoral programs" (p. 12). Another narrative account details the journey of mothering of a woman who returned to college after a twenty-year absence. "Coupling a return to college with the obligations and responsibilities that come with mothering requires a community effort on the part of mothers, families, and institutions of higher education, if mothers are to successfully navigate academia" (Grassetti, 2013, p. 20). This theme of support was also present in my journal entries.

I want to provide a counter-narrative that focuses less on the tensions, conflicts, and challenges that exist, and more on the positive aspects of being a student mother. I plan to achieve this by sharing journal entries and stories of transformation, specifically those during the first three months of my son's life. I try to approach my life with an appreciative lens because I feel blessed to be a studentmotherteacher. I don't feel the need to include a slash between my roles because they are woven together like a patchwork quilt. Bateson (1989) states, "One of the striking facts about the women whose lives I have been examining is that the struggle to combine commitments is really a search for ways to make the combinations mutually enhancing" (p. 184). This quote resonates with me because I see the commitments in my life as positively contributing to one another.

During my PhD summer residency, I tried to journal every other day about how I was feeling and what experiences stuck out in my mind. After reading and rereading all my journal entries, I started noticing themes throughout my experience as a graduate student mother. The themes of role identity, support, vulnerability, emotion, and transformation started to permeate each entry. Each theme will be discussed further at the end of my paper. When deciding which journal entries to include, my criteria focused on submissions that defined my experience wholeheartedly. I looked for raw honesty, emotion, and questions that still force me to think about the societal pressure placed upon parents to do it all. My personal journal entries from the summer are included below in italics, and my reflections upon reading them are included afterward.

Journal Entry – July 2, 2014

The first day of my second PhD summer residency is over and I am left feeling stimulated, tired, grateful, and anxious. It was nice to have intellectual adult conversation this morning; I missed my colleagues over the course of the year. Today was the longest time I have been apart from my three-month-old son, so it was a bit emotional and difficult to do. He was a champ and was very well behaved for my husband. My cohort hosted a baby shower after class for me and another colleague who had a baby. It was wonderful to see my husband and baby boy included in my academic world and I was thrilled for everyone to meet them. I am grateful that my husband is able to stay home for the month because I couldn't continue on this journey without him. He has been an amazing support and has really stepped up to the plate. It is exhausting switching from mother, to wife, to student, so I am looking forward to whatever sleep is coming my way. Some of my anxieties were eased in class when the announcement of "flex time" to hand in the big assignments was made; however, I still feel anxious about who my supervisor will be and what my research question will be. I need to slow down and appreciate the process as I still have lots of knowledge to learn and absorb. I hope I can stay motivated after this month is over as life happens and research/reading gets put on the back burner. I have nothing profound to end with as sleep is beckoning....

As I reread my journal entry now there is one sentence that stands out for me: "It is exhausting *switching* from mother, to wife, to student...." Am I really switching roles? I am always a mother, wife, and student and I love how each role seeps into the other(s). Echoing this sentiment, Brown (2010) states, "Because true belonging happens only when we present our authentic, imperfect selves to the world, our sense of belonging can never be greater than our level of self-acceptance" (p. 26). The author reminds me that belonging does not mean trying to fit in to academia; I feel comfortable bringing who I am to the table. I don't try to hide my motherhood status while on campus, and I proudly show photos of my son to students and faculty. Becoming a mother has enriched my relationship with my husband because I see him in a different light. Watching him in his fatherhood role makes me smile on the inside and outside; our son brings out a fun-loving and silly side of him. I find my passion for research has increased since having my own child because I see the world through his curious little eyes.

Journal Entry – July 6, 2014

As I sit on the comfortable brown leather chair in our living room breastfeeding my three-month-old son my mind starts to wander. Staring off into the abyss I am inundated with thoughts about what to research and how to develop my all-important question. My thoughts are turbulent as I try to make sense of where my paradigm fits and how to articulate it. Suddenly my thoughts are brought back to the present as I am interrupted by the reality of where I am and what I'm doing. I can see milk spraying in an arc formation and when I look down my son is looking up at me smiling from ear to ear. As I relish in the moment all I can do is laugh and tell my son that he is funny as I try to stop the milk from flowing. It is here during this organized chaos that my "aha" moment arrives and my topic becomes crystal clear. My lived experience of motherhood has been lying in front of me the whole time and it is time to acknowledge it and start writing. I can see the working title now, Dirty Diapers and Dissertations: The Balancing Act of Female Professionals. *Questions flood my mind; however, they will have to wait until later to be written on paper as I must attend to my son. I now understand what just being means as I hold my son against my body after breastfeeding and he nuzzles his head between my ear and shoulder. In this moment we are both content and breath a sigh of relaxation as I feel his tiny chest expand and contract. I close my eyes and enjoy the moment we share together with no other thoughts in my mind. This state of just being is so peaceful and I am filled with love for this little person my husband and I created. After putting him down for a nap I return to the questions I had earlier regarding motherhood. Why is the term maternity leave utilized? It has a negative connotation that implies you are not returning to work. I much prefer the term maternity break. Why do I feel so much pressure to return to work in September? What would happen to my career aspirations if I decided to stay home? How do professional women balance their work and home life? Will the feelings of guilt and selfishness go away this month while I am pursuing my PhD? How has my identity changed since becoming a mother? How will this affect my teaching pedagogy? Why does everyone feel the need to give his or her two cents about parenting? Why is the first question from people who see me with a baby about taking a year off? Why is breastfeeding advertised as such a beautiful and natural process when in reality my experience has been an uphill battle?*

I had a few friends express their shock to me upon finding out I was in class for the month of July with a three-month-old baby at home. Honestly, I didn't think much of it because I knew my baby was at home bonding with my husband. As the month progressed, I did not feel guilty leaving in the morning because it was my decision and I would do it again in a heartbeat. Working within the context of mothering helped me get through the month, as I accepted the fact that my grades wouldn't be as high and my writing time would be choppy at best. Instead of spending an entire afternoon sitting down writing a paper, I was forced by my son to take much-needed play breaks. His curiosity and laughter make my day and I feel more productive after playing with him.

When he naps I try to use my time wisely and accomplish something small. Embracing my role as mother provides new purpose and meaning in my life, and I think it has made me a more passionate and motivated scholar and teacher. Bateson (1989) reminds me, "Composing a life involves a continual reimagining of the future and reinterpretation of the past to give meaning to the present, remembering those events that prefigured what followed, forgetting those that proved to have no meaning within the narrative" (pp. 29–30). I see my university students through a different lens now, and I feel more empathy and understanding since having my own child. Instead of looking at my university students as teacher candidates, I now see them as my son's future educators.

Journal Entry – July 10, 2014

As I drove to school this morning with my baby boy babbling in the background, I felt a sense of ease and relaxation that we would be together at school this morning. It has been difficult to leave him each morning; however, I am eternally grateful to my husband for taking the month off. It has been amazing watching the bond develop between my husband and our son. I remember how nervous my husband was when I was pregnant, as he had no exposure to babies. He was worried and had many questions about how to hold a baby and change a diaper. Now he is a professional diaper changer and I love watching him interact with our son. I have witnessed a side of him I didn't know existed, as he is constantly singing and reading him books. Our relationship has been strengthened through the whole process and I am more in love with him now than when we got married. Seeing him as a father warms my heart and gives me goosebumps. I love waking up and seeing the two of them sleeping side by side each morning. As I sat in class this morning taking notes about research ethics, I couldn't help but feel proud of my baby boy and how content he was. Our bond is special and I love gazing into his eyes, as the love we have for each other is unconditional. He watches me so intently and I feel present in the moment as he naps on my lap. His smile makes me feel joyful and I can't help but stare at him. My facial muscles were sore at lunchtime from laughing and smiling so much. It was wonderful to have him with me this morning and I am grateful for the flexibility built into the PhD program. Despite what other people think or say about me returning to school so early, I am at peace with my decision. My mantra since teaching yoga is "no judgment … just love" and this couldn't be more true since becoming a mother. Everyone has an opinion and wants to give you their two cents about parenting, and I have learned that I have to do what feels right for my son, my husband, and me.

Rereading my journal entry from July 10, 2014, really solidifies the importance of place in a narrative inquiry. "Places and people are inseparable. Places exist only with reference to people, and the meaning of place can be revealed only in terms of human responses to the particular environment used as a framework for daily living" (Violich, 1985, p. 113). The author reminds me how connected I feel to the country home my husband and I built together because it is a place full of love, learning, home cooking, and gardening. I felt at ease being at school while my husband took care of our son because I trust the relationship we have and the place that our son is growing up in. Before we got married, my husband and I lost our house to a devastating fire. Losing all your material possessions makes you appreciate the relationships in your life. Bateson (1989) writes, "You keep a house, but you make a home" (p. 119). I fully understand this quote after rebuilding our home, and I look forward to fostering new growth and relationships with my family.

The summer residency was held inside a newly constructed library on campus that contains floor-to-ceiling windows. Natural light streams in and there are beautiful spaces to meet and collaborate with peers. The library as a physical space is symbolic of what the PhD is all about—learning, growing, reading, and discovering how you can contribute a small piece to the research puzzle. Relph (1976) discusses our relationship with place as essential and compares it to our close relationships with people. The significance of place is highlighted by the relationships that take place in a particular space. I attribute my positive relationship with the library to my experiences as a child. When I was in elementary school, my class would walk down to the small rural library for a book exchange, and the librarian would read a book out loud to the class.

I always looked forward to this walk because I loved reading and listening to stories. The sheer wealth of knowledge contained inside a library always astounded me, and throughout my life I have kept a membership to whatever library was closest to my house.

Journal Entry – July 25, 2014

As I reflect on my residency experience, I am left with a variety of feelings and emotions. I feel emotionally and mentally exhausted but proud of myself for making it through. This summer has been very different for me with having a three-month-old son at home; however, my thinking has been pushed and challenged in a positive way. I was tested emotionally each morning as it was difficult to leave my baby boy, but I felt reassured knowing that he was well taken care of by my husband. I was tested mentally in the doctoral seminar to examine my lens and understand who I am and where I come from. My theoretical framework is constantly changing and my paradigm continues to evolve as I read more. My new reality involved pumping breastmilk on break and feeling disconnected from my peers but I wouldn't change anything. I felt pressure socially to go out with everyone but my priority remained getting home to feed my son. My connections with everyone from my cohort were not as strong as last summer; however, I think they understood why. I was tested physically as my body still doesn't feel like my own and I am working each day to feel comfortable in my own skin. I never imagined that the recovery after giving birth would be so long, but I need to be patient with myself and check my self-criticism at the door. My body is not accustomed to sitting for such long periods of time reading, researching, and writing, so I look forward to spending more time walking, biking, and swimming this summer. My greatest fear moving forward is not finishing my doctorate. I want to keep the momentum going as after last summer life got in the way and I didn't make research a priority. Setting realistic goals is important to me because I realize my number one focus right now is my son. He will be small for only a short period of time, so I want to enjoy and cherish each day we have together. We are on this journey together and I look forward to learning and growing alongside him. As he learns to crawl and sit up on his own I will be right there beside him journaling and looking at the world through his eyes.

In order to push beyond my personal experience, I want to return to the themes identified earlier. The themes of role identity, support, vulnerability, emotion, and transformation have helped me use my personal experience as a lens through which to understand greater life experience. Role identity is something that all parents deal with throughout parenthood. Feelings of guilt crop up when one identity is in conflict with another. Through my journey of motherhood so far I have learned that feelings of guilt don't serve me. My identities are not separate entities; in fact, they are woven together to create my whole self. When I am a graduate student, I am still a loving and caring mother, and when I am playing with my son, I am still a curious graduate student with many unanswered questions. Bateson (1989) views the continuities and discontinuities that women encounter in life. Composing a life involves attending to multiple dimensions of one's life and celebrating the differences that exist. I admire this view and I want to continue to look at my life with an appreciative lens.

The second theme present in my journal entries was support. I understand that my PhD experience would not be possible without the love and support of my husband. This brings me to question the experiences of single-parent graduate students. What supports need to be in place for them to be successful? I often find myself wishing my family lived closer to help out with childcare. I want the support my husband is providing to be sustainable for the long haul, and the university providing quality childcare would certainly help with this. Is the theme of support similar for graduate student fathers? Are spouses making sacrifices in order for graduate student fathers to complete their studies?

The themes of emotion and vulnerability go hand in hand. I opened myself up to being vulnerable and sharing my feelings and in return heard many wonderful stories from other parents about their experiences. Being vulnerable encourages others to be vulnerable, and in this space deep, authentic relationships can be formed. Brown (2010) writes:

> Owning our story can be hard but not nearly as difficult as spending our lives running from it. Embracing our vulnerabilities is risky but not nearly as dangerous as giving up on love and belonging and joy—the experiences that make us the most vulnerable. Only when we are brave enough to explore the darkness will we discover the infinite power of our light. (p. 6)

We are generally taught by society not to be vulnerable, to hide our feelings because it is a sign of weakness. From my experience as a graduate student mother, I have gained strength from being vulnerable and have learned about how I deal with adversity. I am not afraid to be vulnerable as a mother, teacher, student, wife, or any other role I occupy because it keeps me authentic and accountable.

When I hear the word "transformation," my mind immediately goes to a caterpillar transforming into a beautiful butterfly. I feel as though I have transformed into a more authentic version of myself. Motherhood has helped me shed my cocoon and spread my wings to new opportunities. My transformation is not complete—I have many more lessons to learn and stories to tell. "Professional people are reluctant to tell stories that may identify what could be perceived as lack, gap, or fault in professional practice or in difficulty with the act of teaching itself" (Fowler, 2006, p. 57). The author reminds us we can learn a lot by sharing who we are and opening ourselves up to the power of vulnerability. I hope that other parents feel supported in combining multiple identities into their lives after reading my story.

References

Bateson, M. C. (1989). *Composing a life.* New York, NY: Grove Press.

Brooks, R. (2012). Student-parents and higher education: A cross-national comparison. *Journal of Education Policy, 27*(3), 423–439.

Brown, B. (2010). *The gifts of imperfection: Let go of who you think you're supposed to be and embrace who you are.* City Center, MN: Hazelden.

Brown, L., & Watson, P. (2010). Understanding the experiences of female doctoral students. *Journal of Further and Higher Education, 34*(3), 385–404. doi:10.1080/0309877X.2010.484056

Carter, S., Blumenstein, M., & Cook, C. (2013). Different for women? The challenges of doctoral studies. *Teaching in Higher Education, 18*(4), 339–351. doi:10.1080/13562517.2012.719159

Castaneda, M., & Isgro, K. (Eds.). (2013). *Mothers in academia.* New York, NY: Columbia University Press.

Connelly, R., & Ghodsee, K. (2014). *Professor mommy: Finding work–family balance in academia.* Lanham, MD: Rowman & Littlefield.

Eisenbach, B. (2013). Finding a balance: A narrative inquiry into motherhood and the doctoral process. *Qualitative Report, 18*(34), 1–13. Retrieved from http://search.ebscohost.com.roxy.nipissingu.ca/login.aspx?direct=true&db=eric&AN=EJ1005511&site=ehost-live&scope=site

Evans, E., & Grant, C. (Eds.). (2008). *Mama PhD: Women write about motherhood and academic life.* New Brunswick, NJ: Rutgers University Press.

Fowler, L. C. (2006). *A curriculum of difficulty: Narrative research and the practice of teaching.* New York, NY: Peter Lang.

Grassetti, M. (2013). Navigating academia while balancing motherhood: A reflective journey of a circuitous path. *Journal of the Motherhood Initiative, 4*(1), 9–20.

Grenier, R. S., & Burke, M. C. (2008). No margin for error: A study of two women balancing motherhood and PhD studies. *The Qualitative Report, 13*(4), 581–604. Retrieved from http://www.nova.edu.ssss/QR/QR13-4/grenier.pdf

Lynch, K. D. (2008). Gender roles and the American academe: A case study of graduate student mothers. *Gender and Education, 20*(6), 585–605. doi:10.1080/09540250802213099

Mason, M., Wolfinger, N., & Goulden, M. (2013). Do babies matter? Gender and family in the ivory tower. New Brunswick, NJ: Rutgers University Press.

Mason, M. A., & Mason Ekman, E. (2008). *Mothers on the fast track: How a generation can balance family and careers.* New York, NY: Oxford University Press.

McClusky, H. Y. (1963). The course of the adult life span. In W. C. Hallenbeck (Ed.), *Psychology of adults*. Chicago, IL: Adult Education Association of the U.S.A.

Moreau, M., & Kerner, C. (2015). Care in academia: An exploration of student parents' experiences. *British Journal of Sociology of Education, 36*(2), 215–233.

Relph, E. (1976). *Place and placelessness*. London, England: Pion.

Springer, K. W., Parker, B. K., & Leviten-Reid, C. (2009). Making space for graduate student parents: Practice and politics. *Journal of Family Issues, 30*(4), 435–457.

Violich, F. (1985). Towards revealing the sense of place: An intuitive "reading" of four Dalmatian towns. In D. Seamon & R. Mugerauer (Eds.), *Dwelling, place and environment: Towards a phenomenology of person and world* (pp. 133–136). Dordrecht, The Netherlands: Martinus Nijhoff.

Ward, K., & Wolf-Wendel, L. (2012). *Academic motherhood: How faculty manage work and family*. New Brunswick, NJ: Rutgers University Press.

I've Been to Me

Jennifer Barnett

The notion of motherhood as constitutive of feminine gender identity, of women's social role, and as desirable and fulfilling for all women remains entrenched in industrial, urban, and rural societies ... studies have shown that increasing numbers of women in Western Europe and North America are rejecting motherhood and choosing to remain childfree ... only a small proportion of women make this choice while the majority continue, at some stage in their lives, to become mothers. (Gillespie, 2003, pp. 122–123)

I love children. I love to watch little babies when they first find their hands; the expression of uninhibited joy on the face of three-year-olds as they blow bubbles on a warm summer's day; the momentary look of shock on the faces of twelve-year-olds when they experience success for the first time in a difficult task—or get asked out for their first date. All these instances are little pieces of heaven.

I love children. I became a teacher and worked for years in an elementary school. I spent day in, day out surrounded by other people's children—but for the year they were in my class, I referred to them as "my kids." My job as a teacher was to teach more than subjects—more than books, history, mathematics, and music. I cared enough to worry and advocate if I noticed a need. I gave my job my heart and my soul—I gave "my kids" every ounce of my energy. It was common for my students in grade seven and eight to say, "Ms. Barnett, you would be a great mom. Why don't you have children?" Modernity may have "given rise to wider possibilities for women to shape a fulfilling gender identity that is separate and uncoupled from the hegemonic ideal of motherhood" (Gillespie, 2003, p. 134), but the message "women should have children" still existed in the consciousness of these early teens.

I love children. I pursued my master's degree in education. This pursuit was complicated by a vice-principal who informed me that I was too young to be doing a master's degree and that I should be doing what other women my age did—specifically, finding a man and having children. After "accidents" such as surprise parent meetings being scheduled by the vice-principal on nights I had reserved for master's classes, I learned how to lie. If class was on Tuesday I would tell everyone it was Wednesday and the "accidents" stopped conflicting with my graduate class schedule. The pressure to quit, however, did not. But I didn't want to find a man and have some children; I wanted to obtain my master's degree.

I love children. When I graduated with my master's degree, the teachers at my new school had the grade ones wish me a happy master's day. Generalizing, as kids will do, they started wishing all the adults they ran across a happy master's day. I am sure some went home that night and wished the adults in their lives a happy master's day as well.

My love of children, my love of my job, and my love of learning took me into PhD studies. Teaching full-time during the day, I would drive two and a half hours to the city and take courses at night. When class was done, I would drive back home and then get up at 5 a.m. to get ready to teach. I love children but I could not have done these classes if I had children.

I applied for a long-term appointment at a university teaching in a bachelor of education program. I took a leave of absence from teaching, moved to a new city, and began a new job—that of the university professor. Here I am years later—a tenured professor, five years from retirement.

I still miss teaching children in the elementary classroom because I love children. When asked to write this narrative, I originally started to talk about all the obstacles I encountered to explain why I am still childless. I then deleted everything I wrote because they were not the reasons why I chose not to have children. While it is true that I have never had a partner I wanted to have children with, this too is not the reason. Besides, as a single woman I also know there are options available to me to have children if I so choose. I love children, yet I have chosen not to go down that road. Why did I make this choice? Was it a choice? In thinking on this I have to admit that the choice not to have children was neither planned nor conscious. It was simply a matter of keeping my focus on the brass ring. I wanted the PhD, but I certainly did not choose not to have children as a means of securing the PhD. Rather than considering myself as childless, I prefer Gillespie's (2003) notion of "childfree." Smith and Smith (2008) point out that the word "childless" implies that to have children is the natural state and to be without children is deemed less. I do not consider myself less of a woman for not having a child or being married.

A friend of mine told me not to use the word "selfish" in this chapter, as this is something we single, childless/childfree people are often accused of being. The word "selfish" is often defined as being totally absorbed in yourself and in your own good, and being fixated on your own desires. I will readily admit that wanting the graduate degrees and holding them aloft as a goal for attainment does appear to be a fixation on my own desires. But, I beg to question, what is wrong with that? As the word "selfish" has negative connotations and I do not feel one ounce of guilt, I guess it is not the right word in my situation. Childfree may frequently be "seen as deviant, unfeminine, and an unhealthy choice for women, one that transgresses traditional constructions of femininity" (Gillespie, 2003, p. 124), but I do not feel deviant or unfeminine. I feel that I am simply a childfree woman professor who has made the choice to be such.

Maushart (2003) argues that the rise in childlessness figures is a corrective swing to culturally deal with the atypical fertility pattern that occurred during the baby boom (p. 127). It is a fact that "not all women want to be mothers. Not all of them believe that a woman's only route toward the fulfillment of her destiny is to bring up children. Although the maternal urge has always been regarded as a universal trait, we are now finding out that it is not" (Smith & Smith, 2008, p. 118). Motherhood and childcare are cultural constructions and, defined through that lens, not an innate female capacity. The meaning culture embeds in the understanding of motherhood and womanhood often is centred on women's reproductive role. I believe there are other social concepts of womanhood—such as being a successful woman professor—that are just as viable (Ramazanoglu, 1989, p. 70) and in essence need to be ingrained just as heavily into our culture as motherhood is with being feminine.

I love my life. It is in this simple sentence that the truth can be found. I love my job and I love teaching. Trimberger (2005) notes that "fulfilling work can foster autonomy in women—autonomy that does not arise out of isolation or individualism … such a woman enjoys a high degree of self-determination and self-definition and feels that she is a whole person" (pp. 115–116). In my job I spend hours preparing lessons and trying to model good teaching practices. Every minute of every workday is consumed with teaching, research, or service to the university. If I had children, I could not do my job to the standard that I hold for myself. In fact, I have very little life outside of work. My friends all work with me and are also professors. Sociologists see friendship as a key component of building a community rooted in companionship and support, and one that provides a sense of belonging (Trimberger, 2005, p. 230). My friends are my family and work is where we congregate. I get a great deal of satisfaction being at work, working or just being present in the work environment. I could not be at work as much as I would like if I had children. I fear I would come to resent these children as my heart belongs to my career.

But perhaps this is all an excuse, as how would I know I would resent the time a child would take away from my work—I've never had a child. I have never actively sought to have a child. Mind you, I also have never made the conscious decision to be childfree. Having children just took second place to the master's, the doctorate, and tenure. To be honest, having children also took second place to travelling and being able to purchase things I want, including fragile knick-knacks and light-coloured furniture. I like my freedom and I love my life just the way it is.

If it appears that I believe having children means giving up other things in life, that is because I do in fact believe this to be true. I remember a friend of mine, who was a fabulous teacher and mother of five, commenting that she could get a master's but did not have the money or the time, and with this comment she sounded angry. I turned to her and asked if she could go back in time, would she choose not to have children and instead create time to undertake a master's degree? She appeared stunned and then smiled and answered no. That's when I noticed that this is where we differed. Unger (2003) notes that "it can be misleading to speak of the focus of our lives as something that we value ... it is more accurate to say that the focus of my life is a *precondition for certain things that I value*" (p. 185). In her study of those who chose to remain childfree, Gillespie (2003) found that *freedom* was a predominant theme, and the push away from motherhood came from the perception of losses motherhood would cause. If I had children I would not have travelled to Russia, Africa, England, or Italy. I believe that I would not have attained my PhD and possibly not even the master's. The majority of the women in my graduate programs were older with grown children or younger with no children. I look at my female colleagues at the university—a significant number who are on tenure track and have tenure do not have children. Those who came to the university after retiring from the education system frequently have grown children. The young children who frequent our faculty get-togethers belong to the male professors. And yet, please do keep in mind that never once did I consciously decide I would not have children so I could get my PhD. I did not make a conscious choice to not have children so I could have this life.

Back in the early 1980s the singer Charlene had a hit song that I loved, but not for the intended message of the songwriter. In the lyrics of the song one woman is addressing another woman. The woman who is speaking has travelled and lived a life full of excitement. She said she did this because she "had to be free." The woman she is speaking to is married with children. In comparing lives, the singer states that she is "all alone today," has "a weary heart," is now "bitter," and feels incomplete owing to "unborn children." She tells the mother and wife that paradise is a lie, and explains, "I've been to paradise but I've never been to me." Though the intent of this song was to promote motherhood, at sixteen years of age I found the freedom the singer was lamenting appealed to me instead. The idea of travelling the world sounded marvellous, and seeing "things a woman isn't supposed to see," though slightly frightening, was also exciting! (That line in the song drove my mind to all kinds of places and imaginings.) I remember listening to this song and thinking the singer was crazy not to appreciate the wonderful life she had.

I love children, yet to this day I have never cried "for unborn children that might have made me complete." Sorry, Charlene. I will admit when I play with my nieces and nephews I sometimes feel that I missed out on something, but this feeling is short-lived. In truth, I am complete and continue to make myself complete daily. I follow my heart, my gut, and my dreams. By doing so, I find sturdy roots in me. I happily remain a single, bisexual woman in her late forties. When I retire in five years I hope to work with the United Nations, building schools and educating teachers in other parts of the world. I would love to see the children have the advantages of an education. I love children. I love learning. And I love my life.

I find it odd that people search for a reason to explain why I am the way I am. As a young person I told my mother that I was never getting married, to which she responded, "What did I do wrong?" I have heard my age used as a reason for my marital status and my lack of children (e.g., "She's too old now to have children, so why would she get married?"). In 2003 Maushart notes, "Marriage without children is still widely regarded as a social aberration" (p. 127). In 1995 Wallerstein and Blakelee claim, "Marriage needs children. That's what makes a marriage. Otherwise it's just a date" (p. 70). I do not believe either of these statements is true. I simply love to learn and have been true to my love. I have been told that my love of education and learning is abnormal (e.g., "You've gone to school enough"); this is usually tied with the perspective that I need to move forward (i.e., have children and find a man). What these individuals do not realize is that "being alone can be a wonderful soul-nurturing state—if you enjoy your own company. There is tremendous pleasure in giving yourself the luxury of time to mull and muse about your feelings and reactions to the day's activities—in peaceful solitude" (Smith & Smith, 2008, p. 76). Those who are aware of my sexuality assume I will not marry because I would be forcing myself to choose a man as a solo partner for the rest of my life and thus would not get what I need—the assumption is that I cannot be monogamist to a man (never a woman) or that I need both men and women in my sex life. These statements are very heteronormative, assuming life can be lived in only one specific way, assuming one way to be "normal." In discussing moral meaning making, Kegan (1982) states, "It is this kind of absolutism, practically excluding from the human community those who fall outside the ideological or social group, which can come to an end when the evolution of meaning transcends its embeddedness in the societal" (p. 65). Often individuals with this perspective of normal as defined by the societal try to isolate the one instant in my life that caused me to pursue learning and forgo marriage and children. They forget (or choose to ignore) that "persons are not processes, and there's no one natural way to break up a person's life into discrete events" (Perry, 2008, p. 10).

It can be argued there are many biological, cultural, and social categories that did work together to influence my current life. In fact, those who believe in the sociological feminist theory of intersectionality (see Collins, 2000; Crenshaw, 1991) could have a field day when attempting to explain why I turned out this way. I was born female to traditionally minded parents. As such, there were things I was not allowed to do because I was a girl. I was raised Roman Catholic and had to endure additional catechism lessons after school hours as my mother thought it would be beneficial. My mother was a stay-at-home wife who got much of her self-identity from keeping a good house and preparing good meals and raising good kids. My dad worked as a professor in a faculty of education and travelled. Using intersectionality, one could argue that I rebelled against the image of womanhood presented in my family and chose to emulate my father. It could be assumed that I desired the economic freedom and authority illuminated by my father and sought to secure the same for myself. In fact, this argument could even be used to claim I wanted to be a man, but since I couldn't alter my sex I instead sought to incorporate masculine traits into my life. This stupidity could even be applied as an explanation of my bisexuality—I could not deny my womanhood though I wanted to be a man. They could base their claim on the fact that I had witnessed "gender inequality: economic dependence based on women's lesser labor force participation ... dependence on men's greater authority and power over decision making in both the family and most workplaces, [and] dependence on men's power to define social reality" (Kane, 1998, 612–613). I witnessed the transformation of "biological males and females in discrete and hierarchized genders ... mandated by cultural institutions (the family, the residual forms of 'the exchange of women,' obligatory heterosexuality)" (Butler, 2006, p. 100). It could be argued that the interrelated cultural patterns of oppression were made manifest in the life my parents created for me as a girl child. It could also be argued that my rebellion against the traditional roles has resulted in me not wanting to have children. By my own admission I love children, so it could also be argued that I do not want to bring a child into this oppressive world.

I have to admit, having written out these arguments, that even I can see how my experiences growing up could be used to explain why I turned out the way I did, why I did not marry, remained childless, and pursued my education.

While it is true that these situations did influence my understanding of the world, my choice to remain single and childfree cannot be explained away so easily. Though I hate gender oppression in any form, I love being a woman; I do not want to be a man. In terms of my sexuality, I knew I was different when I was still a little girl who thought the world was perfect. Except that one time to my mother, I have never said that I will not marry, simply that I did not marry. Who knows what the future may hold. And when it comes to my "choice" to pursue my education and career instead of having children, it was not a conscious decision so it cannot be called a choice. I simply followed my heart, which directed me to pursue my love of learning. Being a university professor is the embodiment of learning. I share knowledge with and learn from my students. I research and read as part of my job. I attend conferences and talk to very bright people about a whole host of interesting topics. I did not choose to be childfree; it's just the way my life turned out. And it is a wonderful life. I love being me.

References

Butler, J. (2006). *Gender trouble: Feminism and the subversion of identity*. New York, NY: Routledge Classics.

Charlene. (1977). I've never been to me. On *Charlene* [Record album]. Los Angeles, CA: Motown Record Corporation.

Collins, P. H. (2000). Gender, black feminism, and black political economy. *Annals of the American Academy of Political and Social Sciences, 568*, 41–53.

Crenshaw, K. W. (1991). Mapping the margins: Intersectionality, identity politics, and violence against women of color. *Stanford Law Review, 43*(6), 1241–1299.

Gillespie, R. (2003). Childfree and feminine: Understanding the gender identity of voluntarily childless women. *Gender & Society, 17*(1), 122–136.

Kane, E. W. (1998). Men's and women's beliefs about gender inequality: Family ties, dependence, and agreement. *Sociological Forum, 13*(4), 611–637.

Kegan, R. (1982). *The evolving self: Problem and process in human development*. Cambridge, MA: Harvard University Press.

Maushart, S. (2003). *Wifework: What marriage really means for women*. London, England: Bloomsbury.

Perry, J. (2008). The problem of personal identity. In J. Perry (Ed.), *Personal identity* (pp. 3–30). Berkeley: University of California Press.

Ramazanoglu, C. (1989). *Feminism and the contradictions of oppression*. London, England: Routledge.

Smith, C. S., & Smith, H. B. (2008). *Why women shouldn't marry: Being single by choice*. Fort Lee, NJ: Barricade Books.

Trimberger, E. K. (2005). *The new single woman*. Boston, MA: Beacon Press.

Unger, P. (2003). Fission and the focus of one's life. In R. Martin & J. Barresi (Eds.), *Personal identity* (pp. 184–198). Malden, MA: Blackwell.

Wallerstein, J., & Blakeslee, S. (1995). *The good marriage*. New York, NY: Houghton Mifflin.

PART THREE
Parenting within Academia: Friend or Foe?

Fatherhood and the PhD
Time Management, Perfectionism, and the Question of Value
Geoff Salomons

When I started my master's in political science at the University of British Columbia, my daughter was just over half a year old. I was often asked what it was like being a parent and a graduate student. I would often reply—half-joking, half-serious—that I spent much more time just sitting on the couch, but that just sitting on the couch was infinitely more entertaining. But the truth it is, it is a constant struggle. It seems as though I'm stating the obvious when I write that, and yet that is precisely what it is. The key to this struggle is that while it is a juggling act, the most important and the most difficult lesson to learn is to know when to let a ball drop. Doing so requires an immense amount of self-knowledge about your own capabilities, mood, and energy level, but also intimate knowledge of those things in your partner. Academic work ingrains a certain sense of perfectionism within people, if it is not there to begin with. Becoming a parent has forced me to resist some of those perfectionist tendencies. Being a parent while a graduate student is not just adding another ball into the mix, but asking you to start to juggle in a whole different way, without stopping. This narrative will discuss my experiences of being a PhD student and a parent through the lens of feminist political economy. I choose this lens because the biggest struggle for me has been determining priorities of competing demands. The decisions I make concerning my time and energy are decisions of what I value. Feminist political economy highlights the fact that within our current economic context of late capitalism, we more easily value what earns or saves us money.

I am a thirty-five-year-old heterosexual male. My partner and I have been married for ten years (April 2006). We had our first child, a girl, in January 2011 and our second daughter in July 2014. My partner is an elementary school teacher, which makes things easier as it is a profession that easily travels. We have not come across the issue other couples have had to deal with where we face a decision between one's career or one's relationship—a common problem that faces academics, especially in relationships with other academics. Nevertheless, I have taken a more circuitous route to my current program, a political science PhD at the University of Alberta, the result of which has put additional strain on my relationship with my partner.

When we first met I was enrolled at the Vancouver School of Theology, a seminary for the Anglican, United, and Presbyterian denominations. In addition, approximately half the student body was composed of "others" who were there for other theological or personal spiritual exploration and not ordained ministry. I had entered hoping to go on to teach theology. I was the son of a conservative Dutch Calvinist minister, and when I broke out of that bubble and discovered more "liberal" theological approaches I wanted to share with others what had been for me a life-altering discovery. However, by the time I graduated in May 2008 I had realized that the job prospects for teaching theology in Canada were incredibly slim, as there were only three or four progressive theological institutions in Canada and many of those where unlikely to be hiring or expanding in the foreseeable future. During my time at VST, for example, the school experienced a financial crisis and a third of staff and faculty were cut. In the wake of this, VST was deemed one of the most financially stable theological institutions in Canada. The 2008 financial crisis made things even worse. Additionally, I was attending an Anglican church and had considered ordained Anglican ministry as a potential option. However, the Diocese of New Westminster was embroiled in a global controversy over its decision to bless same-sex unions and reminded me of my father's denomination's debates over female leadership—primarily focused on ordained leadership—which frustrated me to no end. These debates were about erecting boundaries: who is in, who is out; who counts, who doesn't. The man I spent the past number of years studying—Jesus—seemed more about breaking down barriers than anything. By the time I was done seminary I knew I did not want to work for the church. I still wanted to teach so I thought philosophy would be the most plausible transition at that point. So I spent that next year studying for the GRE, reading, working what odd jobs I could, applying to graduate schools, and doing the majority of the household work. That fall, however, was the 2008 financial crisis, and in 2009 when rejection letter after rejection letter came back they all said the same thing: every school had had an unprecedented number of applicants, often double or triple the average of the previous years, thus making the application pool that much more competitive. Combine that with the fact that I was applying to philosophy programs with a master of divinity, from a school with an unusual pass/fail grading scheme. My applications were obviously not on the top of anyone's pile.

Between the Vancouver School of Theology and the University of British Columbia I worked a couple of jobs as a bartender, something with which I was familiar. I was fortunate to land a job at a new restaurant at the University of British Columbia, which paid union wages plus tips. On good nights, I was making more than my partner. I also decided to switch into political science, studying public policy. I could at least get into a master's program and then work for the public service or an environmental NGO/think tank, or continue the academic route if that opportunity presented itself. My partner continued teaching, getting increasingly antsy about starting a family while I figured out a new life trajectory. During this gap period we had our first child. This gave us an opportunity to get used to being parents before I dove back into graduate school.

The reason I give all this background is that during the gap period, I was gainfully employed and I contributed as much if not more to our household finances. Prior to and since that period, my partner has provided the lion's share of financial support for our household. While I was able to gain significant funding from the University of British Columbia and the University of Alberta, it was nowhere near the amount that my partner brought in. This provided significant tension within our relationship as she, at times, felt trapped because she had to keep working since I wasn't making as much money. At the PhD level this remains the case, despite the fact that this program is and should be treated as an actual job. And yet, for my partner, it remains "school." As a result, the biggest tension that we have had to deal with is what is considered actual work—the kind that brings in money—and other work—the kind that does not bring in money.

For feminist political economists such as Marilyn Waring (1999), this distinction between paid work and other work is more adequately described as the formal and informal economy. Waring's central point is that national accounting systems (GDP, etc.), upon which most policy decisions are based, are systemically biased against the informal economy. Feminist political economy highlights this distinction because it is often the men who work in the formal economy—paid employment—whereas women often work within the informal economy—housework, childcare, and so forth. Such tasks are informal so long as they are simply carried out by individuals who are not paid for them, despite their necessity. This lack of a formal price on such labour systemically undervalues care work (Kershaw, 2005). This value can be both a matter of status of the activity—domestic tasks historically reserved for the servant class in aristocracies—or an actual financial undervaluing of the labour simply because it is not part of the formal economy. If, for example, one hires a maid and/or a nanny, those tasks become part of the formal economy. As women increasingly enter the workforce, the domestic tasks are transferred to those willing to do them, in some cases, with detrimental effects as the domestic tasks that are outsourced *must* be valued less than the other work done by an individual—otherwise it is not worth it, financially speaking, to do that work. Paying a nanny ten dollars an hour to work at a job that pays eleven dollars an hour is not, in the end, worth the time (Ehrenreich & Hochschild, 2004).

In my own situation, this issue has played out in two different ways. First, I do the majority of the domestic labour in our household for a number of reasons. I enjoy cooking to such an extent that cooking dinner is my own "me" time. In addition, I feel as though my partner has a higher clutter threshold than I and so I will tidy, do dishes, and wash clothes more often. But more importantly, my partner works full-time as a teacher. When she comes home after a day with her students (she teaches special ed so some days can be especially trying) she is exhausted and needs some time to just decompress. So once our daughters are home from daycare I am often responsible for dinner, while my partner winds down. If we are lucky our daughter will occupy herself with floor puzzles or colouring; other days she wants to watch television to which we give in more often than we would like—but more on that later.

The second way this has played out is by way of the fact that I am a graduate student and thus I have the "time" to do these tasks. Here the distinction between formal and informal economic work comes into play. As a PhD student I am, in a sense, formally employed. I have research assistant work to do as well as my own research. However, it is not like a typical nine-to-five job as it grants me much more flexibility with regard to my time allocation.

This question of time is particularly vexing for students who essentially make up their own schedule, even more so for students, such as myself, who are in the comprehensive exam stage of the PhD program. While this is a stage that every academic goes through, with the explicit goal of gaining sufficient knowledge of our field to qualify us to teach, I am finding that an implicit learning goes along with it that is almost equally important: time management. Gone are the classes, syllabi, weekly readings, and assignments. Now we have an enormous task placed in front of us—learn your field—with a significant amount of time to do so.[1] If other things come up that take away time from my school work (such as the car breaking down), I can make up the work by skimming my readings more or not having as much time to dedicate to editing a paper and so on. The comprehensive exam stage thus operates as a transition stage from short-term to long-term time management, an essential skill necessary for the completion of the dissertation.

This transition from short-term time to long-term time management is undoubtedly a tricky transition for many students. We have to balance a large future project against the immediate demands of everyday life. I have a significant amount of reading to accomplish and two forty-page papers to write, but I also need groceries, I need to cook, I need to do laundry, I need to get the car repaired, and so on. The difficulty with doing this as a parent is you have a multitude of other immediate demands on your time that easily overcome the distant vague project you are working on. This issue is nothing new. Philosophically speaking, the term for the fact that we care for what is immediate is "propinquity" (Aristotle, trans. 1998, p. II.iii).

Now I have a child to pick up from daycare at a certain time each day, and once that child is home the likelihood of being able to continue working is much less. Even if I try to work I will likely be interrupted because someone just wants to see what I'm doing and sit on my lap or show me her stuffed animal. Dinner still needs to be cooked, and after dinner and a bit of playtime the bedtime routine begins. Unfortunately, like many children our daughter is not a fan of bedtime. The world is just too interesting a place to waste time with sleep. We follow the advice of all the parenting help guides to stick to a consistent routine: bath, stories, and lights out. However, this process can still take a few hours, with the final stage being the most difficult for us. Often we try to get lights out between 8:30 and 9:00, but the time from lights out to her actually falling asleep is often an hour, with each parent trading off as the other gets increasingly exasperated. Last night, she fell asleep just before 10 p.m. Since our alarm is set to go off at 6:45 a.m., I am pretty much ready for bed by this point. So from 5:00 p.m. till bedtime is occupied with parenting, leaving 8:00 a.m. to 5:00 p.m. free for "actual" work.

Yet as easy as that may sound, this is hardly the case. My time is more flexible and so I do make a concerted effort to do the majority of the housework. Part of it is because I can, but part of it is this distinction between formal and informal economics noted earlier. Like many couples, my partner and I fight about finances. While I am funded for my PhD, the amount is barely above the poverty line. This leaves the majority of our finances to come from my partner's work. In addition, and the reason I provided so much background earlier, my partner at times feels resentful for the fact that she has had to work to fund my education. This is exacerbated by the fact that I am on my third graduate degree (MDiv, MA, PhD). Because of the history of how my partner has supported me financially to achieve my career goals—even when they were in flux—I try to make more of an effort at home to make up for the lack of financial contribution. And so some of my work time is taken up with other tasks, some of which I do because they are easy to fit in—like laundry—others

because my flexible schedule makes them significantly easier to do—like bringing the car in for repairs. If I want to do any exercising (I am an avid cyclist),
that comes out of this eight-to-five block as well (although during the winter
months on the bike trainer I can sometimes get an article read).

The resulting struggle then is about defining priorities. While defining
priorities is something everybody does, we often end up defining our priorities
based on urgency. What we should be doing, and the reason I have turned to
feminist political economists to help analyze this narrative, is defining our
priorities based on what we value. It is here that the biggest lesson I have
learned, and am still learning, has to do with a sense of perfectionism with
regard to both my academic work and the work of parenting. As a student you
are constantly graded on your academic work. For those successful enough to
get into a PhD program, they have or have had to learn (as I have) a certain
level of perfectionism in order to get the grades that grant them admission
to such programs. Some of it is natural aptitude, but much of it is hard work
and determination. My grades in high school and undergrad were not very
stellar. Once I discovered something I was passionate about—theology—my
grades shot up. Prior to this I had bought into a mindset that aptitude was all
there was. Now, with hard work and a certain level of perfectionism, I could
get exceptional grades. I could spend additional time working on a paper
tweaking phrases and rewriting sentences, which might, in the end, push the
grade from an A– to an A or even an A+, or not. In the end, I need to be
satisfied with the work I was able to get done in the time I had to do it. I will
always feel as if I could have done more, or done something better, but at the
end of the day I need to let that go and try to do my best to be a parent and
an academic at the same time. In economic terms, the marginal return is not
necessarily worth the investment.

The same thing goes for parenting. With hard work and a certain level
of perfectionism, I could be father of the year, or at least be the father that I
hope and aspire to be. Unfortunately, the perfectionism of academia and the
perfectionism of parenting are constrained by a finite resource: time. We let
our daughter watch more television than we would like because it lets us get
other stuff done like cooking dinner, doing the dishes, folding the laundry,
writing book chapters and papers, reading for my comprehensive exam papers,
or even sleeping in a little on a Saturday morning. We know that passive screen
time is not terribly beneficial for young children, and, if we were able, we
would be less dependent upon such devices. My partner and I have an idea of
what kind of parents we would like to be, but constraints on time and money
get in the way. We have to make choices about what we value more: sleeping
in on a Saturday morning or making sure our daughter's playtime is always

interactive and engaging, even at seven in the morning. To be clear, we have not always made the best choices. We have given in to our daughter's demands more often than we should have and, as a result, are now paying for it as our daughter increasingly throws tantrums when she does not get her way. Part of this is just her age (they call it the terrible twos for a reason), but part of it is also the result of our parenting as we see other children much more obedient.

Setting priorities highlights the problems between informal and formal economies. Doing so forces us to ask the question of how we value the different things in our lives. One of the most common recommendations about time management of long-term projects is to establish a schedule that breaks up the larger project into smaller, more manageable pieces. Doing so makes the distant proximate. Putting a price on things is a way of making those vague trade-offs more immediate because it translates different values into a common, commensurable language. The question is whether that is even desirable when talking about parenting.

My area of research is environmental policy. Within this field, debates abound about how to properly "value" nature (O'Neill, 2006; Sagoff, 2007). The ecological economic answer is that nature is undervalued because it isn't properly priced, it is not part of the formal economy. Two approaches are often presented for how to include the environment into the formal economy: establish real markets (privatization) or establish theoretical markets (inquiring about people's "willingness to pay" for an environmental good). The question has obviously strong parallels to what has been discussed thus far. Does determining people's willingness to pay for an undisturbed landscape really capture how that is valued? What about differences in socio-economic status? Does a multi-millionaire who is willing to pay one million dollars to maintain a landscape value that more than a homeless person who is willing to pay five dollars? Or how do we reconcile culture differences in valuing the world? In an article in *The Province*, anthropologist Wade Davis highlights the cultural importance of the Sacred Headwaters to the Tahltan First Nation (the birthplace of the Stikine, Skeena, and Nass Rivers in British Columbia). He suggests that "to put a copper and gold mine on Todagin Mountain [in the Sacred Headwaters area] is like drilling for oil in the Sistine Chapel" (Luke, 2014).

These questions are also present with regard to parenting. Do we want to start putting a price on our time with our children? Would different activities be priced differently? Is taking my daughter for swimming lessons worth more than a walk in the park? Is a bike ride worth more or less than a family movie night? How do we then compare these things to the other demands on our time? Work on a puzzle with my daughter or go read an article? Cook a dinner with fresh ingredients that takes an hour and is healthy and delicious or order a pizza? While these are always the questions and trade-offs we are faced with, I resist trying to think about them in economic terms, just as I resist talking about environmental goods via "willingness to pay." Many of these trade-offs are incommensurable, but nevertheless decisions must be made. It is a constant balancing act and there are no easy answers to "How do you do it?" I am learning more every day and constantly making mistakes or having regrets. As with any task it is about taking those lessons and improving each and every day. I'm nearly done the comprehensive stage and I wish I had done things differently. I'll just have to try to do better during the dissertation stage. But for now I'm off to watch my daughter during her first swimming lesson, and then groceries, and then shovel the snow on the sidewalk, and then laundry, and make a lasagna, and then ... and then ... and then ... It is Saturday, after all.

Note

1   While different institutions do the comprehensive exams in different ways, the overall goal is the same. At the University of Alberta Political Science Department, the comprehensive exam takes the form of a paper and a syllabus for each of our two subfields. We are assigned a mentor and with that individual develop a reading list. The end goal then is a forty-page paper on the state of the subfield highlighting three major debates or issues. A syllabus for a second-year intro to subfield is also required. Finally, an oral defence of the paper—justifications for what was included and what was excluded—and syllabus complete the process. This process, of course, has its strengths and weaknesses, as do other comprehensive exam processes. The major one with regard to time management is that the open-ended nature of this process makes it much more difficult to specifically plan out the process as a whole. In comparison to comprehensive exams where you are given a set list and then have a closed-book exam (the process currently employed by the University of British Columbia Political Science Department), you can much more easily plan how much time you need to get the readings done in order to process and retain the information.

References

Ehrenreich, B., & Hochschild, A. R. (2004). *Global woman: Nannies, maids, and sex workers in the new economy*. New York, NY: Metropolitan Books.

Kershaw, P. W. (2005). *Carefair: Rethinking the responsibilities and rights of citizenship*. Vancouver, BC: UBC Press.

Luke, P. (2014, January 5). "The world is not dying. It's changing": Anthropologist and explorer Wade Davis has hope for the future. *The Province*. Retrieved from http://www.theprovince.com/technology/world+dying+changing+Anthropologist+explorer+Wade+Davis+hope+future/9348268/story.html

O'Neill, J. (2006). *Markets, deliberation and environment*. New York, NY: Routledge.

Sagoff, M. (2007). *The economy of the Earth: Philosophy, law, and the environment*. Cambridge, England: Cambridge University Press.

Waring, M. (1999). *Counting for nothing: What men value and what women are worth*. Toronto, ON: University of Toronto Press.

Going In and Coming Out
Understanding Ourselves as Mama Scholars

Lisa J. Starr and Kathleen M. Bortolin

We have to begin with women's own experience if we are to understand how profoundly it influences our perspectives, values, attitudes, and role in society. (Glazer-Raymo, 1999, p. 1)

Many of our colleagues—graduate students, faculty members, session-als, staff—are probably mothers and fathers. We think this because, on occasion, we glimpse a photo, arranged neatly on an otherwise messy desk, of a smiling, gap-toothed child. Or we witness a colleague or two climbing out of a minivan in an adjacent parking space, causing us to wonder briefly about their life beyond the ivory tower. Sometimes, and only if time allows, at the conclusion of more pressing dialogue, we inquire after a colleague's family—a polite curiosity. But we seldom dwell, preferring to quickly move our discourses along, focusing on more appropriate topics like book chapters, committee meetings, SSHRC applications; mothering, fathering, parenting is messy and best kept on the fringes of more serious academic-ing. Is it hushed because as parents we need to compartmentalize our commitments? Is it only vaguely hinted at because we fear being seen as less … less what? Committed? Intelligent? Sane? Insane? Here, however, in the pages of this chapter, we invite ourselves and our identities as parents into the academic landscape. We climb out of our minivans, exposing ourselves as academic parents, as *mama scholars*, in ways in which we have not often been invited to do. Through our narratives we tell our stories, and through these stories we hope to further our understandings about the tensions we face attempting to bridge the worlds of motherhood and academia.

Our struggles are not unique; much has been written about the challenges and tensions of being a woman, parent, and burgeoning academic (Acker & Armenti, 2004; Raddon, 2002). However, we choose to represent our challenges through the use of narratives because of their potential to engage the reader as a way of telling and a means for knowing (Bruner, 1990, as cited in Sparkes & Smith, 2008; Richardson, 2000). Among the many values of the narrative, in this analysis, we attempt to make sense of our own lives while creating a vehicle for questioning preconceptions directly tied to motherhood and academia. Our stories are intended to give access to our identities but also to create a sense of meaning in the emotional process of self-construction (Sparkes & Smith, 2008). Additionally, we are committed to creating writing that is meaningful to ourselves and others but also, as Richardson (2000) describes, is *accessible*:

> Research written in the narrative form could be more accessible … to other people who may not have access to social research written in a more conventional positivist style … and even to those who do not have access to these conventional forms of social science research but who could interact with the material in a different way—in a storied way. (cited in Tsang, 2000, p. 45)

Sharing our personal narratives serves two purposes: first to gain understanding of the process so that we may facilitate the type of deep, personal reflection required for transformative learning that enables people "to short-circuit the social currents that run through them and make them who they are" (Ryan, 2007, p. 349). Further, Davis-Manigaulte, Yorks, and Kasl (2006) assert that such a transformation includes a holistic change in how a person both affectively relates to and conceptually frames his or her experience; thus, it requires a healthy interdependence between affective and rational ways of knowing (p. 27). Austin and Hickey (2007) go further in their description of the importance of transformative practice and the role of the constituents:

> Socially transformative education draws both student and teacher into a consideration of their own positioning within the social dynamic, one that provokes the conscientisation necessary to understand the power of contemporary socialization processes that support structures of inequality, oppression and exploitation as achieved largely through the colonizing of mass or popular culture by the dictates and imperatives of global capital. (p. 22)

It is through the creation and articulation of our own narratives that we inquire into a space where method and representation come together, and in which form, function, and meaning are constructed through text. What follows are six vignettes that illustrate our different experiences as mama scholars. We have organized the vignettes around themes of identity and gender.

Following the first three vignettes we provide a brief discussion of how our notion of identity emerges through our stories. Following the fourth, we discuss the competing roles of mother and academic. We conclude with a brief insight into our own understandings of how our stories shape who we are as mama scholars.

Identity: Beyond Playdough, Laundry, and Sweatpants

Coming Out (Kathleen)

I slip the child-friendly earphones carefully over her head and plug them into the iPad. Ah … the iPad. I agonized over spending money on this gadget but am thinking that today alone makes it a worthwhile purchase. I notice a few faculty members and graduate students also using their iPads. I wonder if they're using the same apps as my daughter. Cutting Santa's hair? Playing Bejeweled? Dressing up Hello Kitty in a cutesy-pie dragon costume? More people file into the classroom for our late-afternoon PhD writing group. Today we're talking about narrative inquiry. I seldom get to attend these extra-curricular events, notices sent endlessly and almost painfully through my department's graduate student listserv. Each invitation stings a little when I read the time and realize it's during swim lessons, school pickup times, that playdate, this doctor's appointment. I take out my archaic pen and paper. No iPad for me. I pull the earphone gently from my daughter's head and remind her for the fifth time that if she needs to speak any time during the next hour she has to whisper. I pull out a snack and place it carefully beside her. We have already peed. Twice. Friends and colleagues take note of her existence in the room. Well, some do. Some ignore her completely. Which I almost prefer. Is that awful? Because those who notice her and smile at me betray an ambiguity that I can't quite decipher. Annoyed? Empathetic? Confused? I tell whoever will listen that I had to bring her; my partner (I call him my "partner" only when I'm at university) couldn't come home early today, and I've called in all my favours from the neighbours. All true. I laugh nervously and say things like, "Thank goodness for iPads," and "Oh, she should use narrative inquiry to explore her phenomenological study into monkey-bar accident survivors." No one laughs. Chewing my nails, I am already plotting my escape plan. I have to leave ten minutes early to pick up my son from daycare. I was given a stern warning when I dropped him off that morning that I cannot come past 5:20. I can't remember now what the consequence would be if I were late, but it was akin to selling him to the circus. A part of me is proud to have my five-year-old daughter sitting beside me. She gets to see me in this role—a grown-up with a life beyond playdough, laundry, and sweatpants. Will she remember this one day, when she's older and can make sense of it? "Oh yeah ... Mum toiled and sacrificed to do her PhD when I was a kid while I spent time dressing up Hello Kitty ... digitally." But another, bigger part of me is just worried. Worried that these two worlds—that of an unpredictable five-year-old and a group of no-nonsense narrative inquirers—don't quite mix. I don't want her to disrupt the group, and I don't want the group, or certain important members of the group, to see me in this role. Mother. It almost feels like a dirty word. Synonymous with baggage, lack of commitment, unknown priorities, can't-make-it-to-department-gatherings-because-she-doesn't-want-the-boy-sold-to-the-circus. I realize that I have tried hard to keep these worlds separate. Mother. PhD student. And now they are crashing into one another, as they do all the time, every day, every hour in my own head. But sitting here with the charged-up iPad, evading smiles, I feel like I'm coming out to this community as a mother. And it makes me nervous.

The Birthday Girl (Lisa)

I am forty-two years old and am haunted by perfection or, more accurately, the constant need for it: the need to do more, write more, be more. I think, I discuss, I share, I work, I write, I say yes, I make dinner, load the dishwasher, read stories, wash hair, but am haunted by the voice of the birthday girl taunting me, "You haven't done enough ... you need to work harder."

When I was a child, a small ceramic figurine of a birthday girl sat on my grandmother's dresser. I thought she was beautiful, so pretty in her pink dress with her cute little cherub face and pretty blond hair—everything I was not. I could wind it up and listen to the tune to "Happy Birthday," the song everyone gets on the one day of the year when they are special.

"You need to take care of yourself, because you cannot take care of anyone else until you do...." What am I teaching my daughters about being a woman, about being a mother—that nothing they do will ever be enough? But it won't be enough. In the secret society of motherhood, no one tells you how unimportant you become. You are not a priority; you are not valued or rewarded for your ability to rear little functioning members of society. No one cares that your children are polite, kind, caring because you have spent countless, repetitive hours showing them, helping them, reminding them. You are expected to do this, and do it well ... that's what mothers do. There are immeasurable unspoken expectations for mothers but you cannot possibly meet those. And once you start being a mother, you can't back out, you are in for life. If you do back out, you are vilified.

I want to be me and I don't know who that is. I want to sing and laugh and write and read ... and become someone that is cherished ... not someone's someone who doesn't even have a name. How did I get lost in here?

Today (Lisa)

The alarm rings at 7:05 but I am already awake thinking about what I have to do today. Drive to work [Please let the traffic be light. I don't want to be late again]. Meet Kathleen at 9:30 to talk about writing a paper [I hope I don't have to tell her that I have to leave early. That will really impress her]. Meet Kathy at 10:30 for the association meeting [I do have to leave early because I have to walk back over to MacLaurin to teach. Did I remember to let her know?]. Teach English at 11:30 [Unit planning, maybe I can squeeze out more from the last PowerPoint because I don't have anything else, or maybe I will make it a work class; they will like me for that. Impart wisdom, share stories, bullshit my way through it for today]. Teach Instructional Strategies at 1:00 [Presentations—thank God—I have something ready for after. I wonder if these presentations are working for them, if they are learning anything. I should ask].

I hear my daughter getting ready downstairs and I drag myself out of bed, get in the shower, and get dressed so I can drive Emma to catch the ferry for school. I come home, put waffles in the toaster for Madeline and go to wake her up. She gets dressed, I dry my hair, put makeup on while thinking about what has to go in what bag and who has to be where and when. [I have to respond to Mark today and probably follow up with Nina because they are three hours ahead, but I can probably put off replying to student teachers at least until tonight or maybe tomorrow. Shit, did I post the link to the article for the presentation? I have to check before I leave]. I pack Madeline's lunch [Is a fruit cup really a healthy snack?]. I remind her to hurry up because I have to go by 8:15. Have you put your dishes away? Brushed your teeth, washed your face, brushed your hair? [I don't want to get stuck in traffic and I want to make my first meeting on time. I am late for everything, but if I get all the green lights then I can save about five minutes and maybe get to my first meeting on time, or I will have to use the traffic excuse again. Have I used that one with her yet?]. I pack myself a lunch [if I don't start eating healthier, I will just get fatter... that will really attract someone. Plus I need to save the money. Five dollars a day adds up to about twenty dollars a week, eighty dollars a month ... about six hundred dollars a year ... half a mortgage payment ... two credit-card payments ... Madeline's singing lessons each month ... five months of car insurance]. I load up the car and Madeline, remind her to go to Yvonne's after school and that we have soccer tonight, then drop her off at school. Love you, have a good day [Can I U-turn right in front of the school to get back on the main road? No, I should drive around ... it is the responsible thing to do]. I meet [A paper about motherhood and academia, that pretty much sums up my life ... if I had time for academia]. Take notes at the CSSE meeting trying to keep up with what everyone is saying [God, I wish I could type faster. I have no idea who they are talking about. I'll have to catch up with Kathy later. I've gotta go]. I teach the first class, then the second. I go upstairs and reply to emails, post notes to Moodle then realize I am late [Crap, I have to go. I'll drive the back way to get around the traffic on Mackenzie. No time for lunch again, maybe I will have time to eat it at the red lights]. Drive home. Pick up Madeline at 4:00. Go home to change and pick up the soccer stuff [God, I need caffeine. Do I have time to make a cup of tea?]. Pick up Emma from the ferry at 5:00 [Just keep going]. Drive to Madeline's soccer practice at 5:00. Drop her off. Drive to Emma's soccer practice at 5:30 [Just keep going]. Drive back to pick up Madeline from soccer to take her to singing lessons. Drop Madeline off at singing lessons [Just keep going]. Go to McDonald's to buy dinner. Drive back to pick up Madeline then over to pick up Emma from soccer. We eat dinner in the car. We drive home [I have marking to do, two papers to write, transcripts to read, classes to prep for and … oh yeah … a dissertation to write]. Does anyone else understand how hard this is?

Embedded in our narratives is the notion of identity and the struggle to define and even accept who we are as mama scholars. Juggling the roles and responsibilities required of motherhood and academia shape how we identify ourselves but also define our interactions. The measuring stick that is created as a result may be two-sided but its length far exceeds what can be measured. In our work as graduate students, we have been tasked with exploring identity as a concept, but at arm's length in an effort to prove or justify what we know. Only now, as we reflect on our experiences over the past few years, do we really begin to contextualize identity as a means of understanding ourselves. Looking back at past writing, we described identity.

The theme of identity, as central to knowing, exists regardless of the lens from which we view it because who we are is a construction of what we have experienced, with whom those experiences have taken place, and the context in which those experiences have occurred. The resulting identity is a complex construction.

In terms of knowledge, I believe that it is a social construction for which we are immutably contributors to and receivers of. Our cultural norms, points of reference, and habits of mind serve us and constrain us while simultaneously representing us and are indicative of what we contribute to the interactions that take place day by day, minute by minute. In order to understand identity, I proceed as though who we are, like knowledge, is never a fixed point or a final product; instead, I continue as though identity is a process that cannot be achieved in isolation; it requires participants and participation.

Identity fits within the constructivist paradigm where knowledge is an active construction, one that is "culturally and historically grounded, as laden with moral and political values, and serving certain interests and purposes" (Howe, 2001, p. 202). Postmodern thought demands a process of infinite interpretation and reinterpretation of experiences, circumstances, and conditions (Slattery, 1995). Of importance here is that meaning does not become a fixed or end point as a result of the search. Meaning can be a marker of understanding but one that will be changed as a result of further interactions and movement. Thus, identity becomes a matter of form made distinct by its connection to others (Martusewicz, 1992). Through such a process, ideas and knowledge are created by people who exist in "particular contexts, and who are influenced by particular histories" (Rorty, 1999; Said, 1994, as cited in Sumara, Davis, & Laidlaw, 2003, p. 158).

We spoke of identity, knowledge, and culture in the abstract, applying them without consideration of their position for/of/about us, metaphorically putting the cart before the horse. Being a mama scholar is a complex construction at times built on the backs of our children, partners, friends, and loved ones with the expectations of being a writer, scholar, and researcher, contributing to building a foundation while simultaneously putting pressure on the very pillars holding us up. We find as graduate students and mothers, we are often forced to navigate the waters of our identities in a leaky lifeboat in constant need of bailing to stay afloat. The external pressure to be a good mother or worthy academic is not uncommon among women. Acker and Armenti (2004) share the experiences of women in roles similar to ours where those women were required to create the illusion of "coping well" (p. 13) and to constantly justify their existence to those around them, including deans, supervisors, colleagues, friends, and family. Upon reflecting on this same dilemma in our own lives, we identified other women, our perceived support network, as having a critical and sometimes unfriendly voice.

Gender: Stylish Mid-Century vs. Polyester Slacks

The Part Where Feminists Start Throwing Things at Me (Kathleen)

One of my biggest challenges as a mama scholar is understanding feminism's role in accepting or rejecting mothers in the academy. My first instinct is to think that the feminists, in my department and beyond, would celebrate mothers in the academy. Why do I think that? Because that's what feminists do. Right? They celebrate other women. Especially ambitious smarty-pants women like me. Right? Mothers, however, are a messy brand of woman. They're kind of 1950s, but not in the stylish mid-century kind of way. As a mother in academia, I feel more a tacky polyester-slacks kind of 1950s. For years feminists, and other women, have worked hard to raise awareness of inequality and the damage it causes in the academy, an institution dominated by men for centuries, known for keeping ladyfolk on the fringes. But thanks to our hard-working feminist predecessors we ladyfolk are now crashing the party, and have been for quite some time. Yay for us. But it's 2 a.m. now, the keg is still full, and guess what? Someone else is crashing the party. The modern academic mommy. And I'm not sure if the original party crashers appreciate our dance moves. Unlike mommies of yesteryear, this new brand of mommies are embracing their identity as mother, not hiding it under their pantsuits. They are demanding things that challenge the "let's be just like men" ideals that, like it or not, still prevail among some women in the academy. These newish mommies demand privileges like mat leave, breastfeeding spaces, daycares, extensions, understanding. Privileges that reek of weakness. These requests appear to make some female academics uncomfortable, many of whom are mothers themselves, and they did it without all this fuss. So why can't we? Personally, I've found it intimidating to approach some women in my department with issues of my motherhood. Will they have time for my pre-bra-burning-era requests? They're busy, you see. Busy carving out our niche and acting like men to help women. And guess what? It's not helping that much. Is this how the revolution was supposed to go? The keg was supposed to be full of beer, not breast milk. Mothers, with their maternal paraphernalia, dirty up the academic landscape like giant energy-generating windmills. Alas, even the feminists have been known to shuffle us into limited places, reject our demands, turn their heads as we wheel strollers through the department. Their own assumptions about the unpredictability of the child-bearing academic often cut us mama scholars out of sweet academic deals. But will they be able to stop this new brand of woman from emerging, women pressured by research-based evidence (which appeals to the likes of us) that breast is best, that we need to spend time with our kids, that we need to be spending time reading and exploring the environment and growing community gardens, that we need to be there for them. This is research that comes out of departments like mine. Can we devote the time we want to devote to our families and be TAs, RAs, sessionals, committee members, journal editors, SSHRC winners, and all-around amazing non-men scholars? To be a non-man scholar you have to be just like a man, with a vagina. Not a man with a breast pump, stroller, or PAC commitments. I've spent two (three?) years occupying an isolated place on the fringes among researchers who research women on the fringes. I'm figuring out slowly that I'm not going to be a traditionally impressive non-man scholar with a vagina. I'm going to be a mama scholar with all the messiness it entails. A messiness that informs both worlds—that of mother and scholar—in powerful ways. And I'm realizing I'm not quite alone in this world, but am carving out my own niche, screaming toddlers in tow.

Kathleen's story challenges the notion that mothers, and their increasing commitment to family, are accepted or welcomed in academia. When academic women become mothers they seem to send out the message that they are less motivated, less committed, and less ambitious (Williams, 2007). Indeed, when women became visible in academia in the 1960s and 1970s, they were given a space in which they were expected to emulate and prove they were equal to academic men (Pillay, 2009). Pillay further argues that feminists, as academics,

> have often not allowed motherhood to infiltrate the spaces of our lives and being, as it is wont to do. Instead we fight this by allowing our mothering to live alongside us, and at times outside us, instead of allowing it to flourish as part of the interwoven fabric of who we are, as fundamental to the art of quilting our lives. (p. 513)

Indeed, feminists have worked hard on "the quilting of our lives," yet the quilt is forever evolving. This story draws attention to the emerging ownership of motherhood, and how that ownership is only just being invited into text. Furthermore, this narrative wonders how owning our motherhood will be, and is, taken up by feminists, especially those feminist mothers, influenced by the sixties and seventies, who prevail in the academy. These academic mothers govern the modern academic woman's life as supervisors, deans, and upper administrators. Will they be able to embrace the new mothers by finding a place for them within the frameworks that fuelled their own ambitions? Or will they continue to demand that all women scholars strive to be amazing non-men scholars with vaginas?

Eyes Focusing Ahead ... It All Just Clicked

Being Strategic as a Mama Scholar (Kathleen)

As a mama scholar, I identify as someone on the fringes. I play the game but at odd hours, when the department is hushed and childcare is free. It's true I miss out on opportunities like ad hoc brainstorming sessions at the water cooler and the chance to throw my panties at whatever rock star visiting professor is speaking this term. I toil in quiet offices and look out the window as campus security does it third (fourth?) sweep of the courtyard below. Despite missing out on productive collaborations and juicy gossip, I love this routine. Truthfully, I came back to school to do a PhD because I was a mom. After spending a year and half at home with my first child, and (gasp) enjoying it, I wanted to find a path that would allow me to do something engaging, something that would challenge my intellect, but that would afford me the flexibility and freedom to spend time with my kids—quality time. Being a mama scholar in the arts is not lucrative. Somehow I've kept afloat by piecing together bits of funding, teaching one course per year, and having been trained in a keen thriftiness that comes from growing up in lean times. I'm stressed most of the time. I grapple with feelings of inadequacy when clearly I cannot be as productive and/or chummy as my contemporaries. I walk home in the dark most nights, long after my children have wrapped their sausage arms around whoever is tucking them in. I fall into bed exhausted and worried and writing text in my head, hoping to remember it in the morning. But then the morning comes. And I'm still not rich and my data analysis is still not finished, but I've got the whole day ahead of me to hang out with two sets of sausage arms (three if you count mine). And yes, my children do drive me nuts. But when they do, I remember that I can retreat at the end of the day or on the weekend into my deserted department and into my quiet office and work away, uninterrupted and with free childcare. There is a sacrifice that comes with being a mama scholar, but it may be less of a sacrifice than other sacrifices mothers have to make in an effort to keep it all together.

I Am My Daughter (Lisa)

I drive down the hill, turn around the corner, park, and wait.

Only a few months ago, my daughter was convinced that she would be the only seven-year-old in her class and even in the world who could not ride a bike. I rationally tried to convince her that this was highly unlikely; I sympathetically tried to bond with her over my own frustrations as a seven-year-old learning to ride a bike. I promised that we would continue to practise, but it did not matter. With her chin down and through clenched teeth, she stubbornly stated that she would never learn to ride a bike.

Her sister said, "Watch me" and cycled away like it was the easiest thing in the world. I ran alongside holding the seat, breathlessly uttering words of encouragement. At one point, I thought a Zen-like strategy might work better, so I got her to just balance on the bike while I held it in one place so she could feel what balance was. Each practice yielded more tears and another firm declaration that she would never ride a bike.

Then, as with most kids, the complexity of riding a bike that seems so effortless came together. Moving, concentrating, balancing while not over-thinking, her feet pedalling, right side working together with the left side, hands tightly gripping the handle bars, eyes focusing ahead ... it all just clicked.

I see her push her bike up the hill of the crosswalk, jump on, and take off. She rides that bike with such confidence and pride, sitting tall on the seat, navigating the bumps and breaks in the sidewalk as if they aren't even there. She looks ahead as if no obstacle could possibly prevent her from forging ahead as fast as she wants to go ... quite literally like nothing could stand in her way. As I sit in the car out of sight, I feel her joy, her pride, and know that while she rides her bike, she believes in herself more fully than in any other moments.

After I have taught a class when I have helped students connect to what is happening in classrooms, or when we have a discussion and I know they really understand how important and complex being a teacher really is and in that moment they reconnect with why they want to be a teacher, I am my daughter riding her bike. During a research meeting when we are stuck on what the data are telling us but we keep circling and an idea comes to me that helps us break through, I am my daughter riding her bike. After spending hours in front of the computer searching out ideas and research and finding exactly what I need and I think to myself, I love what I do, I am my daughter riding her bike.

Hirakata and Daniluk (2009) note that in addition to feelings of isolation, pressure, and stress, academic mothers also identified positive aspects of combining their mother-scholar identities. These positive gains included feeling like a more well-rounded and interesting individual, as well as feelings of being pioneers in making positive changes for other academic mothers (Hirakata & Daniluk, 2009). In a similar way, our concluding vignettes illustrate our own understandings of the positive gains of being mama scholars. For Lisa, the positive gain is seeing in herself that which she celebrates in her daughter: learning something, getting something, achieving something and the innate sense of pride and accomplishment that comes with it. Her daughter's journey to not be the only seven-year-old who cannot ride a bike is mirrored in Lisa's own struggles with inadequacy and ambition as articulated in "The Birthday Girl." Yet both Lisa and her daughter overcome and "get it," leading to a sense of acceptance of the struggle. For Kathleen, the positive gain of being a mama scholar is a sense of autonomy and flexibility that enable her to live deeply in two of her favourite roles—that of mother and that of scholar. Furthermore, Kathleen acknowledges that by being a scholar she is perhaps more easily able to balance the world of work and family than if she were, for example, a nine-to-five working mom.

The End as the Beginning

> The agency of the academic mother lies in her courage to rewrite and transform scholarship so that motherhood is written into her intellectualism, into her scholarship and into academia. (Pillay, 2009, p. 513)

With these vignettes, we attempt to fuse our scholarships—the scholarship of our academy and the scholarship of our motherhood. In writing about our overlapping identities, we bring our motherhood, in all its messiness, into our academic landscapes. Like the windmills noted in the fourth vignette, mama scholars are interrupting a somewhat rural scene, hoping to generate a new kind of energy by changing our ways of knowing and our ways of being.

Recycled throughout these vignettes is a struggle to separate our identities, as mothers and as scholars, and a struggle to bring them together. In his discussions of the "lived curriculum," Ted Aoki (1993) explains how identity is not something that is necessarily present, but something that is produced through our "becomings in difference" (p. 205). Indeed, our identities as mama scholars are informed by how we live between the differences in those identities—dichotomies that are constructed and often kept separate by others. But here we grapple with owning those differences and accepting that they crash into one another in both challenging and empowering ways. Furthermore, Aoki explains, our identities are multiple and our multiplicities grow from the middle (p. 205). For us, our identities are not easily one or the other. We are not mamas *or* scholars; our multiplicities, those that we struggle with and those that we celebrate, are what make us ... mama scholars.

References

Acker, S., & Armenti, C. (2004). Sleepless in academia. *Gender and Education, 16*(1), 3–24. doi:10.1080/0954025032000170309

Aoki, T. T. (1993). Legitimating lived curriculum: Towards a curricular landscape of multiplicity. *Journal of Curriculum and Supervision, 8,* 255–268.

Austin, J., & Hickey, A. (2007). Autoethnography and teacher development. *International Journal of Interdisciplinary Social Sciences, 2,* 1–8.

Davis-Manigaulte, J., Yorks, L., & Kasl, E. (2006). Expressive ways of knowing and transformative learning. *New Directions for Adult and Continuing Education, 109,* 27–35. doi:10.1002/ace

Glazer-Raymo, J. (1999). *Shattering the myths: Women in academe.* Baltimore, MD: Johns Hopkins University Press.

Hirakata, P. E., & Daniluk, J. C. (2009). Swimming upstream: The experience of academic mothers of young children. *Canadian Journal of Counselling, 43*(4), 283–294.

Howe, K. R. (2001). Qualitative educational research: The philosophical issues. In V. Richardson (Ed.), *Handbook of research on teaching* (4th ed., pp. 201–208). Washington, DC: American Educational Research Association.

Martusewicz, R. A. (1992). Mapping the terrain of the post-modern subject: Post-structuralism and the educated woman. In W. F. Pinar & W. M. Reynolds (Eds.), *Understanding curriculum as a phenomenological and deconstructed text* (pp. 131–158). New York, NY: Teachers College Press.

Pillay, V. (2009). Academic mothers finding rhyme and reason. *Gender & Education, 21*(5), 501–515.

Raddon, A. (2002). Mothers in the academy. *Studies in Higher Education, 27*(4), 387–403.

Richardson, L. (2000). Writing. In N. Denzin & Y. Lincoln (Eds.), *Handbook of qualitative research* (2nd ed., pp. 923–948). London, England: Sage.

Ryan, J. (2007). Dialogue, identity and inclusion: Administrators as mediators in diverse school contexts. *Journal of School Leadership, 17*(3), 340–370.

Slattery, P. (2006). *Curriculum development in the postmodern era* (2nd ed.). New York, NY: Routledge.

Sparkes, A. C., & Smith, B. (2008). Narrative constructionist inquiry. In J. A. Holstein & J. F. Gubrium (Eds.), *Handbook of constructionist research* (pp. 295–314). New York, NY: Guilford Press.

Sumara, D., Davis, B., & Laidlaw, L. (2001). Canadian identity and curriculum theory: An ecological, postmodern perspective. *Canadian Journal of Education, 26*(2), 144–163. Retrieved from http://www.csse

Tsang, T. (2000). Let me tell you a story: A narrative exploration of identity in high performance sport. *Sociology of Sport Journal, 17*(1), 44–59.

Williams, S. (2007). *Graduate students/mothers negotiating academia and family life: Discourses, experiences, and alternatives* (Doctoral dissertation). Available from ProQuest Information and Learning Company. (UMI No. 3260100)

Longing to Belong
Parenting and Self-Realization within Academia

Ilka Luyt

Introduction

A fly lands on a pool of condensed water near the glass by my computer. As I grade essays in a hot tent trailer, my spouse and two children are enjoying rodeos and cotton candy at the Calgary Stampede. This was the summer of our epic camping trip across North America. Dinosaur bones, the Rocky Mountains, and Mount St. Helens beckoned us. Yet some of these vacation highlights are a blur in my memory since I always had work to do. This summer I taught two online courses from two separate universities, and most nights I had to log on and manage coursework. I never planned on teaching online courses, but the economic realities of life compel me to provide for my family. My journey in online learning and my return to doctoral studies have been largely shaped by my gender. Years ago, as a tenured English teacher at a small college, I did not mind the hour-long daily commute; however, when I became a parent for the second time, the physical stress of endless driving and grading papers was too demanding, so I abandoned tenure to spend more time with my children.

As a heterosexual, middle-aged, married mother of two, I made life choices that were informed by my own desires and reified by a North American culture that glorifies motherhood. What happened in the years following this decision made my re-entry into academia slow and tenuous. The events that I experienced are not unique, but they have been informed, I believe, by a neo-liberal culture that emphasizes self-regulation, hyper-individualization, and market freedom. This narrative explores how my own parenting, teaching, and learning choices are located within the conflicting ideas of freedom and economic forces as understood through a Foucauldian lens. I use Foucault's (2004) *The Birth of Biopolitics* as the framework for our current North American culture and the neo-liberal influences on women who work, teach, and learn in post-secondary schools. I define neo-liberalism as an amplified, over-identified concept of the individual. In neo-liberalism, people have a personal obligation to self-preservation and corporate interests manipulate these ideas. Finally, I offer hope to other mothers who are returning to school by showing how parenting can provide access to other discourse communities through positive and hopefully transformative learning experiences.

How Parenting Choices Changed My World View

When I became a parent, I changed my identity, my teaching priorities, and my world view. My decision to leave a tenured position was framed around the inherent belief that choosing to become a stay-at-home mother would provide a more enriched environment for my young child. I made this choice freely, but this freedom was entirely different from what I had imagined. The notion of personal freedom is an economic choice emphasized by a culture that hyper-individualizes success and the free market. Foucault reminds us that "liberalism formulates simply the following: I am going to produce what you need to be free" (p. 63). However, individual choices also occur within larger cultural forces of gender and class.

When I had my second child almost a decade ago, there were societal trends glorifying motherhood, specifically the stay-at-home mother. Feminist advances of the 1960s and 1970s announced that women could "have it all" in terms of a career and family. As a latchkey child myself, I remember growing up to be more self-reliant and resourceful while my mother was at work. Within the past decade, however, the trend toward hyper-motherhood has redefined parenting to be more labour intensive. When women who work continue to do most of the housework, they rarely have any free time, but mothers of newborns are now adding even more time-consuming tasks to their day. On-demand breastfeeding, cloth diapers, and co-sleeping are just a few trends that leave not only mothers but also spouses consumed with the daily care and nurture of infants. These daily chores take time and energy and in some instances, have spawned micro-markets within the economy such as natural cleaning services and baby products. Combined, the allure of the glorified stay-at-home mother–child bond requires vast resources of time and money.

Foucault foreshadowed a time when social relationships are intertwined with economic decisions. In order for there to be a free market, Foucault (2004) claims there must be an investment in human capital. A strong economy rich in the production of goods requires land, capital, and labour. Neo-liberals would argue that human capital is an investment that involves far more than an education. As Foucault writes, "Time spent, care given, as well as the parents' education—because we know quite precisely that for an equal time spent with their children, more educated parents will form a higher human capital than parents with less education—in short, the set of cultural stimuli received by the child, will all contribute to the formation of those elements than can make up a human capital" (p. 229). What is best for the infant? Current ideologies stress that a child will thrive when there is a single parent who forms a strong attachment to the child and who meets that child's human and emotional needs. These stories and ideologies inform entire populations and ultimately become "regimes of truth" (p. 18). Foucault goes on to argue that "everything comprising what could be called, if you like, the formative or educational relationship, in the widest sense of the term, between mother and child, can be analyzed in terms of investment, capital costs, and profit—both economic and psychological profit—on the capital invested" (p. 244). As primary caregivers, women provide their children with rich educational experiences, and they also benefit with societal praise by being labelled as engaged, socially active soccer moms. For many, this privilege is available only if the mother is able to live on one income, presumably the higher wage earner, which in middle-class circles often refers to the male partner. The mother does not need childcare since she has few expenses and can find cost savings through food, clothing, and gas bills to live on one income. A political economy generates a whole structure of practices; when people are constantly bombarded with the idea that we are responsible for ourselves, how we see ourselves is no longer in community but in isolation. The "regime of truth," or the idea that only a mother can provide what is best for the child, is woven into discursive practices into which we are all invited to participate.

How Parenting Changed My Role as a Teacher

The day I left my tenured position I felt a deep sense of loss. I surrendered my career achievements and the sanctuary of a collegial community for part-time work and reduced benefits. Part-time work, particularly online work, enabled me to care for my children and work when they slept. Little did I know that joining this adjunct community would be a time-consuming and isolating experience. Women continue to make up a large portion of the part-time labour force in post-secondary education. The 2011 almanac of the Canadian Association of University Teachers indicates that in 2010, women made up approximately 60 percent of the temporary full-time and permanent part-time workforce in universities, and more than 50 percent in colleges and vocational schools (p. 22). Female adjuncts reflect an ever-expanding pool of qualified part-time instructors who must also manage their time and fiscal responsibilities in order to make a living. With few benefits and lower pay (Betz, 2014; Fulton, 2000), part-time faculty have fewer incentives to interact with students

(Schuster, 2003) and colleagues. Limited office hours and few institutional supports means that adjuncts interact with students intermittently. I found such limited social interactions amplified in my asynchronous online courses where I was chronologically and conceptually removed from my students. Adjuncts who teach online courses participate in a "game of economic freedom guaranteed by the institutional framework" (Foucault, 2004, p. 83). Adjunct instructors who participate in this economy determine their own financial outcomes and poverty. Commenting on Foucault's notion of neo-liberal social policy, Lemke (2001) suggests, "By encoding the social domain as a form of the economic domain, cost-benefit calculations and market criteria can be applied to decision-making processes within the family, married life, profes-sional life, etc." (p. 200). I encoded this impermanent, temporary status of an adjunct faculty by teaching courses at two institutions, and spending a lot of time online or commuting. Time became more compressed, and free time was certainly a luxury.

Women are especially susceptible to weighing the costs and benefits of employment, especially since they continue to be the primary caregivers of the very young and the very old. When researching the influence of motherhood on post-secondary full-time faculty, Armenti (2004) discovered than many women considered child-bearing before tenure detrimental to their careers, and child-bearing influenced women's decisions to leave teaching entirely. The demands of full-time academic work are difficult for both men and women, but women routinely make life-altering career decisions based on economics and family dynamics. For me, part-time online work was a source of reve-nue and a small but persistent link to my learning and work community. The transition from full-fledged assistant professor to a humble adjunct raised my consciousness to my own voice as a thinker and writer. I was lucky. I had two children and contract work, but the loss of community and connectedness created a profound silence in my psyche, which I was not able to articulate until returning to graduate studies and starting to think, reflect, and write about my experiences.

How Parenting Choices Changed My Academic Opportunities

While the endorphins release when I held my infant son healed my sense of loss over tenure, I felt other frustrations. Spending time and energy nurturing my children ensured that socially, I would not receive the stigma associated with a mother who works outside the home. Instead, I faced increasing neglect in my professional interactions. Collegial interactions were rare, and as an online instructor, I remained a hidden teacher, unnoticed by colleagues and a silent force among my students. I was insignificant in a larger academic structure that emphasizes economic growth in a free market. Part-time instructors are cheap labour since they do not have compensation packages, retirement plans, or any other extra costs associated with full-time employment (Adams, 2010; Sammons & Ruth, 2007). This division of labour is necessary in a capitalist society where "there must be those who work and those who don't, there must be big salaries and small salaries" (Foucault, 2004, p. 143). In order for the market to thrive, there must be competition among workers based on the individual's ability to produce in an innovative manner. Part-time instructors, many with similar credentials as full-time faculty, struggle to find tenure-track work and resort to term or contract teaching at much lower rates than full-time faculty (Feldman & Turnley, 2004). The cost savings of part-time employment were made easier with the advent of online courses. Once trained in the technology, teachers could deliver the same course each semester by pouring the content into a new term's course shell. Producing online courses at the post-secondary level has diversified what and how learning is achieved.

According to Foucault (2004), what drives a market is "obtaining a society that is not orientated towards the commodity and the uniformity of the commodity, but towards the multiplicity and differentiation of enterprises" (p. 149). The rapid evolution of online technologies requires more human resources to manage the differentiation of technology. This specialization in information technology requires hiring non-teaching support positions in already streamlined academic budgets, while adjunct faculty who aspire to the economic prosperity of their tenured colleagues assume part-time employment longer than anticipated. Adjuncts' specific skill set makes them complacent, often exhausted workers in an educational field that relies on cheap labour. Not only was I tired from child-rearing, but I was tired from working late at night grading online. The terms and the conditions of my work were convenient but also wearisome. In subtle ways, technology shifted the boundaries of work and leisure time and forced me to renegotiate how I spent time in my other social roles. I quickly recognized a dissonance between what I envisioned as a practical way to earn money and the reality of parcelling out time in every area of my life.

This dissonance between time, social roles, and work is complicated in higher education, where my adjunct status largely contributes to my marginalized economic status. With fewer tenure-track positions and a constant supply of educated instructors, part-time employment seems like a simple solution for the needs and wants of the academic market. I realized my own limited economic mobility and I looked for more ways to earn a wage. I know friends, myself included, who must work more than one part-time teaching job just to pay their bills. Many institutions limit how many courses a part-time instructor may teach, so some individuals teach multiple courses at various institutions. Adjunct faculty provide supposedly free and voluntary work, but they are bound by a system that exploits their marginal status. As Foucault (2004) points out, "There must be a free labor market, but again there must be a large enough number of sufficiently competent, qualified, and politically disarmed workers to prevent them exerting pressure on the labor market" (p. 65). Part-time instructors are free to work, but they have few choices. Teaching many courses at multiple institutions is tiring work, especially composition courses, which carry heavy marking loads. Part-time teachers may be so busy grading essays that in-depth, focused time on one course or even one student is limited. Giroux (2002) argues that while technology has its proper place in education, when it is used for the "downsizing and deskilling of faculty" and when administrators frame online learning as a cost-effective means of production, true learning is sacrificed (p. 446). He claims, "Of the greatest importance here is how the culture of instrumental rationality shapes intellectual practices in ways that undermine the free exchange of ideas, mediate relations in ways that do not require the physical relations of either students or other faculty, and support a form of hyper-individualism that downplays forms of collegiality and social relations amenable to public service" (p. 448). Online learning employs adjuncts and provides both teachers and administrators with an economic output, but at what cost? Even though I was trained in online technology, my true heart remained in the live classroom, where I could meet and engage with my students in person. Nevertheless, like my students, I exchanged the transformational experience of live learning for the convenience of part-time online work.

Different Junctures for Hope

I continue to teach online and part-time writing courses. I'll continue to pick up my children after school, help them with their homework, and participate in my local community; these are privileges. Coupled with the chores of daily life, I am also enriched by the daily opportunities to engage in dialogue with other parents and at night, to read and grade. The social dynamics of my new-found role have opened overlapping discourse communities. I share my experiences with my students who are also trying to earn an undergraduate degree while working full-time, and I continue to learn from women within higher education who have outwardly managed to balance work and family roles. Relinquishing tenure enabled me to be more receptive to my own identity as a mother and clarified my desires to return to school. My doctoral journey taught me that I really know so little about the world, which is humbling and transformative. I hope that my children will learn to be transformed through reading, thinking, and writing. This occurs best in contexts where learning is a process of dialogue and community-building. The classic book *Women's Ways of Knowing* (Belenkey, Clinchy, Goodberger, & Tarule, 1986) reminds me to be aware of my own voice, silence, and subjectivity as I write essays in the academy. Writing, in itself, is a transformative activity, and writing this article helps me to clarify what has changed in my life since becoming a parent. Parenting has taught me to slow down, and I try to apply this skill to all my social interactions. When I really take the time to engage in critical reflections about my own knowledge and transformation, I see how my life is a network of learning, linked to various people, communities, and cultures. I am aware of my own longing for connectedness and the importance of exploring knowledge through dialogue, both online with my students and in person with my family, friends, and colleagues. Innovation is inevitable in our market-driven, neo-liberal culture, and innovation in the form of online learning has enabled me to provide for my family. However, I am ever mindful to use innovation, particularly technology, as a support but not a substitute for the unique teacher–student, parent–child interactions that nurture compassion and kindness. What transforms me is more than a single event, but a conjunction of experiences and people that change my frames of reference and make me revisit my previous identities in new contexts. I belong to my family, but I also belong to a larger learning community, which continues to define my life in profound ways.

References

Adams, N. M. (2010). Another digital divide? Instructional delivery and pay scale inequity among traditional and online lecturers: A labor market analysis. *2010 4th International Conference on Distance Learning and Education* (pp. 91–98). doi:10.1109/ICDLE.2010.5606031

Armenti, C. (2004). Gender as a barrier for women with children in academe. *Canadian Journal of Higher Education, 34*(1), 1–26.

Beleneky, M. F., Clinchy, B. M., Goodberger, N. R., & Tarule, J. M. (1986). *Women's ways of knowing: The development of self, voice, and mind.* New York, NY: Basic Books.

Betz, M. (2014, January 14). Contingent mother: The role gender plays in the lives of adjunct faculty. *Hybrid Pedagogy.* Retrieved from http://www.digitalpedagogylab .com/hybridped/contingent-mother-role-gender-plays-lives-adjunct-faculty/

Bruner, J. (1996). *The culture of education.* Cambridge, MA: Harvard University Press.

Canadian Association of University Teachers. (2011). *CAUT almanac of post-secondary education in Canada.* Ottawa, ON: Author.

Feldman, D. C., & Turnley, W. H. (2004). Contingent employment in academic careers: Relative deprivation among adjunct faculty. *Journal of Vocational Behavior, 64*(2), 284–307.

Foucault, M. (2004). *The birth of biopolitics: Lectures at the Collège de France, 1978–1979* (G. Burchell, Trans.). New York, NY: Picador.

Fulton, R. D. (2000). The plight of part-timers in higher education: Some ruminations and suggestions. *Change, 32*(3), 38–43.

Giroux, H. A. (2002). Neoliberalism, corporate culture, and the promise of higher education: The university as a democratic public sphere. *Harvard Educational Review, 72*(4), 425–462.

Lemke, T. (2001). "The birth of bio-politics": Michel Foucault's lectures at the Collège de France on neo-liberal governmentality. *Economy and Society, 30*(2), 190–207.

Sammons, M. C., & Ruth, S. (2007). The invisible professor and the future of virtual faculty. *International Journal of Instructional Technology and Distance Learning, 4*(1), 3–13.

Schuster, J. H. (2003). The faculty makeover: What does it mean for students? *New Directions for Higher Education, 123*, 15–22. doi:10.1002/he.116

"Dad and Mom Do Not Want to Get Zeroes"
Parenting in Academia

Mildred T. Masimira

> ME   *Come on, girls, let's go upstairs and Mommy will help brush your teeth so you can get ready for bed.*
>
> OUR OLDEST DAUGHTER   *Are you going to sleep too?*
>
> ME   *No, honey, Mommy needs to study. I have some work to give my teacher next week.*
>
> OUR OLDEST DAUGHTER   *Dad and Mom do not want to get zeroes. Wow, you never stop! Dishes, laundry, work, and now homework. Now I see how hard it is to be a grown-up.*

Introduction

I was just marvelling at how fitting the call for papers was; initially, I thought I would not have time to write this paper. This was the beginning of the semester. Naturally, things were already pretty hectic. I knew I had plenty to write about this subject. It was personal to me because like many other parents who also happen to be students, I was living the topic. But why did I feel so compelled to write it, even with the major time constraints? I write my story because I have talked to several mothers in graduate school as we pored over our books in study groups. All totally exhausted, we often veered off our academic focus to talk about our own lives and struggles as mothers and students. Most of the time, we immigrant mothers have no family supports in this country, something that other mothers may take for granted. I write because of the countless times I have consciously chosen particular group members in my courses, with a preference for parent-students. Only they could truly understand if I needed to reschedule a meeting for a class project. I also chose them because I knew if I asked them to come to my house because I did not have (or could not afford) a babysitter, they would comply without hesitation. I write because it helps me process my own struggles and triumphs as a parent in academia. After all, most days I do not even have time to think because I am constantly on the go trying to get things done. I write because like Anzaldúa (1981), "I am scared not to" for fear that our struggles as parent-students may be easily overlooked. Why not when it was our choice to get into graduate school despite our family situations? Surely we must have had some kind of foresight to make such big decisions in the midst of all our parenting responsibilities? Right?

We do have a mammoth task, being full-time parents, full-time students, and, in our case, employees as well. Sometimes I feel that there are not enough hours in a day to do all that I need to do. Hence, some days I resort to studying well into the wee hours of the night. The only uninterrupted time I can find is when the children are in bed, the toys are neatly packed in the toy boxes, the last dish has been put away, and the clothes for the next day are neatly laid out. At other times, I want the day to end because it has stretched out too long or I am experiencing writer's block as I try to thread thoughts together for my research proposal, and when my kids are particularly active and I cannot concentrate. At that point, I almost always just take time out, sing, dance, or read a story to my children because I realize that this is one moment with them that I will never have again. And, when they are finally asleep, I want nothing more than to have a bit of time to myself. But I must wearily trudge off to bed, only to wake up and go through a similar routine again.

Such experiences compel me to write because I wonder if these stories are heard enough in the academy. Is there a place for such stories? The little vignette that begins this paper indicates that my daughter understands just how busy I am. Her almost nightly question when I leave their bedroom is, "Are you going to sleep or to study?" for she knows I am almost always pre-occupied with either one, the former when I am exhausted or the latter when I have work to accomplish. I am by no means asking for special treatment. But when my single counterparts, or parent-students with older children, or those with available family supports are talking about and packing up to go to conferences in other provinces, or even out of the country, I cannot help but notice just how different our lives are. They too have responsibilities, almost all of them channelled specifically to furthering their studies, and ultimately careers. I and other parents have responsibilities too, a variety of them, and they do not solely have to do with school, such that the balancing act is a mammoth one.

Background

I am at what I would call a crucial time in my doctoral studies in education, a third-year international student enrolled in my last class and in the middle of writing my candidacy proposal. I am also the wife of a third-year doctoral student in biotechnology, whose waking hours are mostly spent at school or at work. A couple of years ago, the decision for both of us to simultaneously go to school did not seem as daunting. Back then, we did not realize the extent of work that would be involved. We did not foresee constantly needing to prevent our gruelling schedules from clashing.

We have been blessed with two beautiful daughters, aged six and two, who are in grade one and daycare, respectively. I mentioned earlier that I consider the extension of the call for papers timely. Just recently, I was on the telephone with my mom in Africa. I had requested her to visit us in Canada for a while to help me care for the children and handle some of the housework so I could put more time into my writing for school. The need for my mother's help speaks to the complexity of the life of married parent-students who are also immigrants with no immediate family supports.

In 2009, four years after graduating with my MA degree in the United States and moving to Canada, I realized that if I ever wanted to go back to school it had to be sooner rather than later. I knew there would always be something going on in life that would sidetrack that goal. My husband also wanted to go back to school. Together, we weighed the advantages and disadvantages of being graduate students at the same time. The overarching factor was that we both wanted to be done with our studies while our children were still in elementary school. That way we could devote more time to helping them with their school work as it got progressively more challenging. We also knew we wanted to have another child. But I was positive that if I waited until the projected four- to six-year doctoral study period, I would not be prepared for motherhood. I had my first child at twenty-eight. I did not want to have another child after thirty-four.

So we both applied to our prospective doctoral programs and got accepted. We were also blessed with our youngest daughter in August of the following year. I was still on maternity leave when my husband and I began our PhD programs. While he became a full-time student, I could do my studies only part-time because of the baby. In the fall of 2010, when our doctoral programs started, our oldest was four and our youngest only four weeks old. Many of our peers thought we were out of our minds. Of course, I could see why. But, at the same time, I also knew that they did not understand that these were goals both I and my husband had set for ourselves, individually. Even when we met and later married and started a family, our individual academic goals did not change.

In the second year of both our studies, I had to start mentally psyching myself to begin looking for a job. Acquiring financial support for my academic expenses was difficult since I had started as a part-time student. I was told funding would not be guaranteed. A few attempts at available scholarships and awards were finally thwarted because I did not seem to have most of the requirements for particular awards. If I thought I did and applied, I never received an award. I decided to stop wasting time on awards I was unlikely to receive and get a job instead. After all, I was an international student with children to look after and tuition to pay. I did get partial funding, which took me through the second year. Financially, I was somewhat set for a while. At least the funding allowed me another year with my children. By then the oldest was in kindergarten and the youngest was still at home full-time with me.

Finding time for study was another issue though. It was a rough two years. Initially, the baby did not sleep through the night. Though my classes were in the early evenings, I still needed to sleep during the day so I could be awake with her at night. Most times, I studied with her on my lap. It was then that I fell in love with the Acer notebook that I have owned for a couple of years. The computer is so compact that it allowed me to hold the baby and do research at the same time. I also found it helpful to have a tape recorder on the bed beside me to record my thoughts since I could not write for lengthy periods of time.

My husband's schedule, from the beginning, did not give him much time at home. He was required to be in the lab doing experiments. After that, he had to go off to work to earn enough to cover our bills and my tuition. For a while, I took on the lion's share of caring for the children since I was not employed and could stay with them at home most of the time. Things changed when I found full-time employment. I was forced to go back to work after my meagre academic funding dried up. Our family life became even more hectic. As parents, my husband and I had to find ways to coordinate our school, work, and the children's schedules. Our typical day began with taking the kids to school in the morning. Then we would each go to school or work. Early evenings involved taking care of the household chores. Late at night, we studied while the children were in bed. On some days, we needed to attend school-related activities: our own as graduate students and our children's as parents. A few times we were able to attend meetings at our children's schools together, but usually one of us had to go while the other studied or worked.

As I write this paper, the fall semester of our third year is well underway. My husband is teaching a class, taking a class, doing experiments for his research project, and still working at his regular job. As I mentioned earlier, I spend most of my days at work, studying and preparing my candidacy paper. So far, we have survived our rigorous routine, and our children are thriving within the hectic environment. We consciously set aside time to focus specifically on them so they realize that our focus is not solely on school. Our schedule has not slowed down; the only difference is that we are now both done taking courses and are focusing on candidacy. We are also actively planning to put in time at conferences and writing for publication, and we hope this will be accomplished.

The Balancing: Negotiating Life's Demands

Parenting while in school is quite the challenge. We love our children dearly and we will always make time for them. But there are also the competing demands of work, school, and other activities that are important for us individually and ultimately for us as a family. After picking up the kids from school, we make dinner, read stories to our girls, catch up on the children's day and our day, and then put them to bed. It is only at this point that we are able to get some time alone to catch up on school work.

Conference attendance so far has been limited to those organized within the city. We cannot afford a babysitter to watch our children for more than a day at a time. Sometimes we make plans to travel with them. Then, something comes up and we have to change our plans. Recently, I was chatting with a fellow colleague—another mother and student. She noted that the single PhD students at the university were able to attend conferences and anything else that came up to develop their portfolios for jobs after graduation. We mused together about job prospects for parents like us who graduate and have not put in as much time at conferences and in publication during our academic years.

Some research (Crittenden, 2001; Hewlett, 2002) has indicated that female professionals who are both academics and mothers are disproportionately affected by difficulties in finding jobs and maintaining or elevating their status in academia. It has also been revealed that women who have babies early in their academic careers are less likely to achieve tenure than women who delay having babies or choose to have none at all. Based on conversations with colleagues, these statistics already project a not-so-rosy future for mothers who pursue careers in academia. As a negotiating tactic, I have been rethinking how to put my doctoral degree to use by actively searching for alternative career opportunities.

In the foreword to *Parenting and Professing: Balancing Family Work with an Academic Career* (2005), Andrea O'Reilly mentions that "the prevailing ethos of academic culture is that the career is to be prioritized above all else. To do otherwise is to risk being perceived as not committed to your profession, or worse, to risk not being taken seriously as a 'real' scholar" (p. xv). This perception results in what Bassett (2005) calls discrimination avoidance, meaning behaviours intended to minimize any apparent or actual intrusion of family life on academic commitment. These behaviours can include making the already identified decision to delay having children or choosing not to have children at all (Cohen, 2002). In our case, we decided to have our last child before starting school so we would not wait too long.

Often, I have seen people roll their eyes when a parent gives an example in class and refers to her children. It is almost as if there is an unspoken code dictating that children should be left out of "academic" discussions and that parents should somehow be ashamed to bring that part of their lives into the classroom. I have noticed how some graduate students (those with children) do not talk about their families at all. They seem also to censor the fact that, like me, they are forced to miss a conference because of babysitting issues or other scheduling issues around their much-needed jobs and children's activities. Jiron-King (2005) learned not to bring her "maternal" examples into the classroom. She writes, "A female professor laughed at me and said I'd better speed up on the learning curve. I learned that there is clearly a bias in graduate school against bringing personal experience as an example or as evidence for an argument in theoretical discussions, especially if that experience is maternal" (p. 30). Clearly, such perceptions in academia indicate that there needs to be a shift in attitude regarding parenting in academia. There has to be an understanding that parents' work ethic is the same as their counterparts', albeit with different responsibilities.

In Christensen's discussion on language and parenting (2005), he writes, "The real problem is that both roles, professor and caregiver, presuppose total preoccupation and commitment, making them feel like mutually exclusive domains" (p. 36). The truth is that the roles are not mutually exclusive. They trip over each other all the time. Hence, the examples that parents may give about their children in class, as well as the struggle presented by Jiron-King (2005) about whether or not a graduate student who is a parent is a "serious and committed scholar" (p. 25). Unless proven, it seems highly unlikely that parents, especially those with very young children and jobs outside academia, such as ourselves, will be taken seriously as academics.

Olsen (1978) is known for her statement that "work interrupted, deferred, relinquished, makes blockage—at best, lesser accomplishment. Unused capacities atrophy, cease to be" (19). Though I believe this to be true in some cases, in my case, having young children has allowed me to make more efficient use of my time. It is highly unlikely that I can sit at home and finish a project without paying attention to my children the whole time. Thus, when I sit and write, I am fully aware that I need to do the best work I can in the limited time I have to focus on my own work.

Conclusion

Despite the challenges of parenting while in graduate school and in the workforce, many parents have completed their educational programs. In some instances it may take them a little longer than others. Still, they get it done. Being in a doctoral program and doing well is itself a feat of no small magnitude. Doing it in the midst of parenting as well takes great effort. A friend once said, "You may gain a degree and lose your family, or you may sustain your family and lose out on a great academic opportunity." We strive daily to find a balance so that when all is done our children understand that despite it all we were still great parents. We hope the academic (and career) worlds recognize us as professionals with the resilience needed to accomplish all three without totally falling apart. Personally, I believe what my husband and I have been able to do so far is commendable. And the vignette at the beginning of this paper is proof that if anything, we have raised an awareness of and instilled the value of hard work in our children as well.

References

Anzaldúa, G. E. (1981). Speaking in tongues: A letter to third world women writers. In C. L. Moraga & G. E. Anzaldúa (Eds.), *This bridge called my back: Writings by radical women of color* (pp. 183–193). Berkeley, CA: Third Woman Press.

Bassett, R. H. (2005). Introduction. In R. H. Bassett (Ed.), *Parenting and professing: Balancing family work with an academic career* (pp. 1–16). Nashville, TN: Vanderbilt University Press.

Cohen, H. (2002, August 4). The baby bias. *New York Times, Education Life Supplement*, p. 25.

Christensen, M. (2005). The language of parenting. In R. H. Bassett (Ed.), *Parenting and professing: Balancing family work with an academic career* (pp. 34–43). Nashville, TN: Vanderbilt University Press.

Crittenden, A. (2001). *The price of motherhood: Why motherhood is the most important—and least valued—job in America.* New York, NY: Henry Holt.

Hewlett, S. A. (2002). *Creating a life: Professional women and the quest for children.* New York, NY: Miramax.

Jiron-King, S. (2005). La estudiante caminante: My motherwork is here, my otherwork is there. In R. H. Bassett (Ed.), *Parenting and professing: Balancing family work with an academic career* (pp. 21–33). Nashville, TN: Vanderbilt University Press.

Olsen, T. (1978). *Silences.* New York, NY: Seymour Lawrence.

O'Reilly, A. (2005). Foreword. In R. H. Bassett (Ed.), *Parenting and professing: Balancing family work with an academic career* (pp. 21–33). Nashville, TN: Vanderbilt University Press.

Of Diapers and Comprehensives
A Feminist Exploration of
Graduate-Student-Mothering in the Academy

Anita Jack-Davies

Mothering, Identity, and Graduate School

When I began grad school in 2002, motherhood was far from my mind, as I was not yet married. Truth be told, I was not even engaged. I would meet my current partner at the start of grad school, toward the end of my first year. At the time, I was teaching grade eight in Toronto's Jane-Finch community and taking night classes while working full-time during the day. Thoughts of motherhood invaded my psyche years later when I was accepted into a doctoral program in education. My partner and I often spoke about having children. A trip to our family doctor, where she and I discussed my fertility concerns, prompted my partner and me to have "a serious talk" about starting a family. At the time, I was thirty-four years old. My doctor told me that my ongoing medical concerns, coupled with my age, meant that I should consider starting a family sooner rather than later. I feared that if I waited until I completed my PhD, I might not be able to conceive at all.

Equipped with this information, I sat with my partner weighing the pros and cons of having a child at that stage of my academic career. It seemed that a long and winding road lay ahead of me. We volleyed ideas back and forth, periodically stopping to ask ourselves whether we were crazy for even considering starting a family. I wondered out loud: Will I be taken seriously as an academic? Will my colleagues think that I have lost my mind? Will this cause me to drop out? Will I be treated with disdain if I walk around with a big tummy? Asking these questions caused kernels of doubt to dart to and fro in my brain. However, this self-doubt was swiftly interrupted when my partner said, "Who cares what people think? It's what we think that matters!" To this I replied:

Right, like you would know what it feels like to be ignored when
walking down the hallway or after saying hello to one of my colleagues in the grad lounge. Like you would know what it feels like
to be the only black face in the entire building and to be stared at
like I am an alien from outer space. Can't you see, I am the only
black person for miles, and if I have a baby, everyone will think
that having a baby is the only thing that I can do. Get it: black
girl, baby, stereotype, single mother—lots of black girls having
babies, even a smart black girl is having a baby! You don't get it!
You are white! You don't get it. You are not only white, but you
are a man. Privilege is coming out of your ass! No one looks at
you and thinks these things. They don't judge you. I, on the other
hand, am not so lucky. At best, they think that I am dumb and
stumbled upon the academy by accident. My having a baby is
only going to reinforce every single stereotype that exists in this
world about black women.

Recognizing the complexity of my social location in the physical and conceptual space of the academy, he held me and reassured me that everything
would work out as long as we loved each other and were committed to making
starting a family work. By his touch, I knew that we were making the right
decision, despite the fact that questions about the intersecting nature of my
"race" and gender identity continued to haunt me.

Being racialized on a predominantly white university campus is always
fraught with tension. The simultaneous visibility and invisibility (Collins,
2000) of my identity as a black woman meant that, in thinking about starting a
family, I also had to consider what the changes to my physical self would mean
in a space that rewards the activities of the brain, instead of the activities of the
body. This is especially true when the body that is experiencing these changes
is a body that McKittrick (2006) argues is a body of racial-sexual knowing:

> For black women, then, geographic domination is worked out through read-
> ing and managing their specific racial-sexual bodies. This management effec-
> tively, but not completely, displaces black geographic knowledge by assuming
> that black femininity is altogether knowable, unknowing, and expendable:
> she is seemingly in place by being out of place. (p. xv)

This sexuality is based on a "set of effects produced in bodies, behaviours,
and social relations by a certain deployment deriving from a complex political
technology" (Foucault, 1990, p. 127). My being pregnant, in that space and at
that time, was neither conceptualized as neutral nor value free. Hooks (1992)
writes that popular representations of black female bodies "rarely subvert or

critique images of black female sexuality which were part of the cultural apparatus of 19th-century racism and which still shape perceptions today" (p. 62). In other words, it was difficult for me to divorce myself from common media representations of black women as mammies or "wild sexual savages" (p. 67).

When I became a mother in 2008, my identity as a black woman took on new meanings simply because I existed in an academic space where my blackness was already being read in a myriad of ways. Despite awareness of the deeply disturbing images about black women that circulate widely within the culture, becoming pregnant forced me to internalize the meanings of these images for my own life. Collins (2000) suggests that black women in the academy have always occupied the status of outsider. She writes that the exclusion of black women's ideas from "mainstream academic discourse" means that they often straddle that curious space of the outsider-within in many of their academic pursuits (p. 12). They are outsiders and perpetually seen as the Other. They are insiders because they are physically present despite being invited to remain silent. As outsiders-within, black women must constantly carve out spaces for themselves, spaces that weren't meant for them.

It is this outsider-within framework that shaped my experiences as a graduate-student-mother. Chacon (2006) suggests that in the academy, women's bodies matter, especially when such bodies are marked by race and gender. Magda Lewis (in conversation) emphasizes that women in the academy are never divorced from their bodies. Their bodies are under constant scrutiny and surveillance. Women's bodies are too thin, too young, too old, and never good enough. Chacon (2006) believes that this notion of a mind/body split is an illusion and that bodies matter in the academy: "The emphasis on the Cartesian separation of mind and body ... is of course an illusion; it is, moreover, a profitable illusion.... Although the teacher, or scholar, rather, has been historically framed through this critical lens, we are never separate from our bodies, particularly in the classroom" (p. 385). In the academy, she writes, the white male body is read as a text that is both rational and professional. Conversely, the racialized female body is read as a body of surplus visibility, as unprofessional, and as less intelligent (p. 38). This creates a sense in which the white male body becomes the body of belonging, of knowing, of theory, of study, and of research. I worried that my growing belly would justify my un-belonging in the academy and would inflict further punishment on my already fragile existence. And while my body grew and the love for my unborn child increased with each passing second, this same growth made me feel more and more out of place in a space that had not prepared itself for a woman with child.

Writing the Comprehensive Exam

I wrote the take-home comprehensive exam on December 1, 2009. Weeks leading up to the exam, I prepared myself for a question that I did not know. Each day I left my daughter with her caregiver and secretly reassured myself that I was leaving her behind for a greater good, obtaining my PhD. Overwrought with guilt, saddened, and resentful, I kissed her goodbye and dreamed of a day when I would not have to leave her. On the morning drive to my desk, saddened by her tears and her screaming as I said goodbye, I reminded myself that my daughter would benefit from having a mother with a doctoral degree. To prepare for the exam, I made several trips to the library and signed out books to read. I searched online blogs to learn from the successes and failures of virtual graduate students around the globe. I made and remade to-do lists. I spoke to colleagues at the faculty about their experiences with the comp. At times, I reassured other colleagues who were preparing for their upcoming exams. I contacted my thesis advisor via email when I could not meet with her in person. I read and reread academic papers that focused on my main dissertation topic and created a work plan to keep my daily progress on track. Despite this preparation, I worried myself sick about the upcoming question. I agonized over what it might be: How might my dissertation committee structure the question; what would they ask me to do? I racked my brain thinking about the different angles that my committee might take with it, reassuring myself that I had a good handle on my area of study, teacher education and inner-city schooling.

At the faculty the exam seemed to be shrouded in the utmost secrecy. I heard horror stories about students failing the exam and having to rewrite it several months later. I warned myself that as a mother with a young child, I could not afford to fail. At the time, there were no formal courses or workshops to demystify my questions surrounding the exam. I wondered why the exam was never truly unveiled, except for the fact that it had a take-home format. To this day, I continue to question who benefits from structuring a high-stakes exam in such a way that a graduate student's entire life is turned upside down in order to write it. I wondered if this was the price that I had to pay in order to be an academic. I questioned whether passing this exam would prepare me to become a scholar or a better thinker. As a graduate-student-mother, I could not afford to lose control. In fact, I could not even afford the tears that came anyway. I had a daughter to take care of and she needed me to be sane, complete, and whole. I wondered if the creators of the exam actually had children.

Three Weeks to Submission

I remember well the day that I picked up the exam question from the Graduate Studies office. I had exactly three weeks from that moment to submit my response. Standing there, outside the office, I ripped the envelope open in maddened haste. I skimmed the question and my heart sank. The only word that I made out was the term "Foucault" and my heart began to pound. I reread the question several times, never looking up to take stock of my surroundings. My mind raced back and forth in the realization that this was the moment that I had been preparing for. I reminded myself that Foucault's writing was difficult and needed considerable attention, and that I had no time to mess around. I headed straight to the library to sign out another bagful of books, this time centring on the themes of discourse and power.

That day, upon arriving home, my daughter did not seem to be her exuberant and boisterous self. After putting her to bed at 8:00 p.m., I began work on the question on the first floor of our house. At approximately 10:00 p.m., hours after my daughter had gone to sleep, my partner yelled that our daughter was vomiting in her crib. Laptop, headphones, and blankets flung aside, I dashed upstairs to a weeping baby whose clothing was wet from head to toe. Overcome with concern and worry, we decided to divvy up the tasks that awaited us, as I comforted her. I started a warm bath and my partner began to clean up the colossal mess in her nursery: towels to mop up the mess were strewn everywhere, along with a bucket, Fantastic cleaner, and washcloths, as well as my partner's exasperated sighs. As he cleaned, my daughter only seemed to get worse. She vomited approximately each hour until 2:00 a.m. Her upset stomach meant that she could not settle down to sleep.

After calling Telehealth Ontario and answering a series of questions, we were told to give her clear liquids, keep her off her formula for a few hours, and monitor her progress throughout the night. At approximately 4:00 a.m., I decided that it made no sense to continue working and called it a night. Riddled with fatigue and worry, I settled down to sleep knowing that the clock was ticking away on my exam. In that moment, I knew that despite my daughter's illness, I had to make up the time that I had missed looking after her. I felt that no one at the faculty could relate to what I was going through. However, I was reluctant to approach anyone in the program because I was desperate to succeed, in spite of my decision to have a child. I did not want to use my daughter as what would inevitably be constructed an "excuse." And so I chose to remain silent.

Silence as Discourse

The discursive practices that stem from being a graduate-student-mother are constructed to suggest that the academy is not responsible for the ways in which raising my family might have an impact on my progress through the doctoral program. These discursive practices include silence or an absence of blatant and open discussion about motherhood, parenthood, and graduate school. In speaking of women's subjectivities, Lewis (1993) argues that there is "an active discourse of silence which is politically grounded as well as politically contained" (p. 31). This silence is deliberate because it has particular implications for the experience of women with respect to power. Women are invited to remain silent about experiences that are unique to them and about women's way of knowing. She explains that discourse never exists outside of the social locations that women occupy and is never divorced from power:

> Power is having access to those processes which legitimate and enforce meaning as it is inscribed in language and supported by concrete practices. This discursive/power relationship is not just a handy theoretical construct; one never just makes up discourse in the abstract or in a solitary moment outside of the social locations we occupy. (p. 114)

In speaking about the discourse surrounding sexuality, Foucault (1990) insists that rules of propriety surrounding sexuality dictate the ways in which sex is talked about, with whom it is discussed, and where it is discussed. I argue that the rules surrounding the discourse of parenthood in academia work in similar ways. Of discourse and silence, Foucault (1972) insists that they inform each other:

> It is supposed therefore that everything that is formulated in discourse was already articulated in that semi-silence that precedes it, which continues to run obstinately beneath it, but which it covers and silences. The manifest discourse, therefore, is really no more than the repressive presence of what it does not say; and this "not-said" is a hollow that undermines from within all that is said. (p. 25)

The discourse of silence about women deciding to become parents while in graduate school sent a clear signal to me that these two worlds do not meet. There were no meetings, there were no support groups for women, and the graduate student handbook mentioned little about formal processes surrounding becoming a parent while studying in the program. As my pregnancy progressed, I explored what was available to me in terms of resources at the faculty and on the larger university campus. In finding very little, I felt alone, despite the fact that I was keenly aware that I was not the only one who was experiencing what I was going through. Despite the fact that formal processes have been developed in universities today, at the time, I would have benefited from more tangible and visible signs that suggested the normalcy and acceptability of starting a family in graduate school. I needed to know that choosing to have a child as a woman making my way through graduate school was not a deadly kiss on the cheek of my academic career.

In speaking of discourse, Hall (1997) explains that it cannot simply be reduced to a statement, a book, an action, or a single source. It appears in many different forms, across a range of texts and "rules in" how we speak about certain things (p. 44). It dictates what is considered acceptable speech, intelligent speech, and appropriate ways of behaving. Discourse also "rules out" and narrowly defines how certain topics are spoken of. In the academy, the discourse of motherhood rules in "polite" talk about becoming a mother: How old is the baby? What is she saying now? Is she in daycare? The opposite is also true. The discourse of motherhood also rules out out formal discussions about the challenges faced by graduate-student-mothers attempting to make their way through competitive programs. Such practices might include meetings, pamphlets/brochures about becoming a parent, discussion about such issues in graduate student governance, female-led graduate student support groups, written policies included in graduate student handbooks surrounding funding, taking leaves of absence, and accommodations for graduate-student-mothers that require them.

I was desperate to never use my daughter as an excuse if I required additional time to meet deadlines. I was invited to believe that I could meet the same academic expectations that are met by other graduate students without children, despite the fact that having a young child at home placed additional challenges on me. I was invited to believe that motherhood should not make any difference for my academic progress with respect to teaching and prepping for classes, publishing, working on research projects, and planning the completion of my dissertation. As a graduate student who occupied a curious space as a professor-in-training in the academy, I was always aware of the ways in which I was simultaneously powerful and powerless. I was powerful because my presence in the academy provided me with a voice. I was powerless because I was not a faculty member and my voice was unknown.

The faculty formally recognized my impending motherhood by freezing the graduate student funding that I was entitled to, such that I was not financially penalized for taking two terms off to give birth to my child. I was both grateful and relieved that the program recognized my circumstance in this regard. Because I was unsure about any formal structures in place that would recognize the impact that mothering might have on my progress through the program, the invisibility of support for graduate-student-mothers silenced me even before I could feel comfortable enough to advocate for myself. This lack of knowledge was as much about my being unwilling to appear incompetent as a new mother as it was about the discursive practices that made my silence inevitable.

Silence as discourse, in relation to graduate-student-mothering, dictates behaviour. Foucault (1972) explains, "There is not one but many silences, and they are an integral part of the strategies that underlie and permeate discourse" (p. 27). The silence surrounding formal accommodations for graduate-student-mothers suggests that I chose to have a baby while in graduate school. In choosing to have a baby at this time rather than after completing the program, it is my responsibility and not the academy's if I face additional burdens during the program. This was the hidden curriculum of the program or the informal truths that I came to know and experience. In choosing to have a baby while in grad school, I was signing an invisible contract that said, if I fail my comprehensive exam because of my situation, it is my fault; if I fail to hand in final papers for courses on time, it is my fault; if I fail to publish papers or to attend conferences, and do all the things that I am evaluated on as a graduate student, again, it is my fault. I chose to have a baby.

As I worked feverishly to finish the exam on time, I spent considerable amounts of time away from home. This meant that my partner shouldered much more of the child-rearing responsibilities than I normally feel comfortable with. I gave up simple tasks such as grocery shopping and running errands at our local mall. Cooking responsibilities were also managed by ordering takeout from a local Thai restaurant, which became an easy but expensive fix. Often, after leaving my daughter early on a Saturday morning, I vowed that I would spend each and every weekend with her when the exam was over. There were times when I felt resentful and sad that I was working at the faculty on a Saturday or Sunday morning, when I could have been playing with her. I often wondered if anyone would recognize the tremendous sacrifice that I was making. I felt that the university could never appreciate the time and effort that I made in order to keep some semblance of sanity at home, while trying to tread water in the PhD program.

Accommodating Graduate-Student-Mothers?

Fatigue seemed to be my constant companion throughout the writing of the exam. Additional challenges included stress due to juggling motherhood and graduate school, and additional feelings of loneliness and isolation that exacerbated my marginality as a black graduate student. I learned to live on little sleep and simultaneously binged on an unhealthy diet of research and study. I stopped going to the gym and began to rely on the Tim Hortons drive-through and meals delivered to me by my partner when I worked late or on weekends. I watched as dark circles moved into the deep crevices of my eyes.

The constant fatigue and pressure of having to submit the take-home exam left me worried and anxious. Pushing myself to the limit, I often rationalized that I would sleep after the exam was submitted. However, illness was inevitable owing to neglect for my mind, body, and spirit. In retrospect, stress was also caused by my being unable to contact any member of my dissertation committee to determine if I was on the right track with my answer. My indecision about the structure of my answer caused me to rewrite major sections, which reduced the overall effectiveness of my answer. During this three-week examination period, I felt more alienated than at any other time in the doctoral program.

Moving Forward, Looking Back

Formal and informal strategies that might create less-stressful circumstances for graduate-student-mothers pursing doctoral studies include providing additional time to complete exams, enabling graduate-student-parents to opt out of teaching responsibilities (if desired) one term before the exam, and creating a support group for graduate-student-mothers. The three-week examination period was set by the grad school for all students, regardless of our individual circumstances. This was a written rule that seemed to be carved in stone. All graduate students know of "the rules" and are expected to follow them, no questions asked. However, the writing of my comprehensive exam was not all negative. The exam enabled me to focus on my dissertation and on general readings for my area of study in ways that I may not have done otherwise. The exam also solidified consistent and daily writing habits, which contributed to my ability to complete my dissertation. With respect to having our daughter while I was a graduate-student-mother, we chose this path because of our dream of starting a family. Despite the challenges that starting a family posed, our daughter remains our greatest accomplishment. Now that I have completed my doctoral work, I am proud of the fact that I persevered through the difficult moments of being a graduate-student-mother. My new identity as a mother will continually develop as my daughter grows and as my relationship to the academy changes.

References

Chacon, R. M. (2006). Making space for those unruly women of color. *Review of Education, Pedagogy and Cultural Studies, 28*(3–4), 381–393.

Collins, P. H. (2000). *Black feminist thought: Knowledge, consciousness, and the politics of empowerment* (2nd ed.). New York, NY: Routledge.

Foucault, M. (1972). *The archaeology of knowledge.* London, England: Tavistock.

Foucault, M. (1990). *The history of sexuality: An introduction* (Vol. 1). New York, NY: Vintage Books.

Hall, S. (1997). The work of representation. In S. Hall (Ed.), *Representation: Cultural representations and signifying practices* (pp. 13–74). Thousand Oaks, CA: Sage.

Hooks, B. (1992). Selling hot pussy. In *Black looks: Race and representation* (pp. 61–77). Boston, MA: South End.

Lewis, M. (1993). *Without a word: Teaching beyond women's silence.* New York, NY: Routledge.

McKittrick, K. (2006). *Demonic grounds: Black women and the cartographies of struggle.* Minneapolis: University of Minnesota Press.

He Told Me "Babies Sleep"
Expectations and Realities about
Maternity Leave Productivity

Tarah Brookfield

What are your plans during maternity leave?" The question was posed to me by a senior administrator in Research Services when I was nine months pregnant. We were chatting before a faculty research talk began, and the question was asked in a rather casual manner, the way one might inquire about a friend's holiday itinerary. Given that the administrator was appointed to mentor tenure-track faculty like me, I suspected his question had a less friendly point. "Take care of my baby," I replied awkwardly. His response was to lean in close, as if to impart some carefully guarded wisdom. "Babies sleep," he stated, implying that I would have hours of free time during my leave that should be devoted to academic pursuits. I regret that my response was not to remind him that maternity and parental leaves were neither vacations nor sabbaticals but rather my legal right to temporarily stop work while I recover from birth and am the primary caregiver for my daughter during her first year of life. Nor did I remind him that my university's collective agreement allowed new parents to stop the tenure clock while on leave, so there was no need to use that time to build my CV. Instead I listed off some projects I could work on because in that moment, a week away from giving birth, I felt incredibly vulnerable about the major life changes from both a personal and a professional perspective. I also feared being judged as unproductive by someone who adjudicated internal grants.

This incident was the most troubling but not the only conversation I had while pregnant about working during my leave. Several colleagues, academic friends, and even a few students told me I would be bored on my leave and would feel compelled to carve out time for academic pursuits. Many expressed surprise that I was taking the entire year off or assumed I would return three months early so I could be on campus in September for "back to school."

Meanwhile, another representative in Research Services encouraged me to move up my plans to apply for a grant so the money would be available during what she referred to as my "year off." In these other exchanges, I candidly insisted that I had no intention of working during my leave or returning early. I was looking forward to taking a break from academia, and besides, I had grand plans for my daughter's sleep time. When I was not catching up on my own sleep, I envisioned finally becoming adept at all things domestic and saw in my future a kitchen full of home-cooked meals and beautifully hand-knit baby clothes. I had no fear of boredom, not when my night table held stacks of unread novels. I even dared voice out loud that I may finally have the time to work on a novel of my own. Therefore, one of my last tasks before I gave birth was to add the "out of office" notice to my work email, alerting the academic community that I would be back in a year.

This chapter, written during my leave, while my baby slept, demonstrates how naive my expectations were about how I would spend my leave. Not only did my daughter's frequent nighttime waking and naptime battles seem to defy the notion that babies sleep for a good chunk of their first year, but I struggled more than I expected with how to handle the professional opportunities and demands that occurred during my leave. From publishing deadlines to reference letters, I never felt very far away from my job, and I used many of those elusive naptimes to catch up on academic correspondence, course prep, conference planning, projects for two professional associations, and other tasks. A part of me enjoyed staying in touch with colleagues and keeping abreast of news from my field and my campus. At the same time, I came to resent the professional and institutional factors that compelled me to work, most notably the pressures to gain tenure, the ability to work from home, and my appointment at an under-resourced campus. I also grew more aware of the gendered dimensions behind my own ambition and desire to please, and the lack of respect given to childcare as a form of work. As a result, I found myself, a year earlier than I anticipated, navigating the work–family balancing act.

Before I continue, I must acknowledge the privileged position from which I write this essay. As someone who has a tenure-track position, a healthy child, and an employed spouse, I am aware of how these aspects make combining child-rearing and paid work a lot smoother. Also, I live in a country that protects women's labour rights and recognizes the caregiving labour of parents by granting fifty weeks of combined paid maternity and parental leave. Evans (2007) classifies the length and provision of Canada's paid maternity and parental benefits as "notable," especially in comparison with the shorter paid leaves in the United Kingdom or the unpaid leaves offered in the United States (p. 119). Nevertheless, as Calder (2006) notes, there is still much room for improving the access and construction of Canada's benefits, most notably that maternity and parental leave benefits are contingent upon participation in the labour force (p. 100). On top of the federally administered benefits, approximately 20 percent of mothers in Canada receive supplemental benefits from their employer or other sources, and most university's faculty collective agreements include such supplements (Bischoping, 2003). My university tops up faculty members' salaries to 95 percent of their regular earnings for half of the leave period. Furthermore, it provides that any faculty member who takes a maternity or parental leave has the option of a one-year extension to apply for tenure.

Most research on maternity and parental leaves within academia focuses on female graduate students and faculty's marginalization, underemployment, and withdrawals from the academy in circumstances where there are no or few accommodations made for maternity or parental leaves. Even in Canada, where paid leaves are available, a 2004 study by Pulkingham and Van de Gaag showed that 35 percent of mothers with infants do not have the employment record to qualify for benefits, a grouping that often includes most graduate students, post-doctoral fellows, and sessional faculty (p. 119). Panofsky (2007) argues that the lack of available paid leaves and other related policies causes an "uneasy partnership" for the "Mother/Professor" where "faculty women remain disadvantaged in academia because it continues to reward early and sustained achievement; a distinctly male model for success that often excludes women as they bear and raise their children" (pp. 72–75). The personal narratives shared by American women at different stages of academic careers in *Mama, PhD* (Evans & Grant, 2008) reveal the consequences of unpaid or unavailable maternity and parental leaves and their effects on real families, including the common choice to delay or avoid motherhood, the challenge of finding affordable childcare, the realities of debt and marital stress, and, in some cases, the decision to phase out of the academy. Yet even in my experience where a paid leave and tenure stoppage was available, academic culture and university practices made it challenging to use those policies as intended.

Having married just after I finished my undergraduate degree, I gave little thought to having children in the years when I pursued my MA, worked for a non-governmental agency, and began my PhD. At first I simply was not emotionally ready to start a family, but once I was midway through my PhD and the precarious academic job market became apparent, financial worries and job stability became the reason to delay having children. In 2009 I defended my PhD in history at York University, and after a year of juggling contract teaching at three universities, I was fortunate enough to be offered a tenure-track job at Wilfrid Laurier University. Amazingly, within a week my husband had secured work in a nearby city, and a month later we purchased our first house. I still look back in amazement at the synchronicity of this turn of events. The only black mark that summer was losing our beloved dog to cancer. While we looked for a new four-legged friend, we also talked seriously about having a child for the first time. Despite deciding we were ready to have a baby, the ticking of the tenure clock overruled the biological clock. I thought it would be better for my career (and sanity) to complete the book based on my dissertation research before a baby made an appearance. I also felt that I would make a better impression on my campus community if I put a few years into the job before disappearing for a year. Still, I was aware that at age thirty-three, I did not want to wait much longer. Approximately two years later, once I had a manuscript draft and a book contract in hand, my husband and I started trying. This waiting period was not unique to me. Sorcinelli (1992) reports that male and female junior faculty on the tenure track experience what she calls less "negative spillover" between their work and personal lives after a few years into the job, making it a more comfortable period to start a family or add more children (p. 27).

At first the timing of conception was important to me. I had seen other pregnant colleagues end or start their maternity leaves early, by choice or from pressure, to avoid disrupting their students with a new instructor partway through the term. I wanted neither to give up the time with my baby nor to be seen as an inconvenience on campus, so I plotted my fertility alongside the academic calendar, a common practice according to Weststar (2012) for academic women anxious for a seamless transition from professor to parent (p. 360). Using a spreadsheet, I found a three-month window where we could try for a summer baby. Unbelievably, we conceived immediately, right on schedule. Our joy at having everything work out was short-lived when I miscarried just past the first trimester. I was devastated and found it hard to shift back into academic mode, planning conferences, research trips, and courses for the time period I expected to have been with my baby. In hindsight, this change in plans prompted a critical shift in my perspective and priorities. Losing the baby made me more certain that rather than trying to fit my personal life neatly into my professional life, I had to acknowledge that these two parts of my life would always overlap and I would need to accommodate them both. The spreadsheet was thrown out the window. I just wanted a baby whenever he or she wanted to make an appearance.

Three months later I was pregnant again, this time with a due date scheduled two days after classes ended. I knew due dates were only best guesses, but it gave me some relief that my baby's term would finish close to my students'. When I asked my dean about what would happen if the baby came early, I ignored his assertion (another follower of the "babies sleep" mentality) that I could just finish marking exams the week after the baby was born. I explained that my students had the right to know in advance what would happen should I leave early, and the dean promised there would be replacement instructors. However, when I passed on the names of recommended graders to the dean's office, it was left to me to check their availability, negotiate their hours and wages, and have them sign a contract. Later, upon more careful reading of the collective agreement, I discovered I was not responsible for finding and arranging suitable coverage for my classes. Despite having policies in place and a baby-booming young faculty, neither my program coordinators nor my dean was entirely confident about how to handle leaves occurring during the term. When swapping stories about this process with other new faculty parents, the confusion or lack of administrative initiative was common, prompting a shared refrain of "has no one ever had a baby at this university before?" Regardless, my preplanning turned out to be necessary as my daughter Juliet was born a week early.

What I remember from Juliet's first few weeks was the tremendous sense of awe (Look at those toes, eyes, belly button! She just sighed! This is love!), combined with equal amounts of terror (Is she breathing? Am I doing this right? Is she breathing?). It was during this period that I felt most able to focus completely on my child, or rather I simply had no time or energy to do anything else and no one expected otherwise. When she was awake, I was feeding, changing, bathing, and cooing, and when she slept I had to fight the urge to research every aspect of infant care. I was surprised at the amount of choices and how sharp the learning curve was for everything from swaddling to nursing to figuring out how to get those delicate hands through tiny sleeves. Eventually my husband and I stopped googling everything and just learned to trust our gut and read our daughter's cues.

Around one month after the birth, I had to make a decision regarding the stack of book proofs that had arrived the same week as Juliet. In order to meet my publisher's deadline, I had three weeks to proofread three hundred pages. I decided to tackle the pages during naptime and again in the evening when my husband was home. The first time I sat down to copy-edit, Juliet slept for two hours and I managed to get through the entire introduction. I still remember that awesome nap, and I clung to the hope that two hours would become the norm. Instead, Juliet turned out to a catnapper, often requiring more time to get her to sleep than she usually slept. Eventually we got into a routine where she went down easily, but up until she was about seven months, she rarely napped for longer than thirty minutes at a time. This could sometimes be stretched to an hour, but only if I held her for the nap in the rocking chair.

If I left her to nap in her crib, I would race around the house with "Flight of the Bumblebee" playing in my head as I tried to clean, eat, shower, and dress while an invisible clocked ticked toward the inevitable thirty-minute mark. I was not getting much editing done, or anything else. I hated having to work while she was awake, but as the deadline crept closer, I would frantically try to get some pages read while Juliet was content in her bouncy chair. Meanwhile, my daughter was still getting up every two to three hours at night to nurse. Exhaustion caused my eyes to glaze over and I knew I was not reading closely enough to catch every typo. It did not help that my book was about children endangered by war and the mothers who moved mountains to save them. It served only to confirm my own inadequacies as a diligent scholar and loving mother. I made the deadline, but my reward was nightmares about reviews pointing out error-riddled pages. Luckily the pages came back one more time, and my indexer turned out to be a thorough reader who caught an embarrassing date mix-up, among other typos.

Why did I put myself through that agonizing editing process with a newborn? Looking back, I see I had many choices. I could have delayed doing the final edits until my daughter was older or I was better rested or I had some form of childcare or even until I returned to work. I was under no illusions that the world was waiting with bated breath for my book. At worst my lateness would have annoyed my publisher, but I suspect they would have accommodated me with a new deadline. A combination of pride, ambition, and anxiety pushed me to make the deadline. It was important to demonstrate, mainly to myself, but also to anyone else paying attention, that a baby had not changed me. Plus my book was already advertised in the publisher's spring catalogue. If I made the deadline it would be out in time to be on sale at the book fair at the annual meeting of my professional association during the Congress of Humanities and Social Sciences, which was being hosted by my home institution. I wanted to attend Congress with a baby and book in tow, proof that one could have it all. To have done otherwise would have fed my lingering imposter syndrome and made me worry that I lacked a serious reputation. If I did not finish the book now, I remember thinking, what else would I fail at accomplishing? So close to Juliet's birth, I can blame some of these emotions on fluctuating hormones. My anxiety was also provoked by being a new professor trying to hit all the critical markers, however vaguely defined in actual qualitative and quantitative terms for tenure, a process that is entirely dependent on impressing your peers. Even though I was perfectly in my right to take time off, my concern about the connection between reputation and job security was definitely one of the reasons I worked hard to finish my book on schedule and continued to work for the rest of my leave during Juliet's naptimes or after she went to bed.

It is also important to acknowledge that the nature of academic work, at least in the humanities and social sciences, namely the flexibility and freedom of where and when we can work, ensured that working during my leave was possible. I am doubtful that my book prep or any other project would have happened if I had to leave home. I had no childcare during my leave, and there were many days in the newborn stage in which my own showering and dressing did not occur. As someone who still is a little giddy about having an office all to myself, I really love working on campus, but I take advantage of the fact that much of my workload can often be completed at home. I also greatly appreciate that outside of classroom time, office hours, and meetings, I am not beholden to a specific schedule. Nor do I often work with anyone but myself, and when I do, collaboration takes place over email or phone. So while on leave, I had most of the resources at home to continue working away from my office.

I know flexible work schedules and workspaces will be greatly appreciated when I have a sick child to care for or a school play to attend, yet at several points during my leave, this freedom felt like a curse. As I am sure many professionals who leave the workplace with laptops and smartphones at their fingertips can attest, taking work home can also mean a workday that never ends. In fact, the very nature of academic work, be it the teaching, research, or service portion, means there is always something that can be done, and it is often entirely up to ourselves to place boundaries on the appropriate time period to work. I know my own judgment was influenced by a work culture that normalized working nights and weekends. Even among my supportive, noncompetitive community of pre-tenure friends there was a certain fetishization of long work hours. Not being able to join in on a social gathering because of work was sometimes worn like a badge of honour. I also knew of colleagues, male and female, who had written and published articles, presented at conferences, and in one case organized an international conference while on parental or maternity leave. Ironically, the research talk where the "babies sleep" comment was made was being given by a colleague on maternity leave whom I had invited to present! Given these pressures and precedents, I felt my willpower would have been stronger if work had not been possible to complete at home. Of course, I may have been tempted to return to work early if I could not have worked from home or if I worked in a time-sensitive research field. A survey of female faculty in Canadian medical schools by Lent, Phillips, Richardson, and Stewart (2000) showed that 46 percent took sixteen weeks or less of maternity leave, and 12 percent took only five weeks or less when at the time of the survey they were eligible for twenty-five weeks. The justification for the shorter leaves was the perception that time away caused a negative impact on their academic work, particularly research, and a negative effect on their colleagues' workloads. The authors of the study concluded that this was partly due "to the culture of an institution that sees maternity leave as vacation time and a 'slacking off' from career advancement, or to both" (p. 575).

I was also aware during my leave of all the deadlines that were critical to planning the work I would do when I returned. Given how long it takes to publish, and the seasonal nature of conferences and funding opportunities, I kept an eye out for interesting calls for papers and submitted proposals for projects I would work on when I got back. (In the case of this collection, I was grateful that the deadline was extended and the new timeframe coincided with my daughter's vastly improved naptimes and nighttime sleep; otherwise I would have never had the time or energy to write.) I rationalized that this legwork was necessary if I wanted to be fully active in my first year back on the job, and not have an even longer gap on my CV. Advanced scheduling was also indispensable for teaching. Admittedly I like to schedule things more in advance than is the norm, but it would have been impractical to start from scratch when I returned, just a few weeks before the winter term started. Beyond the typically early bookstore deadlines, I had one new course to develop and I learned its enrolment cap had tripled while I was on leave, forcing me to entirely rethink the assignments and reading list. I wanted that class to do an oral history project with the local historical society, which required an application to the research ethics committee a term in advance. I also applied for a grant to fund the visit of an author whose memoir my students were assigned to read. Additionally, I kept in touch with students and colleagues who needed reference letters. None of these were onerous tasks, but they added up over the course of my leave to approximately two to twenty hours per week. Under most circumstances I relish the independent nature of academic work, which allows us to pursue research and teaching opportunities in ways that we find most illuminating and useful. Yet during my leave there were times when I felt burdened by the constant need to keep on top of my academic to-do list and longed to have someone who was not only on campus covering my sessional teaching responsibilities, but also taking care of all the loose ends related to teaching and research. Or rather, I just needed someone to tell me it was okay to fall behind in the conference circuit or to have simpler syllabi in my first term back.

Overall, many of the dilemmas I found myself in had to do with the fact that while I may have been on leave from my academic position, taking my employer out of the equation did not mean the work was suddenly unavailable. Yet there were also a dozen circumstances where my employer directly sought my labour. For the most part these requests were prompted by a lack of bodies to complete service and administrative tasks. This problem stems from the common practice of replacing faculty on leave only in terms of their teaching commitment, not any other university responsibilities. I imagine there are some universities where programs and departments are large enough that one or even several persons' leave does not mean unduly burdening your remaining colleagues. In the case of my institution, I work at Wilfrid Laurier's Brantford campus, an interdisciplinary satellite where most faculty have service and teaching responsibilities in at least two programs. In his analysis of my university's Bilateral Committee on Brantford Campus Workload, Warrick (2012) reports that due to the many cross-appointments and a disproportionate reliance on limited-term appointments whose ability to serve on university committees is limited, "FT [full-time] faculty and librarians at Brantford have a service workload that is two to four times that of their Waterloo [main campus] counterparts" (p. 8). At the time of my leave, I was part of the campus's core program contemporary studies, plus history and youth and children's studies. The latter two were small programs with only four full-time faculty members in each, all of whom were cross-appointed to other programs. During the twelve months I was on leave, every one of my full-time colleagues in history and youth and children's studies was at some point on sabbatical, parental leave, or sick leave. For example, all four members of our history program, including the program coordinator, overlapped their leaves for the entire winter term. Meanwhile, in youth and children's studies, over the summer and through the fall term only our brand-new tenure-track hire was on campus. With the exception of the unexpected sick leave, our administration was well aware of the overlapping leaves months in advance and denied the faculty's requests for any appointments to cover these massive gaps. I understand that my university, along with most others in Canada, is underfunded, but this refusal to adequately cover leaves also stems from the invisibility of the service work performed by faculty that keep the university running. As a result, the faculty who were not on leave were stretched beyond a reasonable limit to complete all the administrative duties and service work. It was not until there was literally no one to answer student concerns, represent the program at recruitment events, have the required number of faculty present to vote through program changes, or staff the part-time hiring committees that the scope of problem was realized.

One administrative solution was to apologetically approach the faculty on leave to attend to these matters. I was not sympathetic to this self-made problem and said no to most requests, even if they included the caveat that my daughter was welcome to tag along. On the surface this attitude was baby friendly, but it also assumed that I could juggle my caregiving and professional duties simultaneously. Certainly there was a point when Juliet was highly portable and would have been barely noticed at a meeting, but by the time these requests came in, she was more mobile and vocal, and like all babies, unpredictable in her mood and needs. Regardless of whether she would have been unfazed by her campus visit, I came to view my daughter's inclusion in these invitations as another assumption that babies could or should accommodate the working adults around them. In two circumstances, I brought Juliet to the campus for hiring meetings so I could help out the colleagues left behind to sort out these messes. I also continued to answer student queries and participate in program-development-related discussions and votes over email or on conference calls. Yet I could not help notice that with one exception, my tenured male colleagues on sabbatical answered requests to sit on committees or attend meetings in the negative. Why did I not feel confident to do the same? Why did I, whose supplemental benefits had expired by the time most of these requests came in, meaning I was not even being paid by the university, come to meetings? Why was my leave less valuable to the university or to me?

These questions lingered and bothered me throughout the remainder of my leave. I wrestled with how much I had brought on myself by simply not saying no and continuing to check my work email, and how much was more of a systemic problem within academia, or my campus in particular. In her study of maternity and parental leave experiences at one mid-size Canadian university, Weststar (2012) did not specifically ask her twenty participants about working during their leave; however, in four instances this issue was independently raised, and the work included organizing conferences, revising book manuscripts, writing book chapters, marking papers, and supervising graduate students (p. 360). Meanwhile, Ollilainen's (2012) comparative study of Finnish and American academic women revealed that I was not alone in undergoing desire, confusion, anxiety, and resentment over continuing work while on leave. Whether it was caused by an uncertain academic job market or differing interpretations about what leaves meant from department chairs and colleagues, academic women in both countries "expressed a clear dissonance between the strong feeling of entitlement to not work and the need to maintain a professional image for job security" (n.p.). Since "academia has historically excluded reproduction and care work," Ollilainen positions the expectation about working during these leaves as stemming from "the male-dominated academic tradition" where "the reproductive lives of women faculty have been either overlooked or viewed as an impediment to productivity and getting tenure" (n.p.). Indeed, academia tends to thrive on "the ideal worker model" that seeks and rewards the "professor/researcher without outside responsibilities" who can tackle "expectations for teaching, research, and service [that] far exceed a 40-hour work week" (n.p.).

My desire to prove myself as a scholar has definitely been nurtured not only by academia's competitive environment, but also by evidence documented by Fothergill and Feltey (2003) that female academics are paid less and progress through the ranks slower than their male colleagues. It is also clear from the ways multiple parties encouraged or asked me to work during my leave that staying at home to raise a baby was not considered to be valuable or stimulating work. A cavalier comment such as "babies sleep" explicitly denies the labour involved in caring for an infant, and treats babies like convenient objects that can be put away or toted along while the real work occurs. Considering that women are still the dominant parent to take all or most of the parental portion of the leave in Canada, this attitude is a specific devaluation of women's work in the home. It also undoes the legal and social progress behind the equity laws that established paid maternity leaves (Evans, 2007, p. 119).

One result of my year-long contemplation and frustration was deciding to formally address the mixed message "babies sleep" sends to new faculty parents, particularly women. To that end, with the urging of other female and male colleagues, I decided to make a complaint about the attitude emanating from Research Services. I was tempted to take the suggestion of another academic mother, recently returned from her own leave, to stage a sit-in in Mr. Babies Sleep's office, where we could play the role of a sleepless, colicky baby screaming in his ear and see how much work he got done. Instead, the women's faculty colleague representative for Laurier's Faculty Association, Rebecca Godderis, offered her assistance, first in asking her counterpart at the main campus if she knew of other instances where faculty, male or female, were being pressured to work on their maternity and parental leaves. When Godderis received an affirmative answer, the following recommendations were made in her 2011 annual report:

There needs to be a clear message from administration to all members of campus that when a faculty member (male or female) is on maternal/parental leave that this is not simply an opportunity to do more research; rather, they are acting as primary care giver and, in addition to not legally being able to work, should not feel pressured to do so. It would be particularly beneficial if members of research services on both campuses were regularly reminded of expectations for family-related leaves. (n.p.)

This section of her report received a same-day response from Laurier's vice-president academic, who forwarded it to our vice-president research. I was pleasantly surprised to learn that both individuals were receptive to this feedback, listened to the rationale, and promised to follow up with Research Services. Although it is not clear what changes may come to pass at my own institution, it is critical that university administrations set a tone that bolsters their tenure-clock stoppage policy, consistently communicate accurate information about leaves to faculty, and ensure appropriate coverage of service duties, alongside teaching ones.

On my part, I know there are organizational strategies I can employ when I return to work in order to find a more satisfying work–family balance. Beyond creating stricter boundaries around my work hours and being gentler on myself when I scrutinize my performance as an academic and mother, I am moved by the idea suggested by Bartlett (2006) that academic women, as well as men, "need to find ways of taking our life to work, instead of just taking our work home with us. Perhaps if work/life were represented as slashed, as balancing or colliding, there could be room for other conversations, other policies" (p. 23). In the meantime, I suspect there will be moments where I feel pushed to the limits, but when that happens I will try to remind myself that what I truly value in life is not always present on my CV.

References

Bartlett, A. (2006) Theory, desire, and maternity: At work in academia. *Hecat, 32*, 21–33.

Bischoping, K. (2003). The best you can expect when you're expecting … and beyond: A review of contract language for mothers in the Canadian academy. *Journal of the Association for Research on Mothering, 5*(2), 77–86.

Calder, G. (2006). A pregnant pause: Federalism, equality and the maternity and parental leave debate in Canada. *Feminist Legal Studies, 14*, 99–118.

Evans, E., & Grant, C. (Eds.). (2008). *Mama, PhD: Women write about motherhood and academic life.* New Brunswick, NJ: Rutgers University Press.

Evans, P. M. (2007). Comparative perspectives on changes to Canada's paid parental leave: Implications for class and gender. *International Journal of Social Welfare, 16*, 119–128.

Fothergill, A., & Feltey, K. (2003). I've worked very hard and slept very little: Mothers on the tenure track in academia. *Journal of the Association for Research on Mothering, 5*(2), 7–19.

Godderis, R. (2012). "Women's faculty colleague report." Waterloo, ON: Wilfrid Laurier University.

Lent, B., Phillips, S. P., Richardson, B., & Stewart, D. (2000). Promoting parental leave for female and male physicians. *Canadian Medical Association Journal, 162*(11), 1575–1576.

Ollilainen, M. (2012). *Ideal workers on maternity leave: Family-leave policy and academic mothers' work/family conflict in Finland and the U.S.* Unpublished Manuscript.

Panofsky, R. (2007). Professor/mother: The uneasy partnership. *Femspec, 8*(1.2), 65–74.

Pulkingham, J., & Van der Gaag, T. (2004). Maternity/parental leave provisions in Canada: We've come a long way, but there's further to go. *Canadian Women Studies, 23*(3.4), 116–125.

Sorcinelli, M. D. (1992). New and junior faculty stress: Research and responses. In M. D. Sorcinelli & A. E. Austin (Eds.), *Developing new and junior faculty* (pp. 27–37). San Francisco, CA: Jossey-Bass.

Warrick, G. (2012, December 2). News from your Brantford faculty liaison. WLUFA Advocate [Blog]. Retrieved from https://advocatewlufa.wordpress .com/2012/12/02/news-from-your-brantford-faculty-liaison/

Weststar, J. (2012). Negotiating in silence: Experiences with parental leave in academia. *Relations Industrielles, 67*(3), 352–374.

Legacy and Vulnerability
Queer Parenting in the Academy

Sarah R. Pickett

My mother's gravestone reads as follows: "beloved wife, mother, and daughter." This legacy, with its focus on relationships as the most valued aspects of one's life, has been the backdrop of my career as a professional. It both grounds and haunts my development as an academic.

Voyage

My path to the academic world has been murky, unplanned, and at best tentative. Unlike many of my peers I did not set out to be an academic; I decided to pursue my doctoral studies with the "best opportunity" for my future family in mind. At the time, I had completed my master's degree and was practising as a marriage and family therapist. Obtaining my doctorate with a goal of becoming a licensed/registered psychologist would provide more options for the future.

Womb Urges

I consciously decided, at twenty-seven, that I would put my urges to have children aside for the promise of a career with endless opportunities and greater flexibility for my family plans. My then partner of four years had already expressed her wish for me to carry our future child, and I was more than agreeable—we decided that when I finished my doctorate we would actively pursue pregnancy and parenthood. In support of this decision was a well-developed rationale maintained by the prevailing heteronormative culture. In a heteronormative society, fertility is viewed as a problem that only heterosexual couples encounter. As a same-sex couple creating a family in a heteronormative culture, we recognized the potential for many explanations, choices, and endless vulnerable encounters with physicians and allied health professionals operating from a heteronormative lens. Additionally, there was the financial cost that may be associated with fertility treatments, one that would most certainly have thrown us into an uncomfortable amount of debt. There were relatively few questions from family, friends, doctors, and colleagues about "us" having children; it was 2001, slightly post *Ellen* but not yet *Modern Family*, despite the fact I was the prime "baby-having" age. If by chance our family planning did make it into conversation, the questions were along the lines of "Can you have children? How would you? Why would you want to? What does the research say about lesbians raising kids?" Media images were not targeting the lesbian community and thus me about ticking biological clocks. In fact, within the southern California lesbian community I was a part of, I had not yet encountered anyone who identified as a lesbian and had children within that lesbian relationship. Three of my academic mentors identified as lesbian: two of them had no children, and one had an adult child with her ex-husband. None had embarked on having children with another woman while in an academic context. Throughout the remainder of my studies my womb would urge and I would see my heterosexual colleagues, friends, and family have children, and some struggle to have children. However, I do not recall many sharing a decision not to have children. Most often it was in the plans. Professionals, not academics, mostly surrounded me, and while these non-academic professional environments did not necessarily have policies that were supportive of having children, on the surface there was a general acceptance of heterosexual couples having children as a "predictable phase of life." There were baby showers, congratulations, and "it's about time" floating all around.

Then it happened: I finished my degree in 2005 and my eight-year relationship ended over a glass of wine. Now what? What about our agreement, my plans, my sacrifice, my womb, my aching heart? Family, friends, and colleagues would say, "Thank goodness the two of you did not have kids; what a hassle that would be," but I had been waiting for the hassle. Couldn't everyone see the devastation in my eyes? It was as if I were wearing a billboard no one could see: "Thirty-one-year-old lesbian fears never having children—please help!" I was invisible. In time I would come to think of this early relationship as one in which we "grew up together well." Importantly, over our eight years we learned what it meant to have a lesbian identity; how to walk in a heteronormative world with self-worth, reclaim voice, negotiate multiple roles, and aspects of the self; and how to begin, end, and transform within relationship.

The following few years brought many new personal and career opportunities, including meeting my soulmate, Kathy, and entering an international relationship with the ultimate decision to move from California to Newfoundland and Labrador (initially because of our lack of legal recognition as a same-sex couple in the United States and Kathy's resulting inability, as a Canadian, to legally reside in the United States). When I met Kathy and we were in the process of deciding whether or not to embark on the journey of international couplehood together, the conversation went something like this:

> ME: I would like to have children tomorrow. Can you live with this?
>
> KATHY: I will likely have many career changes and employment uncertainty. Can you live with this?
>
> We both agreed.

Now, seven years later, at thirty-eight (me) and thirty-five (Kathy), we have two small children, almost three and fifteen months, I am in my second three-year term contract in the Faculty of Education at Memorial University of Newfoundland (seeking a conversion to a tenure-track position), and we are both struggling with career and family life balance. Today, I grapple with what it is to be an academic transitioning from a well-developed career as a psychologist and an out lesbian parent with two young children living in St. John's, Newfoundland.

A Beginning Academic

As an aspirational tenure-track faculty member coming from a professional background, I frequently feel as though I have been transported to another country. The language, customs, rules, roles, and boundaries are familiar yet foreign.

Upon my entrance to the academy I was six months pregnant and Kathy and I were expecting our first child. I was grateful that I managed to proceed through the interviews without being confronted about my protruding belly. I vividly remember meeting with the dean of the faculty and wondering how accepting the position offer with a sidebar of "by the way, I will be having a baby in three months" was going to be received. I was overwhelmed by his humanness. He managed to spare me all that he may have known about the spoken and unspoken performance expectations within academia, and with a calm, supportive, slightly spontaneous and gentle smile conveyed his empathy for my colliding worlds. I went on in a fumbling manner to explain how my timing was slightly off and how I didn't mean to deceive anyone by not sharing my pregnancy. I had learned from the professional world enough to know that applying for a job and disclosing a pregnancy (in particular for a contract) might make me seem a less than optimal candidate.

What I remember most about that conversation is that he said something to the effect of "We are a faculty of education. If we cannot support children and families, then who will? Isn't that what we are about?" This was meaning-ful on so many levels. I told him we were expecting and I went on to clarify that by "we" I meant Kathy and I were expecting. Again, his humanity and genuineness softens my heart as I write. In that brief exchange, for a moment, both my desire to be a mother and my identity as a lesbian and partner were made visible, acknowledged, and valued within academia. Maybe this was not the foreign territory I thought, or maybe it was better, different, and more inclusive.

My belly preceding me, I began my first semester as an assistant profes-sor in the fall of 2009. The long hours of course preparation, the struggle to acclimate to an academic culture with which I was quite unfamiliar, and the insecurities of being the only visibly pregnant faculty member (and on contract to add to it) contributed to the isolating, chilly climate I experienced. I was lonely, unsure of myself, and longing for connection. Perhaps the loneliness and insecurity I experienced was confounded by the pairing of our launching into parenting-hood and my academic debut.

Fortunately, I found a safe haven, the newly established faculty writing group. In this space "all of me was welcomed." I felt visible as a mother-to-be, a new faculty member, a novice academic, and an experienced clinician. It was through my connection with this group that I began to find the relation-ships I was yearning for and had hoped to find through my career change, relationships that honoured the "whole me" and the "whole of others" with all our complexities.

Parenting

I was marking furiously to meet my semester deadlines and my pregnancy due date, and then it happened: my water broke.

Phone call

> ME: I think my water may have broken.
>
> KATHY: Oh, okay, I'll stop studying [for final exams]. Are you on your way home?
>
> ME: No, I think that I will just get this Christmas tree first.
>
> KATHY: What? The baby is on the way? I am a little nervous.
>
> ME: It will be fine; we have some time, and besides I need to get our Christmas tree!

Even in that moment I knew my time and our time would soon be spent balanced between lectures, feedings, never-ending marking, and all the new uncharted grounds of motherhood. What were a few more hours? In time this would become a story that Kathy would tell fondly. It highlights my desire to carry my mother's legacy and possibly reveals my survival strategy thus far in academia. It was December, and beyond the marking, beyond the anxiety I knew that I was causing Kathy, was a deep-seated need to bring our beautiful baby home to a space filled with the heritage and the warmth I so fondly remember from my childhood. The menorah was already out for Chanukah but the Christmas tree was absent. Once the tree was purchased, we could embark on this new life journey together. My marks would be submitted late; Kathy would send the prewritten email I had drafted for this exact situation to all my students (while we were in the delivery room), assuring them that as soon as the baby and I were settled at home, I would attend to their needs. For a moment, all that mattered was the three of us.

When we emerged from the first few weeks of parenthood, reality reared its head. On a three-year contract I am privileged with some of the same benefits as a tenure-track academic staff member. Unfortunately, however, in order to be eligible for paid maternity and/or parental leave, you must have worked for a one-year period. This presented quite a conundrum because it would mean I would go straight back to work. How would we do it? Kathy was in the midst of a career change and had returned to school, so my income was our primary source of financial support.

> **Result:** Working odd hours, two hours' sleep at a time, Kohen (our son) taking up residence in meetings and my office, and a much earlier start at out-of-home childcare than we wanted. Eventually, September rolled around and I chose to take the sixteen-week paid leave that I was now eligible for.

September 2010 marked the end of the first year of my three-year contract, and I began my parental leave despite my fears of how this would be perceived by my peers and those with power. No one in a position of power or authority asked if I was taking more than the allotted four months of "top-up"; in fact, they never asked if I was taking any time off. I was granted the leave by the kind dean who himself was struggling with an illness and holding on to life. He wrote a supportive email stating that he too had taken a parental leave a while back and understood how important it was to be with family. I believed his words. I, however, was not in the same place of privilege as he was when he was making the same decision. He was not on contract trying to break into academia. Yet, I am thankful for his support and for sparing me the details of how this decision may or may not have affected my career. Later, I would come to learn at his funeral of the shift his life took when his children were born, of how his wife and two daughters became his priorities. I often think about how lucky I was to have had my entrance into academia as a parent softened through his lens and my naïveté spared for long enough to further strengthen my alliance with my mother's legacy.

Decisions: Second Womb Urge

Now thirty-six, I was keenly aware of my ovaries' expiry date. Given that as a lesbian couple we have to actively create our families and pregnancies, the decision about when to begin this process was ever looming. It had taken us five tries with intrauterine insemination (IUI); numerous drugs, both oral and injections; and two different sperm donors to create our son. Both Kathy and I were all too aware of the fact that one try with IUI was the equivalent of three tries without medical support; thus with our son it took us fifteen months to get pregnant. This is called unexplained infertility. The billboard in my mind read, "Thirty-six years old with the potential of unexplained infertility once again—two children wanted."

Pregnancy, Visibility, and Loneliness

The higher education literature is filled with articles regarding the decision to become a parent, parenting in academia, and the impact of the aforementioned on a tenure-track trajectory and academic career (Halpern, 2008; Mason & Goulden, 2002, 2004; Wolfinger, Mason, & Goulden, 2009). However, there is paucity in the literature around women becoming pregnant, lesbian women parents, and the fictions surrounding these in the academy.

Hello, where am I?

Historically, the literature has been heteronormative, often rendering same-sex/queer couples and/or same-sex/queer couples who are also parents invisible. The themes represented in the literature are of anxiety, decisions around becoming/being a parent, demands made by the academy, career impacts of having young children, and women negotiating being on and off the academic ladder, and are all very relevant, relatable, and representative of elements of my experience (Mason & Goulden, 2002, 2004; Tillmann, 2011; Warner, 2008). Nevertheless, I find that as a lesbian parent and academic, my voice, my identities, and my experience of becoming pregnant are marginalized by the context and the heteronormativity of the academy. When reviewing research on parenting in the academy, frequently I have to read through to the subtext to determine the inclusion and exclusion criteria. Most often the population being discussed is women, but not lesbian women, or the author has not considered the possibility that lesbian women may have a different voice and may be hidden/less visible or marginalized within the dominant social paradigm.

Ticking Clocks

My seventy-eight-year-old father in California had stage-four terminal cancer. He had already outlived the doctors' "expectations," and we were fortunate enough to make several planned and costly trips to visit so that our son, Kohen, and he may know each other. Academia can offer flexibility, the privilege of going on a moment's notice to visit and being able to stay for weeks. But what is the cost of such actions on my long-term academic goals? How does this affect my time for research and writing? Yes, I can teach online, attend to correspondence with colleagues and students, and reschedule classes as needed. Although this is not vacation time or family leave, the work is still there; waiting for me to stop crying, stop attending to my father and our son so that Kathy can take the lead and I can pick up my work 24-7. My father is a pivotal person in my life and career; I felt he must know both our children.

This time, it was much quicker.

> **November 2010:** Returning from parental leave. Dreaded conversation with top administrator, "We're expecting, July of 2011."
>
> **Beginning of January 2011:** Phone call to Dad in the hospital in California, "It's a girl."
>
> **Late in January 2011:** Chemo stops working.
>
> **February 15, 2011:** Dad (Grandpa) sees the ultrasound when we visit him. Dad (Grandpa): "She is beautiful. Sarahdoo, now you have two, a boy and girl, you can stop now. You have it all, the career, partner, and children, be happy. Now, let me see that grandson of mine. Kohen, I love you. Sarah, I love you. Kathy, I love you. Baby girl, I love you."
>
> **February 24, 2011:** Dad (Grandpa) dies.
>
> **January–April 2011:** Three courses, year two of my contract. I must prove my worth if I want to stay.

Parentless Child, New Parent, Expectant Parent, and Unstable Career

Dancing through Discourses

As a (pregnant) lesbian/parent (to be), I am faced with several associated discourses that some heterosexual mothers-to-be are not. The most significant discourse is rooted in the fictions women may have to perform to justify becoming pregnant in academic contexts. Most heterosexual women are privileged with the ability to say, "It was unexpected" or "It was an accident," followed by nonverbal gestures that support this claim to be baffled or surprised. The subtext is that no sane woman would deliberately get pregnant at the outset of an academic career. In this way some heterosexual women are allowed to perform a reaction to an unexpected/unplanned situation. There is a safety in denying the deep desire to have children and begin a family for women wanting a career outside the home. It is not acceptable to say, "Yes, we planned to have a child at this exact moment, when my career is launching and my womb is aching, and my doctor says time is ticking if I want to increase my chances of a healthy baby." Engaging with peers through the framework of either a quasi unplanned or unexpected pregnancy has significant implications related to priority, value, and commitment to the academy that are considerably different from planning a pregnancy. Women in same-sex relationships do not have access to these performances; we are denied access to these fictions because we do not have real or quasi accidents in getting pregnant. There are endless appointments, ovulation tracking, medications, ovulation triggers, insemination, and waiting the never-ending two weeks to see "if it happened." Every step is a conscious one in this process and one that forbids the use of these fictions. It didn't just "kind of" happen, and we did plan, expect, and want to be pregnant.

As a lesbian parent-to-be, I have no access to private decisions to plan actively to get pregnant followed by a plan to act surprised or say things like "We weren't trying, but we weren't not trying—we tried not to think about it too much; we just stopped the pill and thought, if it happens it happens." This is a notable difference: the inability of lesbian women who are pregnant to use the performances some heterosexual women may engage in to function within the discourse and legitimatize their choice to have children. Without access to this performance, this fiction, some lesbian academic women announcing pregnancy to those in power stand to encounter greater vulnerability than their heterosexual women peers. I risk being positioned as someone who is not as committed to academic work when this is not the case. My response of "Yes, that's right, Kathy and I are expecting for a second time" is often insufficient. I feel pulled to answer, explain, and justify my actions.

July 2011: Reghan arrives! This time I take the seventeen-week maternity leave right away.

Cost: Missed opportunities to engage in research (a deeply lacking area of my CV), further struggle with developing my academic identity, fears of possible disapproval from my peers and the incoming dean, worries that this will have an impact on the possibility of conversion to tenure track (for which I begin eligibility this coming year) and/or contract renewal.

Benefit: Bonding with Reghan; successful breastfeeding; time to help Kohen adjust to his new sister and reassure him of his importance, worth, and value; being present and available to Kathy through this transition; sleeping when she sleeps (sometimes); spending time with family when they visit; laughing and crying together; watching our children grow; nurturing each other and our little ones.

Late November 2011: Return to work. My concentration, focus, and interest for work/career-related matters is reduced. My soul's primary distraction, I want to be home, creating irreplaceable memories with our children instead of fearing the time I may be losing. I begin to actively question my decision to transition to the academy.

Aftermath: Deciphering the Consequences

My contract was not initially renewed as I expected. I and those more senior in my circle had assumed that the only question would be if my position would convert to a tenure-track position or my three-year contract would simply be extended. The offer, however, was an unpredicted one-year teaching contract at a substantially lower salary without research time. Through a series of negotiations and significant advocacy from my colleagues, in the end, I did manage to hold on to my three-year contract. It is situations like this that lead me to wonder. My contract not initially being renewed was concerning, and in light of my two pregnancies and childbirths during this time I am left questioning if these may be related. If anyone in a position of power had asked how I was managing or had offered to sit down with me to help me understand my options, I might not wonder. But no one did. When the university faculty association suggested that I inquire about my eligibility to stop the clock in the same manner that the tenure clock may stop for maternity and/or parental leave, advising that the language in the collective agreement is vague and likely flexible enough to allow for this accommodation, I followed up on this possibility immediately. If the clock had stopped, right now I would be beginning the remaining eight months of my prior contract and not up for renewal until well after I submit this chapter, complete an actual research term, and likely present a paper at a conference this spring. All of this I imagine would have reflected positively when negotiating my renewal. I was denied my request.

Result: I Wonder

When I was given the first offer, were my maternity/parental leaves taken into account, my extra teaching, the fact that I was now managing two children under age three while simultaneously learning the new language of the academy? The task of unpacking the meanings of actions and behaviours is mine alone. I am often left with the decision of being visible or invisible. How many times have I had to say, "Yes, my partner, Kathy," when a colleague assumes I have a husband and watch the person's reactions, looking to see if they are friend or foe. In speaking with my heterosexual colleagues, they are often surprised when I describe the luxury they have of sharing with their classes anecdotal stories of their lives which highlight a theory or bring the text to life, without the following fears:

> "How will this change the dynamics of the class? How will the fact that these students know I am a lesbian and a parent affect my credibility in teaching family systems theory, adolescent counselling, and ethics?"

What about when I share with my peers my developing passion for creating cultures of inclusion in our schools for children with same-sex parents and engaging teachers in the importance of not only visibility but acceptance, curiosity, and interest in these children's, my children's, lived experiences? When will I stop wondering if they think that I am on a mission and should just get over it? If I don't do this work, develop this research agenda, who will? How do I articulate the importance of keeping me around, in the faculty, to do this critical work when I am holding on for dear life between peanut-butter-strewn walls and questions of belonging and worth in the academy?

Am I Crazy or Did That Just Happen?

Through broad systemic and societal constructs my experience in the academy has been influenced by microaggressions where "communication of prejudice and discrimination is expressed through seemingly meaningless and unharmful tactics" (Shelton & Delgado-Romero, 2011, p. 210). I hope to contextualize my experience through an analysis of how the subtle nature of microaggressions such as dismissive looks, tones, and gestures makes deciphering the attack a challenge (Shelton & Delgado-Romero, 2011). Microaggression communications are most frequently imbedded within content and syntax and are contextually hidden (Shelton & Delgado-Romero, 2011). They often send a negative, unwelcoming, or demeaning message about the person or group (Sue et al., 2007). Within this framework it has been suggested that the most detrimental form of microaggression is microinvalidation (Sue, 2010). Microinvalidations are outside the aggressors' awareness and serve to "exclude, negate and nullify the psychological thoughts, feelings or experiential reality of certain groups" (Sue, 2010, p. 37). Additionally, these acts may be rationalized through non-biased and convincing arguments since well-intended and thoughtful individuals often communicate them (Sue et al., 2007).

In the academy, as a lesbian parent-to-be I am acted upon through micro-aggressions. I am subject to queries and subtle gestures, such as gazes and lifts of the eyebrow, and silent, intrusive questions for which my heterosexual peers would not be required to respond. An example is when someone is asked, "How did you know you were a lesbian or when did you decide you were gay?" in which the subtext is that I couldn't have possibly always known I am a lesbian. When the question is reversed, "When did you decide or know you were straight?" the absurdity in the question is easily revealed. A more accurate and inclusive question might be, "When did you come out for the first time?" Likewise, the subtext associated with the nonverbal gestures and looks I receive when announcing my pregnancy as a lesbian demands a response. In this way these gestures and the subtext suggest that as a lesbian parent-to-be I have different, more deliberate, and somehow more manipulative intentions than my heterosexual academic peers in deciding to have a family.

Microaggressions are not defined by the occurrence of a particular incident but are related to the frequency of small injustices that support environments of unfriendliness and perplex the target of the aggression (Sue, 2010). Each occurrence serves as a venue that reinforces invisibility and leaves the target confused as to what just happened. I am left questioning/doubting my own experience, often in the face of a system that when confronted denies any harm or hostility. It may be that the struggle surrounding my contract renewal and the thoughts and questions I posed earlier are in my imagination. Undoubtedly, there are other factors that contributed to the difficulties with my contract renewal: a perceived funding crisis, changes in senior administration, changes in contract types, and a movement toward a greater research focus throughout the university. However, in the context of a heterosexist and heteronormative institution, the impact of how microaggressions shape my experience of such events and reality is evident. I question, wonder, analyze, and attempt to decipher the meanings of each occurrence to determine safety, action, and allies.

It Did Just Happen. Now What?

Through the process of identifying the presence of microaggressions within the academy, I realize I am denied the justification heterosexual women have used to defend their choices, wants, desires, and actions around becoming pregnant. I am forced beyond the "double consciousness" that Wallace (2002) describes of asking, "How do straight people see this?" into a "double-bind" of knowing the performativity discourses women engage in when pregnant in the academy without having access to them ("Double Consciousness and the Subtleties of Homophobia," para. 4). Thus, I must ask not only how straight women have performed within this discourse, but also how I as a pregnant lesbian perform in the context of heterosexual women's performances. In making decisions around how I will share my "news," I must consider my audience. Have the straight women who have likely spent time reflecting on what it means to be a woman in an academic environment given any thought to what it might be like to be the only open lesbian parent/parent-to-be in my faculty, let alone the first full-time pregnant woman in the faculty in roughly twenty years? How do the answers to these questions influence how I will reveal myself, navigate this territory, and perform within this environment? My response to the microinvalidations, the unspoken queries, is, "Yes, our family did involve quite a bit of planning, although it happened quicker than we thought, than we expected, or than we planned." I try to access the "fictions" heterosexual women use to operate inside the dominant discourse that frames childbearing and parenting in academia within the discourse that surrounds my lesbian identity.

Mother Legacy: Whole Self

Elrena Evans (2008) shares the following about her daughter and herself: "She is a whole person, a whole woman and she fits in to herself just fine.... This is what I want to do: I want to fit in to myself. Nothing more, and nothing less" (p. 54). I have been blessed through the legacy of my mother, a woman who "fit in to herself." She understood the importance of fostering, nurturing, and building relationships. Her worth was not dependent on the value that others bestowed upon on her, but rather within the context of an identity based in relationship. For me, relationships have become the grounding agents for navigating through the microaggressive minefields that surround my identities. I have always "fit in to myself" just fine; I am just waiting for the academy, society, and the world to catch up. Perhaps for both my daughter and son, holding on to their convictions, belonging, and worth with the knowledge that they "fit in to themselves" just fine will be a little easier. This is my wish for them within the relationships I hold as a mother, partner, lesbian, and academic.

References

Evans, E. (2008). Fitting In. In E. Evans & C. Grant (Eds.), *Mama PhD: Women write about motherhood and academic life* (pp. 49–54). New Brunswick, NJ: Rutgers University Press.

Halpern, D. (2008). Nurturing careers in psychology: Combining work and family. *Educational Psychology Review, 20*(57–64). doi:10.1007/s10648-007-9060-5

Mason, M. A., & Goulden, M. (2002). Do babies matter? *Academe, 88*(6), 21–27.

Mason, M. A., & Goulden, M. (2004). Do babies matter? (Part II). *Academe, 90*(6), 10–15.

Shelton, K., & Delgado-Romero, E. A. (2011). Sexual orientation microaggressions: The experience of lesbian, gay, bisexual, and queer clients in psychotherapy. *Journal of Counseling Psychology, 58*(2), 210–221. doi:10.1037/a0022251

Sue, D. W. (2010). *Microaggressions in everyday life: Race, gender and sexual orientation*. Hoboken, NJ: John Wiley and Sons.

Sue, D. W., Capodilupo, C. M., Torino, G. C., Bucceri, J. M., Holder, A. M. B., Nadal, K. L., & Esquilin, M. (2007). Racial microaggressions in everyday life: Implications for clinical practice. *American Psychologist, 62*(4), 271–286. doi:10.1037/0003-066x.62.4.271

Tillmann, L. (2011). Labor pains in the academy. *Cultural Studies<=>Critical Methodologies, 11*(2), 195–198. doi:10.1177/1532708611401338

Wallace, D. (2002). Out in the academy: Heterosexism, invisibility, and double consciousness. *College English, 65*(1), 53–66. Retrieved from http://lion.chadwyck.comqe2a-proxy.mun.ca

Warner, J. (2008). The conversation. In E. Evans & C. Grant (Eds.), *Mama PhD: Women write about motherhood and academic life* (pp. 3–10). New Brunswick, NJ: Rutgers University Press.

Wolfinger, N. H., Mason, M. A., & Goulden, M. (2009). Stay in the game: Gender, family formation and alternative trajectories in the academic life course. *Social Forces, 87*(3), 1591–1621.

Surviving Parenthood and Academia
Two Professionals Striving to Maintain Work–Life Balance

Rose Ricciardelli and Stephen Czarnuch

Just yesterday we were in Costco with our three kids, our daughter who just turned four and our two-and-a-half-year-old twin boys. Costco has become a necessity for our household, the perfect place to shop for multiple reasons: we can purchase food and cleaning products in bulk—essential for a family that lives off bread or pasta with cheese or peanut butter on top and does an average of nine loads of laundry weekly. More importantly, in Costco two kids can sit side by side buckled into the shopping cart, something that is likely irrelevant to most people but surprisingly rare. Never would we have thought our shopping excursions would be based on "cart" capacities, but now it's reality. We all sat at a table drinking a poor excuse for juice—a very pink Fruitopia available at the concession stand—while we hoped the kids would remain calm and consider eating some food. Two of our three children were fevered, which translates into the potential for these lovely little people to transform into evil demons in the bat of an eye. Yet, before you question our parenting skills by asking, "What kind of parents take three kids, two fevered, shopping?" give us a chance to explain.

The day before, "Mom" had returned from a week-long academic conference in Europe and right before that had been on the east coast of Canada for another three-day conference, with a brief stop in a second province for research. "Dad" had just been away at a week-long conference before Mom left, and, not surprisingly, once Mom was back from Europe Dad started preparing for another academic conference on the west coast of Canada. Thus, in the balancing act of life, Mom had arrived home intellectually fulfilled and missing her family tremendously, Dad was at his wits' end after taking care of the kids for the last couple of weeks, and the house was lacking in supplies (and in need of a good cleaning).

So, we were in Costco when the unthinkable started to unfold. Our young-est, the free-spirited stuntman, leaped/fell off the table bench, followed by his sister. In her defence she was trying to save her little brother. Feeling judgment in the eyes of those around us, we took a quick look around just in time to witness the shaking heads of the other shoppers. The only exception was the woman at the table next to us, our sole ally, who smiled, noting her kids had done the same. Once upon a time, this whole experience would have left us saddened and feeling like complete and utter failures. Nowadays, we are okay with it. We have learned over time to interpret the situation based on the meaning we elect to pull from the gestures around us—our interpretation of the symbols around us—our personal position affects our understanding of how others react or speak to us. As such, we embrace Mead's teachings and remember "one of the great values, of language that it does give us control over this organization of the act" (1934, p. 13). Thus, let the world judge—we view all as witnessing our "survival"!

Thus, we will explain our experience as parents in academia from our personal perceptions and our interpretations of the world around us (Blumer, 1969; Mead, 1934). Indeed, interactions and perceptions fuel interpretations of the world and, more often than not, our experiences have been influenced by how we "feel" we are viewed by others (see Cooley's conception of the looking-glass self [1933]). Thus, in the complex realities on which we base our autoethnographic account of parenting in academia, one must take into consideration how experiences are fuelled by interactions. Perceptions and the influences of others in society and social living shape all our experiences. Many perceived "shortcomings" are based largely on perceived failures as interpreted by interactions in social encounters (Mead, 1934). In this sense, reality itself is questioned, given that it is based on interpretation; however, reality is true given that definitions of the situations (Thomas, 1923) shape constructions of real or even nonreal. Thus, interpretations of interactions and perceptions of self and society influence how we as a couple have tried to negotiate the worlds of parenting, relationships, and academia.

Personally, I—Mom—have struggled with the realization that I will never be a "perfect" mother, as I have been socialized to perceive what a "perfect mother" entails. I meet some requirements according to old-school traditional understandings that lack any social bearing in my world today—I am a mar-ried heterosexual woman—but I value neither sexuality nor marital status in determining what constitutes a "perfect mother," or "mother," for that mat-ter! I had my first child one month after my twenty-eighth birthday, and my next two at twenty-nine, eighteen months later. Today, at thirty-three, I can now admit that I have walked out of a grocery store, abandoning a full cart of merchandise, because I could not handle shopping with the three kids. I have left gatherings prematurely to follow through with poorly thought-out threats (e.g., "one more time and we're going home"). Most recently, I villainously ensure my kids "voluntarily" clean up their toys when I bring out a garbage can and start sweeping the toys into a pile ready to be brushed into my oversized dustpan (a strategic purchase), among many other things. Indeed, the meanings attributed to actions are pervasive, and their frenzy of cleaning demonstrates the power behind such symbolic gestures. Nonetheless, somewhere along the way I came to accept that on this crazy journey of parenting I am an okay mom and my husband is a good dad. I am not a typical mom but I am okay. I do not make fudge; feed the kids only organic, gluten-free foods; or fill their days and nights with "developmental activities." I am not a "stay-at-home" mom, albeit I predominantly work from home and try to spend time with my family as much as I can. I put my family first, but I *love* my job and I work a lot and hard. I spend a lot of time researching and writing, as well as teaching. As a mom I may not be perfect, but I *always* stand by my kids and I empower them. I strive to ensure that they are confident and will be equipped to handle the world we live in. I won't baby them, shield them from life and germs, or let my fears from their prematurity, especially the boys' extreme prematurity, affect their lives. At the same time, I will not give up my career, my research, my collaborations, or myself. It is about balance. And I'm still struggling to figure out just what that means to me—my own interpretations of this crazy reality in which I live.

AS FOR ME—DAD—IN STARK CONTRAST TO MY WIFE, I realized about a year ago, at the age of thirty-two, that I viewed myself as the "perfect" dad. My "primary structure of self" was rooted in the cognitive, rather than emotional, realities that shaped my identity (Mead, 1934) as an aware, hands-on father working toward the best for my children—broadly speaking. I recognized that "the essence of the self is cognitive, it lies in the internalized conversation of gestures which constitute thinking or in terms of which thought or reflection proceeds" (Mead, 1934, p. 173). For me, given that I know all my children inside and out, I care for my family, I support my wife, and though I may be hard on my kids I push them to excel, I identified as the "perfect dad." I can proudly say that almost every action I have taken as a father has been for what I consider the best interests of my children and my family. This was reinforced by those around me; my extended family and friends—or reference group—also viewed my parenting as optimal, and their interactions reinforced my internal dialogue—I was clearly a great dad!

As a husband, however, I think that I somehow lost track of my importance in my wife's life. I became too much of a father, neglecting my duties as a husband and resorting to almost token support rather than the true support a loving husband offers—a real problem considering my wife needs support in an occasionally harsh academic world. My professional life succumbed to the same fate, where I left a respectable field in the prime of my career to pursue a new career because I thought my family could have more of my time and I would be intellectually stimulated. In the process of this change, though, I lost a big part of what defined me as a person—being a professional and a husband—and the balance I had so easily maintained throughout my life was lost. Indeed, my interpretations of my social world were called into question.

Mom: The First Child, the First PhD

During what could have been the final year of my PhD, I became pregnant. Although thrilled about the idea, my husband and I cannot say the pregnancy was expected. We both wanted a child but we had under no circumstances expected it to happen so quickly. Personally, I found being a graduate student timely for having a child. I was finishing off my dissertation, teaching a full course load at another institution, and working on some additional research projects. Pregnancy was not entirely taxing on my body, and it did not seem to affect me emotionally, so I relaxed, worked, and enjoyed the experience. I found that my student status provided me with ample flexibility to work when I had the energy and rest when I felt the need. Also, the hours associated with teaching were relatively flexible and I was able to stay social and involved. I did find as the pregnancy progressed that I had what felt like never-ending visits to doctors and specialists, and as a result teaching became a little challenging. Yet, everything appeared manageable, and my "complete self" (Mead, 1934, p. 144), which derived from the unity of my "professional," "wife," "pregnant woman," and "student" selves, appeared complementary, reflecting a coherent, completed social process where I was able to negotiate diverse realities to present with a positive and healthy self-identity. Indeed, I had found a way to maintain a healthy perspective and to keep everything in check. Dad experienced a similar compatibility of his elementary selves that united to enable his feeling of confidence in his identity. He had finished his master's a few years prior and was now continuing to work full-time in an engineering position. He had a great job, with stable income, the potential for upward mobility, and good benefits. Although he was not "challenged" intellectually in his occupation, it did provide a positive foundation for having a child.

Together, the perspective we strove to maintain was a simple strategy of always recalling what the end goal was—a happy, healthy baby and family—while remembering that despite what our future would hold, most situations were not permanent. We wanted to make sure our family was well provided for and had opportunities. Even when times were hard, we tried to remember it was just a temporary setback as we strove to reach our goals. This perspective is something we have really tried to live by, sometimes successfully and sometimes not—but always manageable given that we were comfortable and aware of who we were, our selves, as individuals and as partners.

For example, we clearly recall the period of high stress we underwent when our daughter was first born. Indeed, Mom is one of those rare individuals who does not feel labour pains, for better or worse (and in our case worse turned out to be an understatement). When our daughter was born six weeks premature Mom was lucky her water broke; it happened at about 3 a.m. At least we knew it was labour. We arrived at the hospital at 7 a.m. (after showers and some house cleaning), where we learned that the contractions were intense and continuous.

To keep it brief, our daughter was born after three relatively uncomfortable contractions, an epidural, and a nap. At birth, she was not breathing on her own; nurses filled her with oxygen, let us hold her for just a second, and then took her to the neonatal intensive care unit (NICU). We were terrified. She weighed an ounce less than five pounds. There was not a single tube attached to her, she breastfed immediately, and she had an oxygen monitor on her foot that she kept kicking off. She gained weight continuously for six days in the NICU (hospital protocol for all premature babies) and then came home. We thought it was a trying, traumatic experience—and it was.

We stayed by our daughter's side as much as we could. Every day we hoped she would be able to come home. For the final three days of her stay we were disappointed each morning when we were told she should stay another day, but we knew she would be discharged soon. It was our first experience in an NICU, a level-two NICU at that, a room full of healthy babies needing to put on some weight in order to be discharged. All the babies were eventually going to go home. Retrospectively, the worst part about the situation was constantly wondering if today would be the day she would come home. Recall always that experiences, particularly first experiences, have emotionality and uncertainties that cannot be discounted—even if in retrospect we can both understand that our daughter was healthy and the NICU was a tedious, arguably even unnecessary precaution we are fortunate to have, being in Canada. Our interpretations of each interaction, our symbolic understanding of simply being in an NICU or the monitors, tubes, and medical staff, enlisted a state of fear for us as first-time parents that can be neither discounted nor trivialized despite our daughter's clear health.

During this NICU experience, Dad continued working at his job—although he was intending to start paternity leave as soon as our daughter was discharged, and Mom kept reading (academically) and doing some mild work. We learned in that first year we had ample time between feedings and while our daughter slept to progress with work, and we did. We recall spending many days with our daughter lying on our belly, typing away at the computer, curled up with a book (or stack of papers, articles, proposals, etc.), or simply watching television and playing video games (we found a way to play games from our youth, Nintendo games, which kept us up laughing at night!). Our trick to keeping up with life was simply to be flexible—to look at the needs of a husband, wife, and daughter and find a way that worked for us to meet them.

Nonetheless, it was during this time that we really had to come to terms with a lot about ourselves as parents. It was here that our understanding of ourselves, particularly given the reflected realities of our social environment and reference groups, started to be questioned. For example, I was never going to be a "happy homemaker," even though I thought I wanted to be. I did not make all food from scratch for our daughter largely because our daughter simply refused to eat it. I did not bake or enjoy the "mom" activities I was often invited to join. I had no desire to do salsa with a baby strapped to my chest or go swimming in cold water holding a baby. I hated spending an entire day cleaning and craved doing research and progressing on papers. Dad also discovered that being an active father was not just up to him. Other mothers appeared resistant to accepting a man doing so-called domestic tasks (e.g., grocery shopping, swimming lessons, or even drop-in play centre outings). Indeed, the harsh realization that playdates are arguably more about mothers getting together than about children playing with each other became all too apparent after several rejected scheduling attempts. Who we thought we were and who society was ready to accept us as were not entirely compatible. Indeed, Dad's experience can be perfectly explained by Mead (1934): "The individual experiences himself as such, not directly, but only indirectly, from the particular standpoints of other individual members of the same social group, or from the generalized standpoint of the social group as a whole to which he belongs" (p. 138). As the excerpt explains, for Dad—as has been the case for Mom—society also indirectly shapes who we can be as persons, and countering that reality is often an uphill battle. We realized our family would not have a "traditional" mom (whatever that is) or a "traditional" dad (however defined). Together, we still remind each other that it is okay for us to choose a non-normative parenting arrangement, although society may not always agree. In retrospect, reflecting on our remembered past (Mead, 1934), we realize this was the start of us, as a family, going through what may be a lifelong process of trying to find balance in our lives, coming to terms with who we are and what we really want in life.

Dad: The Second PhD

When our daughter was about six months old, I decided to apply to a PhD program at a prestigious school in the area. This was a carefully considered decision, based largely on the lack of intellectual stimulation I experienced at work and the desire to have more flexible work hours. The decision was made easily because we felt strong balance was already established in our lives with our single child. We were confident our small family could handle the stress associated with pursuing another PhD and decided we would have more children in the future when our professional lives were established and more stable. A quick acceptance into the graduate program, in conjunction with what we dubbed "team PhD," a group of PhDs (other friends, associates, etc.) behind us, bolstered our confidence in the decision. In fact, we managed to find a new balance where Dad could simultaneously continue to work full-time in his engineering position while "unofficially" entering his PhD as a full-time student over six months early (it seems mildly crazy once we see it in writing).

Then We Were Growing ...

Before Dad had even officially started the PhD and our daughter was just over a year old, Mom started experiencing some pains and discomfort. Due diligence suggested we rule out pregnancy, which we quickly did with negative tests, and we decided to visit the doctor to ensure everything was okay. A second pregnancy test noted that without a doubt we were not pregnant. An ultrasound was ordered to further investigate what was going on with Mom's body. We should explain, we expected to learn Mom had an inflamed appendix that needed to be removed. We received some *very* unexpected news: the ultrasound revealed *three* separate tiny sacs (i.e., fetuses). Three. The pregnancy tests had occurred too early to detect even a triplet pregnancy. We were shocked to be pregnant again. After seeing our obstetrician it was confirmed to our unimaginable relief that it was *only* a twin pregnancy (one sack had stopped growing). Thus, we had a daughter who was just over the age of one and two more on the way, and Dad was undergoing an entire career change, leaving a stable, well-paying, and secure job to enter academia. Our entire reality was in flux ... mixed with disbelief.

For me, Mom, I defended my dissertation when the twins were three months gestational age, returning from my maternity leave to submit the final document—and everyone thought I was at least five months pregnant given the size of my belly. The period of time leading up to my defence was an interesting experience, as I was trying to remain stress free but was about to defend my research and start a highly stressful professional career. Surprisingly, looking back (and even at the time), it was a positive experience. My "complete self" was only slightly unravelling, I was not a perfect mom, but I was okay with myself and thus, despite some less than positive reflections from reference groups, I was learning to manage, life was okay. Following my defence and through the rest of my second pregnancy, I continued to teach part-time at three different universities and I was still actively researching. I found, again, it was about trying to achieve balance—balancing financial needs, career goals, family objectives, and sanity. With one child, I could work during her naps and in the evenings. I had ample time to get things done. However, with a twin pregnancy the health risks were high. I was scared more often than not, and I was in a doctor's office at least weekly for tests and precautionary measures. Finding time and energy to focus on research or teaching became increasingly difficult as family life imposed non-negotiable demands.

Similarly, Dad was now struggling to balance a full-time job, the steadily increasing demands of coursework, and research in an aggressive and competitive PhD program, as well as the future needs of a growing family and the imminent needs of a wife starting an academic career while pregnant with twins. For example, before learning about the twins, neglecting engineering duties in favour of stronger academic performance was an easy decision— this was a period of transition and academia was the future. However, the unanticipated and imminent arrival of the twins created a sense of financial anxiety, making the decision to leave a stable career for a stressful and uncertain academic future much less desirable. It became clear to both of us that we were no longer just striving to maintain balance as individuals; the meanings underlying our understandings of diverse realities were becoming increasingly complex. Rather simple decisions were loaded, in a Blumerian sense (1969); our interactions were shaped by the many meanings embedded in each act (e.g., working represented professional aspirations, our self-identities, our family's financial future, and so on). We were now trying to find equilibrium for an entire family while trying to remain sane or somewhat true to our quickly dissolving sense of self.

Pregnancy and Academia

Being pregnant while in academia was not always easy to negotiate. For myself, Mom, I found I often avoided discussing my pregnancy with colleagues whom I did not have a friendship with per se. This was not due to a lack of support or understanding on their part; rather, it was simply that I did not always feel comfortable disclosing information about my pregnancy. The meanings (Blumer, 1969) I attributed to pregnancy in an academic world left me in a state of mild insecurity. I was concerned about how my pregnancy would affect the way my colleagues viewed my ability to work or my future employability. In reality, I did not want to lose my sessional appointments, since my husband would eventually need to leave his job, and I did not want to lose potential research opportunities. As such, I was trying to balance a lot. How open should I be about my pregnancy? Should I disclose I was having twins, as this fact could have an impact on my future employability? Was it appropriate to not disclose it? Only in retrospect do I recognize that I could have been much more open about my pregnancy, stresses, and experiences. I recognize now that my colleagues were largely supportive and could have provided advice and assistance. Yet, at the time it felt too complicated and risky. I was trying to succeed as a researcher and course director, and I was not certain that pregnancy would be viewed positively; perhaps my interpretations of interactions and language were motivated by feelings of insecurity or the life changes occurring. Not being tenured or even in a tenure stream appointment, I really felt a need to prove myself, and I did not want to be taken less seriously or have my commitment to academia questioned. I now recognize that being younger and feeling I had to prove myself somehow equated to not asking for help. Next time—which there will never be—I would know better.

AS A GRADUATE STUDENT WHOSE WIFE WAS EXPECTING TWINS only a year after having our daughter, my experience (Dad) was a little different. I remember apprehensively approaching my supervisor about a month after officially entering the PhD program to somehow explain that my children would be tripling in number. I also thought this would be a good time to explain that I would like to continue working as an engineer for a period of time in order to financially prepare for the arrival of the twins. His response was somewhat surprising: "Do what you need to do. Just make sure you finish. You will still be able to finish, right?" At the time I was not quite sure what he meant. Was he supportive of me continuing my second job? Did he understand that I likely would not be on campus as much as the other graduate students (if at all)? Thought is a dynamic reality; according to Blumer (1969), it modifies an individual's interpretation of symbols—toward or away from the truth. This time it worked in my favour as the one thing I knew for certain was that he did not know or ask about my wife's career and clearly assumed she would be taking care of the children. So from his perspective why should any of this news affect me? Realistically nothing had actually changed yet, so my wife and I decided that I would try to establish myself as a reliable, hard-working student before the boys arrived and that I would begin to withdraw myself from my engineering duties to prepare for the boys.

Welcome, Boys!

We can vividly recall worrying about how we would manage the third trimester of a twin pregnancy; Mom was teaching at different institutions and researching while trying to be a good, not perfect, Mom, and Dad was researching and working. In retrospect those worries would have been easy to write about, but even now, well over two years later, the real story is remarkably harder to tell. When I, Mom, was just over twenty-six weeks pregnant, I woke up on what seemed to be a typical Monday morning—January 4, 2010—and headed to campus to teach a third-year class. I had seen a doctor only four days prior who had given me and the twins a clean bill of health. I drove in to teach in horrendously cold weather, gave my lecture, and had a coffee. I recall feeling off, for lack of a better descriptor, and by the end of my lecture I knew something was not quite right. On the way home I opted (after talking to my husband, who insisted) to stop at the hospital. I convinced him to meet me at the hospital at 3 p.m., which gave me a few hours to shop and have lunch. In my mind I was being diligent, going for another routine checkup, expecting a few comments from the attending about slowing down and some calming words promising that the babies were just fine.

It was about 3 p.m. when I arrived at the hospital. Surprisingly, the same obstetrician I had seen just four days prior was the attending. An ultrasound allowed us to witness anew the boys' nonstop flips and hugs. I was to be sent home with a pelvic brace (a support belt to assist with "abdominal heaviness" as my baby belly resembled three basket balls!), nothing remarkable considering that my stomach had expanded over a foot forward (if I sat down my belly almost reached my knees). However, though my husband and I thought we were satisfied that everything was okay, the doctor decided to pursue what seemed like an afterthought, and a quick check changed everything. I'll never forget her "uh-oh" as she started to explain that I was dilating. It was too soon, twenty-six weeks and five days. I would need to be transported to a level-three NICU that had three beds available: one for me and two for the babies. If I could not get transferred, a delivery team from a qualified hospital would come and deliver the babies, but that was a last resort because transferring the babies directly following their birth correlated with a lower chance of survival and a higher probability for long-term damage. Yes, I would go by ambulance to another nearby hospital or by helicopter to a hospital farther away—even in a different country. My tears were uncontrollable. I was again contracting but did not feel a thing except being a little off.

To summarize, I felt as though I had somehow failed. I was scared. I was given antibiotics, a patch to slow my contractions, an IV, and a variety of other interventions. I was given steroids to help the boys' lungs and told that I would have another injection in twelve hours, if I made it that long. The injection and IV were the most physically painful experiences of my labour. Twin A was now breach as well, meaning a Caesarean delivery was necessary, which scared me even more. The doctor and nurse stayed with us, giving us updates on the bed situation in different hospitals and trying to calm me down just a little—not an easy feat given that I was close to hysterical. It was a surreal experience.

We were told three beds were being made available at a nearby hospital. Thus, I was transported in an ambulance with sirens, medical staff, and all the bells and whistles. When I arrived, I encountered another brigade of doctors, drugs, needles, and nurses. I was given more antibiotics, swabbed, poked, prodded, and stabbed. I was given new IVs and more steroids—clearly a bad sign as it had been only a couple of hours since my last dose, not the noted twelve hours between doses. I was given an epidural simply to slow my contractions; it hurt as I had no labour pains for distraction. Neonatologists came in to talk to us about the pending birth of the twins; they would be taken away and intubated, and, to be honest, it all sounded like *horrible babbling*. They asked for a waiver to be signed giving permission to resuscitate and give blood transfusions should I or the babies require such interventions. We were scared. When Dad stepped out for a brief second, ironically, the OB entered and noted an immediate emergency Caesarean was required, another terrifying experience. I was given a form to sign (consenting to the surgery) as I was wheeled into the operating room, where I proceeded to have an anxiety attack. I felt as though I could not breathe. I can still close my eyes and see the surgical light that hung above my head. When my husband was allowed to enter he was wearing scrubs. The team of doctors had pried Twin B out from my ribs. Each twin had his own team of doctors and nurses. There was no crying, just *a lot* of emptiness. We were told the first forty-eight hours would be the hardest in terms of their survival—the transition from womb to room. Then there would be a honeymoon stage where it would seem as though everything was going to be fine, and then the roller coaster would start. "Start??" Yes.

My interpretation of each interaction, of each word spoken, of the meaning behind each gesture, piece of equipment, intervention—even that overhead light from the surgery—was trying, loaded with fear-inducing anxieties, and creating discourses of pure panic. Each person who spoke used words that held back promise, carefully chosen words that ensured no false hopes were presented—that made sure we knew survival was *not* guaranteed and complications were an undeniable possibility. The caution in words, the attempts to refrain from creating false hopes or promise, the desire to provide "truth"— formed a symbolic reality (Blumer, 1969) that in essence begins the process of possible grieving for any parent about to give birth to twenty-six-week-old twins in 2010. According to the Quint V Boenker Preemie Survival Foundation (Quint V Boenker Preemie Survival Foundation, 2013), named after a preemie whose life both began and ended much too soon, "micro preemies," "extremely premature," "extremely low birth-weight" babies (less than 1000 grams at birth) have a 50 percent chance of survival (not good odds with twins, no matter how I try to express it). Not a symbol around me equated to comfort or confidence in the health of my babies; the interactions, the gestures, the objects, the words, everything equated to thoughts drawing out terrifying discourses tied to emotions that I still long to forget.

I was wheeled from post-surgical recovery, in my hospital bed, to where the twins were post-delivery. It was the first time I saw them in the flesh. I touched each of their hands. They had plastic bags around their bodies and more tubes than I could count, they were intubated (unable to breathe on their own because their little lungs were not yet developed), they had been given surfactant (to help their lungs), and they were smaller than I could have imagined. At the time I thought a baby could not be that small ... little did I know they would lose even more weight before gaining any. The roller coaster began. They were born on January 5, at 1:31 and 1:33 a.m., at twenty-six weeks and barely six days gestation. Twin A weighed 2 pounds and 3 ounces; Twin B was 2 pounds and 2 ounces. I held one twin for the first time on January 17, twelve days after they were born (maybe I could have held him earlier but I was scared, he was so fragile). The skin was unable to be stroked as it was so tender and fragile it could rip under a finger. At their lowest weight Twin A was 1 pound and 11.9 ounces and Twin B was 1 pound and 11.2 ounces. It was all terrifying. However, as parents we were lucky because the twins followed an expected course. This means that they would repeatedly stop breathing and their hearts would stop beating a few dozen times a day. They would acquire life-threatening infections, need a blood transfusion, and have a whole plethora of other ailments but eventually pull through without long-term complications. Oddly, as parents in that situation we accepted that it is all we could ask or even hope for.

Three months in the NICU taught us a lot about balance. Despite the situation, Mom kept teaching—perhaps not the smartest decision ever made, but it assisted with her sanity. And, whenever someone mentions the paper written when the boys were in the NICU, tears almost flow, suggesting to her colleagues that a mild hint of craziness may be present. During this blur of our existence, we fought for our boys' survival, but we also had to keep ourselves sane. Mom kept writing, kept doing what she normally did. Again, it was those times when the boys were resting, when all that could be done was sit beside them, that Mom, instead of letting her mind wander to potentially negative places, would review articles, read, and write. Work equated to balance, and it was not until years later that she learned that the act of writing academically with hopes to positively affect diverse groups in the community was her version of therapy—what keeps her sane.

Dad ended up contracting some sort of cold or flu shortly after the boys were born. Rules in the NICU were strict, where any symptoms of illness prevented entry. So Dad spent hours in the hospital cafeteria passionately working on research proposals, coursework, and other academic responsibilities. Research became an outlet for all the fear, frustration, and helplessness caused by our situation. However, after about a month, guilt began to set in. We still had a daughter who was passed around to various family members, and she was a very important part of our lives but had somehow become lost to us in our upended world. So, as parents we decided to divide and conquer—or rather divide and try to survive. Dad would move back home, take care of our daughter, and come to visit every day while Mom would stay at the hospital. Now Mom had to learn to be apart from her daughter and negotiate feelings of failure as a mom on many levels; her body had failed the twins, and her daughter did not have her around as much as she needed since she was living in the hospital. Dad had to curb his passion for research and recent progress to come back to the world of parenting, while accepting the fact that he could not be there for the boys because of other responsibilities. What about each other? We both wanted to be there for all members of our family and we wanted to keep our careers on track, but our world was changing daily. For example, in the latter half of January we almost lost Twin B. It was the worst feeling we had ever experienced. Indeed, we were trying our best to survive an unpleasant situation while striving to find some balance. Bills had to be paid, commitments had to be kept, and deadlines had to be met.

Perhaps it was the sheer excessive realities in our lives that played into our current—we were losing our "selves." Mead (1934) metaphorically argues that any individual can become preoccupied in an action such that his or her experiences are "swallowed up in the objects about him, so that he has, at the time being, no consciousness of self at all" (p. 137). He emphasizes this idea metaphorically by explaining that if a person is trying desperately to run away from someone who is chasing him or her, he or she will become lost in that act and lose sight of other realities and, most importantly, his or her "self" at the time and place. In this sense, perhaps the realities of pregnancy, parenting, research, and teaching and the sense of failures on so many levels simply combined to leave us both in state of preoccupation, anxiety, and fear, where we were striving to remain sane. In the end, perhaps unknowingly at the time, we both temporarily lost consciousness of our self. Perhaps this reality also gave us the motivation to keep working while in the NICU, where we cheered when the boys tolerated 1 millilitre of breast milk and we feared their daily bradys (bradicardic arrest) and apneas (apnea of prematurity). We also felt guilty about our daughter and wondered if we were meeting her needs. We were particularly happy when we were given a larger room in the hospital where our daughter could stay the night too. We planned to all stay together every second or third night—although Mom never went home (though she did leave to teach). It was late March when our boys came home. The story continues, with a slew of conditions they were diagnosed with during their first hospital stay and a trail of follow-ups, doctor's visits, eye tests, hearing tests, and many other things that most parents would rather never think about—including us. Thus, in all of this we tried to create and maintain a sense of balance or at least the illusion of having balance—and it was clearly an illusion—all enmeshed in diverse meanings, for better or worse.

Out of the Frying Pan and into the Fire

Soon after the boys were discharged, an advertisement for a full-time (although non-tenure-stream) faculty position was posted at an institution where I, Mom, had been employed as a sessional lecturer. I now had my PhD in hand and had missed out on what should have been my first year on the job market. Thus, I decided to apply for the position. I was hired soon after my interview. I believe perhaps as a family we were too busy to recognize the impact this would have on us, as life was about to become less about enjoyment and more about pure survival.

As an academic, finding balance between a full-time position in academia and a family is a challenge on multiple levels. The strains are physical (e.g., pure exhaustion), psychological (e.g., anxiety and guilt), and social (e.g., where was the time for barbeques, playdates, or lunch with colleagues?). Indeed, to find, create, or maintain balance, I learned that support is essential. In trying to manage a variety of responsibilities, my husband has proven to be a necessary sounding board. He constantly reminds me about our end goals—our desire to have a happy, healthy family and active careers. In itself this provides direction in our lives. Without this shared end goal (i.e., if we were not sure what we wanted in life), we would not even know how to start trying to find balance—at least we are on the same trajectory in life and that helps keep our relationship intact. One consistent meaning gives solace to the root of all our actions, interactions, and interpretations—we share a common directive and allow this to shape our future. However, our sense of self remained fragmented or incomplete during this time—our reference groups and social interactions created doubt and challenged our self-constitution. I (Mom) felt increasingly like a failure as a parent. Why did I not like baking? Why did I get grossed out by supposedly cute baby moments (e.g., smashing food into their hair or food all over their faces)? And why did I feel I was alone in this?

Nonetheless, we always try to keep our goals paramount in our minds and act toward those goals. As a couple, we recognize that our careers require making some decisions, often temporary, that may force us to be away from the family or appear, on the surface, to prioritize our careers over our family. It is particularly challenging when our reference groups fail to see beyond this seeming prioritization of work over family—clearly what kind of mother leaves her children overnight for work? As such, in attempts to negate guilt or other emotions, we try to remind each other that each decision we make moves us closer to the larger end goal—although it may be difficult in the short term. And our interpretations and understandings of our actions as individuals and family are most valuable, as we construct our realities and our own truths in our definitions of our social world and lived experiences (Thomas, 1923).

Nonetheless, one of the greatest challenges with both parenting and academia is recognizing that life changes and new opportunities present themselves, leading perhaps to new goals, new desires, and, ultimately, new guilt. For example, one substantial benefit of an academic job is the flexibility and academic freedom. Yet, with this flexibility life can easily be thrown into chaos. A new research project can send a scholar across the world, a job can transfer a family to another continent, and a new contract can lead to months of extensive work. Thus, the academic freedom and greater flexibility can also disturb balance, a fragile, almost achieved reality. Routine, especially with two academic parents, dissipates rather quickly despite the best intentions. Indeed, the question then becomes, can balance be created when what needs to be balanced is in constant flux? In essence, we would think this is the greatest challenge of parenting in academia—finding balance amidst the potential for constant change.

The Spousal Relationship

Through the course of our relationship, we have learned that it is essential to keep our spousal relationship strong, though this is obviously easier said than done. With three kids, the quest for full-time academic employment, the new status as a student after a decade as a successful professional, job searches, and extensive travel, we have watched our relationship become increasingly strained. We can probably blame it on a variety of reasons that seem obvious to the external observer; however, we never thought we would fall prey to such realities. Things became particularly strained in year three of Dad's PhD—perhaps not an unfamiliar story.

I, Mom, remember year three of my PhD. I almost left the program and changed career paths. I felt I would never make it and that even if I did I would never be a satisfactory, let alone good, academic. It was a year of self-doubt and esteem struggles, and that was before children and before marriage. Dad was now facing the same academic struggles while trying to manage a family with three children in the life stage of "terrible twos" *and* supporting a wife trying to secure a tenure-track position in academia. Whatever the reasons behind it, constant travel and strains on the family caused by job searches, heavy research agendas, and the stress of having minimal sleep and multiple children have forced us to agree that it has been a difficult year. We try to reinforce that everything has to get better. We know, in due time, these stresses will pass too. We rarely spend quality time together (e.g., not working or sleeping) without our children. Talking is not always fun, given that we are stressed, sleep deprived, and short-tempered. Thus, our together time tends to include shared activities—not extensive dialogue. All too often we end up in disagreements or unintentionally hurt each other with our word choices, but we always try to remember this is not a true reflection of who we are. Rather, at this point in time, we have fallen prey to the stresses and strains in our environment and our life situation—it too will pass, and if we really are the couple we see ourselves as, we will find our way back to each other. What we know is simply that relationships are not always easy or simple, and they require effort and work. Moreover, with kids and careers, resentment becomes increasingly plausible, particularly when surrounded by an academic culture of criticism and an almost neurotic scrutiny—with a lack of sleep! We recognize that we have made promises to each other based on how we thought things would be, promises we either cannot keep or do not want to keep, and we are just starting to realize that this too is okay. Parenting strains and academic criticisms do enough to kill our self-esteem and confidence; we do not need that from our partners too.

Personal Balance

Somehow, we are managing a full-time academic position, multiple research projects, one toddler, two infants, a full-time PhD, and a full-time engineering position. We are no longer making small adjustments to maintain balance in our lives. Rather, we are making gross leaps of faith, swinging the teeter-totter back and forth trying to make it through each day and meet the constant demands the different aspects our lives place upon us all.

Mom's Struggle

On a personal level, I think somehow, somewhere I lost myself. I have always been a bit of a free spirit, ready to try anything. I also like to have time to myself, but I become exceptionally anxious if I feel I am falling behind. I like to travel, to relax, and to read, but I have not picked up a novel for pleasure (not work related) in years, I rarely fully relax (I often end up in a semi-relaxed state with some underlying guilt about the things I have yet to finish), and I have just recently started to travel again for pleasure (outside of work). So, somewhere along the journey of parenting I started to lose myself. I became focused on diapers, work, feeding, research, and teaching. Perhaps the fact that all my children are now over the age of two has given me the time and space to notice this; the whirlwind of the life that has swallowed up my existence (see Mead, 1934) and allowed me to lose sight of myself was starting to calm, and this allowed me to notice that I have been lost.

To be clear, I would not trade the last few years of my life for any other experience in the world. I just feel surprised that my identity has become so entrenched in my children and work. I worry about what will happen over time as the kids grow up. So I have started again to intentionally do things that used to come naturally, and now I recognize it has been years since I have thought about myself. A simple example: my husband and I decided to take a quick trip to Paris, something we had not done in almost five years. However, travelling (especially spontaneously) was a defining characteristic of who I (and we) used to be: spontaneous and free spirited. I think now that it is not simply a process of rediscovering who I am. Rather, it is now about negotiating all aspects of my identity, all my roles, and figuring who I have become—for better or worse—and more importantly who I want to be.

Too often I feel I do not quite fit with the people around me. People assume when they see me with three young kids that I am a typical stay-at-home mom, which would be entirely acceptable (even more acceptable) in my reference groups and select social circles. Being completely honest, I become bored if I spend too much time discussing feeding schedules and school supplies, dance classes, violin, and the possibility of French immersion. I cringe when I hear about food allergies, gluten intolerance, veganism, and just about any child-aware dietary restriction simply because I recognize that my children live off "lethal" peanut butter—and often have it with Nutella (not to make light of any food allergy). I can talk for only so long to the same group of people about how my daughter will start school in September. I do feel judged at times because I have no idea if I am going to pick her up from school for lunch or not, I do not want to enroll her (or the twins) in any program where I have to be an active participant, and I have no intention to volunteer on the PTA; given that most people assume I am a stay-at-home mom, the judgment is particularly intense at times. And it does hurt, despite my best efforts—feelings are feelings, and right or wrong they are raw and can be painful, affecting my esteem and leaving me to temporarily question my decision (even if it is short-lived). Mead explains that "all living organisms are bound up in a general social environment or situation, in a complex of social interrelations and interactions upon which their continued existence depends" (1934, p. 228). In this sense, society clearly shapes who we are as individuals, and feelings of "poor fit" or even "failure" do have lasting implications on our constitution of self, particularly when an individual is feeling fragile and in a crisis of self. Indeed, too quickly these interactions tend to make me want to get back to work or talk about something different.

I also recognize that I am able to have a full life at home and in my career because of my supportive husband, who has also chosen a career path with flexibility. I opted to encourage my husband to take paternity leaves. It allowed us both to be at home more. Also, I could still breastfeed (which I did exclusively for all my children) and be there for my kids if I worked a few days a week outside the home. My priority is my family, but to others perhaps it does not seem that way—and they reflect this back onto me (see Cooley, 1933, for a discussion of the looking-glass self). Not surprisingly, I used to take offence and try to prove myself, but I have learned I do not want to do all these things and I do not want to spend time with people who do not accept me for who I am or make me feel inadequate because of who I am and the choices I have made with my family. It is rather simple. I also recognize my own limitations. For example, I cannot commit to weekly get-togethers or to scheduled patterns of meetings. My schedule and, more importantly, my personality do not allow it. I like to have freedom and flexibility. And I have accepted that it is okay; my kids neither notice nor are they worse off as a result. Yes, I am a career mom with a free spirit and that is okay. Fortunately, how we interpret, understand, and give meaning to the realities in our society shapes our lived experience and can enable us to find freedom and positive self-identities despite the feelings of judgment surrounding us. In this context, Mead (1934) notes that "the environment, I had said, is our environment. We see what we can reach, what we can manipulate, and then deal with it as we come in contact with it" (p. 248). In this sense we shape our realities. It is only when we define something as real that it becomes real in its consequences (Thomas, 1923), and if we take caution in understanding and defining real, we create a more positive lived experience for ourselves. The question becomes, why do I interpret it as judgment and feel judged by others? It may not be judgment at all—perhaps approval, support, or even envy?

Dad's Struggle

The struggles we have faced over the past few years have given ample opportunity and motivation to reflect on the last decade of my life. I excelled throughout my undergraduate and master's schooling, developed a highly marketable and unique skill set as an engineer, and progressed professionally for almost ten years. The world made sense to me, and work, social interactions, and relationships could be easily broken down into rules. After our daughter was born, we decided that she would fit into our lives and we found a way to make it work. I do not think the way I viewed life was robust enough to cope with the changes imposed by two more children and a motivated and driven wife intent on succeeding as an academic. My mind, which was previously so good at understanding all the details that shape one's interpretation of the world, became overwhelmed with the constant change. Then, already losing the balance and control I was so used to commanding, I started my PhD.

The characteristics that used to define me were no longer true. I was no longer calm, rational, easygoing, and practical. I was illogically emotional, anxious, and overwhelmed by almost every aspect of life. Perhaps the fact that I had never struggled with anxiety before my PhD prevented me from noting the signs earlier. Maybe it was the fact that after close to a decade as a decision maker I was relegated to the life of a "lowly" graduate student. Regardless of the cause, I began to withdraw from academia and work and start to associate my identity with the only thing I felt I still excelled at: fatherhood. As with everything else in my life, I jumped in feet first, and in retrospect I realize I likely made promises to myself and to my wife that I could not keep. I would quit my engineering job, watch the children, support my wife's career, and still complete my PhD.

Until very recently, I never realized the burden these promises would place on me. I now recognize that I need to feel important, and without my engineering career I do not feel I receive that reinforcement anymore—certainly not from my position as a graduate student. It was important to me to have a reference group (Mead, 1934) that reflected to me I was in a position of control—over myself and people around me. Indeed, academia can be quite the opposite, where feedback is almost entirely critical, pointing out all the things one does wrong. Parenthood also offers little in terms of immediate gratification if one is not in the necessary personal state to enjoy the beautiful gifts children offer. Finally, and most importantly, supporting a highly motivated academic wife is not a job for the faint of heart. Only one person can drive a car at any one time, and I think this is also true for families. As such, I think I inadvertently put my own career and my own professional dreams on hold by committing to supporting my wife and her career. However, despite the pressure society places on a man to work and succeed, I realize that I just might be okay with my non-traditional role. But then again, is it really not a traditional role? I am, actually, preparing to defend my doctoral research and actively collaborating on projects; I also have multiple post-doc opportunities lined up, or even possibly a tenure-stream appointment. So for us it seems the future simply presents the challenge of finding a new balance. And maybe we should also stop to recognize our successes....

Managing Guilt: Self-Imposed Rules

Recently, our attempts at balance often begin with self-imposed rules. The first rule, resulting from much guilt and stress, is that we will not check email during family time. Too often one email turns into hours of dealing with urgent needs, emotional ups and downs, or time demands. Then, instead of spending quality time with our family, we become lost in guilt because either our work or our family—or both—are not receiving the appropriate amount of attention. Yes, this simple rule has allowed some progress toward balance via the ability to have focused family and work time.

Second, we will not fall prey to external parenting pressures. Everyone has an opinion about parenting, and we refuse to try to be supermom or superdad according to everyone else's criteria. Thus, when we are with our kids, we work to maximize and enjoy our time together. This means our home is not spotless, meals are easy, and nothing is perfect. As a mom, I realize I will never make individually portioned fudge wrapped in coloured foil to distribute as a parting treat after playdates (really, in my opinion it is a playdate, not a wedding). But I will dump a bag of goldfish in a few kiddie bowls served with juice boxes during the playdate. Thus, I have lowered my own expectations. And as a dad, I will not abandon Mom with the three kids because I need "man" time with the latest electronic gadget. Thus, we know what is important to us—happy, healthy kids—not fudge, polished silver, or smartphones.

Third is the quest to find balance at work. We have learned that the flexibility and freedom of academic employment is accompanied by the reality that we could work all day and night if we did not set limitations. All too often it seems as if an insurmountable slew of demands are being made. Emails overwhelm us, data ages too quickly to publish it all, and the phrase "publish or perish" echoes all around. We have learned that we will never be caught up on email. We will always have lists upon lists of things that need to be done, each urgent, of course. In days when we set out with certain goals to accomplish, we will spend the entire day dealing with new demands and somehow end the day with a greater rather than a reduced workload. Finding balance in the academic world alone is something we—each at the different stages of our careers—are still trying to negotiate. What is a reasonable amount of work to complete in an evening? When is it okay to stop? To say no? To take a break? How much time is appropriate to dedicate to course preps or research? Here, we are slowly learning about the need to focus and how to say no. It's an ongoing process but essential because otherwise opportunities will overwhelm and eliminate any chance for a healthy balance between work and family life. Moreover, neither of us wants to miss out on watching our kids grow up. We want to witness all the first words, laughs, and experiences. Would either of us forgive ourselves if we were too focused on a contract or manuscript to enjoy our children? Or would we forgive each other? In the same sense, we have come to terms with the fact that we will miss some things, but as long as we are progressing toward our end goals, it is okay.

Finally, our last rule is rather simple: we always do what works for our family. We have learned that different strategies work for different people and we do not have to live with what other people do—only what we choose to do. For example, some people let their babies "cry it out" to go to sleep at night—people swear by it and are sure it will work for everyone. We have even had another mom offer to come to our home and teach our first-born to sleep by crying it out (honestly). However, this strategy did not work for us as a parenting team, although we did not necessarily agree on what would work. Thus, we learned to do what worked for us as parents and as a family.

Now, we use a routine if it works, we feed the kids with whatever works, we use the type of diapers we are comfortable changing—we do things that work for us as a family. For example, as a breastfeeding mom I was told repeatedly that the kids would all sleep better with formula. I smiled, nodded, and appeared grateful for the advice and insight. Then I exclusively breastfed all three of my kids and continued with breast milk when they started solids. With my first-born, this constant nagging advice made me uncomfortable and I felt I was doing something wrong. With the twins, I learned the "smile, nod, and thank" strategy. I still use it all the time.

Indeed, it does not matter if a feeding pattern or strategy worked for others or would do a "world of good" for the child's development. If it causes either of us guilt, unhappiness, or stress or just does not fit our individual personalities or family dynamic, it is *not* worth the perceived benefits. No other person in the world is part of our interactions, our realities, and recognizes what it means to be us in our family. In this mix of loving both our careers and our family, we find that imposing rules helps create balance and negate some guilt.

In the End

When we look at our lives today, we are happy to not have a nanny—not because we have a problem with nannies, but because a nanny would not (and did not) work for our family. As parents we alternate caring for our children. We wanted one of us to always be with our children, and we have done so for over four years. But this September, our daughter is starting school and our boys will go to daycare twice a week. This was a tough decision but necessary because it was what we needed to do as a family to help create balance. We recognize we are becoming strained and are no longer able to keep the promises we made to each other while managing our work and family demands and needing more focused time for both. Thus, we gave ourselves two full days to dedicate to our work each week (beyond evenings and other stolen hours). We both want to enjoy our family *and* our careers. Over time, we keep striving for balance. We try to be flexible because we recognize that our careers and our children demand this flexibility. The hardest part of our life is that we are tired, and when we are tired we have less patience with each other, become sensitive, and are irritable. It's something else we are hoping to work on.

When we think back to the transition from being a family of three to a family of five, from being PhD students to faculty members, we are not sure what we expected but it certainly was not what we got. It also happened very fast, a complete and utterly terrifying blur. Yet, nothing can express the surprise and fear we experienced when our boys arrived over three months before their due date—fourteen weeks premature. At the time the only thing we knew for certain was that we would fight to the bitter end for their lives. We could not fathom the thought, and it still makes us cringe, of losing even one of our boys. We needed them to survive. And now, we can proudly say that they did survive, as did our careers and our professional dreams. Unfortunately, we may never be the same again but overall, with some marital challenges, a lack of sleep, and a *lot* of love, we have found a way to seek (not yet find) balance and make it work as parents in academia (and we recently had a fourth child!).

References

Blumer, H. (1969). *Symbolic interactionism: Perspective and method.* Englewood Cliffs, NJ: Prentice-Hall.

Cooley, C. H. (1933). *Introductory sociology.* New York, NY: C. Scribner's Sons.

Mead, G. H. (1934). *Mind, self and society from the standpoint of a social behaviorist: The works of George Herbert Mead* (Vol. 1). Chicago, IL: University of Chicago Press.

Quint V Boenker Preemie Survival Foundation. (2013). Premature birth statistics. Retrieved from http://www.preemiesurvival.org/info/

Thomas, W. I. (1923). The regulation of the wishes. In W. I. Thomas (Ed.), *The unadjusted girl* (pp. 41–69). Boston, MA: Little, Brown and Co.

Parent-Student, Student-Parent

A Tale of Two Roles

Kevin Black

The first time I was told how profoundly the act of becoming a parent could change a person, I did not believe it. I was a young master's student, single and unattached, with no image of myself as a parent, then, or at the farthest point on my personal horizon. This was in stark contrast to a close friend of mine, who was then a single parent with a precocious toddler. Though over ten years have passed since our conversation on parenting and life choices, it is the only dialogue of ours whose echoes still resonate in my mind.

Our conversation occurred during a late-night drive. As I motored down the highway, she closed her eyes and reclined in her seat, sharing anecdotes about the life she had led before the birth of her daughter. She had been a human-rights activist, had travelled extensively, and to that point had led a unique, exciting, and impactful life. "How did you give it all up? Don't you miss it?" I asked. With only a pause to measure her words, she replied, "All of that was fun, and important, and really very meaningful. But raising my daughter is *the* most important job I will ever have. Nothing else compares to being her parent." I knew she was being truthful. The serious, thoughtful way she spoke told me that. And she was certainly someone I greatly respected. But I couldn't help being suspicious of her answer. *Surely she is exaggerating. She must be compensating.*[1] Try as I might, I just could not make sense of it.

As I recall our conversation now, I laugh at myself. I could chalk it up to being a student of psychology, since many of us learn to doubt someone's immediate answer to emotionally laden topics. But I think it is more accurate to say I had no frame of reference[2] to help me understand what she was talking about. All I knew about parenting was my own upbringing, and at that time I certainly did not feel like I was the outcome of someone's "most important job." Overcoming the solipsism that fuelled my disbelief in my friend's answer would take seven years, by which time I had a daughter of my own to hold in my arms—to sing to, to stare at, to read to, to teach, to entertain, to learn from, to love.

Now when I think about how I would answer my younger self's question about the quality of life before and after parenthood, I am reminded of Sydney Carton and his famous last words from the 1935 version of Dickens' *A Tale of Two Cities*: "It's a far, far better thing I do than I have ever done."[3]

To any Dickensian readers of this piece, please do not draw the wrong conclusions about me. I was never a dissolute cynic like Carton (or if I was, it was a long time ago); becoming a father was not like heading to my execution (not even to the execution of a particular version of myself—the solipsist is still alive, though thankfully his visits are shorter and less frequent); and if I have lost my head, it is, as they say, only so that I can better find my heart (I well recall a colleague admonishing the younger me for living too much of life in my head). What truly resonates between my image and practice of fatherhood and Carton's final words is the inspiration I feel from his actions: the quiet nobility of self-sacrifice; the opportunity for redemption—that is, to strive to become one's best self; and the importance of making difficult choices and standing by them.

Though there are certainly many ways to make sense of the thoughts and feelings I have just expressed in comparison to Carton's last words, I think that my experience of fatherhood is an example of the kind of phenomenon that Deci and Ryan's self-determination theory (SDT; 2000, 2008) was designed to explain. Specifically, I see four SDT constructs in the above example and throughout my years as a father. These theoretical constructs are autonomy (the conscious experience of making meaningful choices); relatedness (a feeling of deep human connection); intrinsic aspiration (to set one's sights on a goal or purpose that is greater than oneself); and competence (the experience of using one's skills, knowledge, and abilities to meet a challenge; this integrates nicely with Pink's 2009 description of the "mastery" motivation as a challenge whose perfect accomplishment is forever just beyond one's grasp).[4]

Many years ago in a highly influential article, the co-developers of SDT expressed their deep-seated belief that human beings have an "inherent tendency to seek out novelty and challenges, to extend and exercise their capacities, to explore, and to learn" (Ryan & Deci, 2000, p. 70). Typically, beliefs like this have been applied to children, based on their intrinsic curiosity and desire to explore the world. But I think that innate pleasure in, if not passion for, exploration, learning, challenge, and skill development can also apply to parents. We parents also experience an intrinsic motivation to explore the worlds *of* our children—and the world *with* our children. And as SDT states, some social contexts are conducive to autonomous motivation toward intrinsic goals, and some social contexts impair that motivation (Ryan & Deci, 2000). On balance, I think that academia has been conducive to developing my autonomous parental motivation. Of the three basic human needs posited by SDT— autonomy, competence, and relatedness—the first is actively encouraged, the second is abundant because of the choices I have made, and the third, while arguably not fostered in academia by design, is not purposefully and consistently thwarted. Let me briefly explain.

I have a high degree of autonomy in deciding how, when, and where I work, thus providing me great latitude in how I schedule my day. This benefits my parenting by allowing me to be with my daughters during important parts of their day and their lives (I will give several examples further on in this chapter). My multidisciplinary studies into father engagement and early childhood development (ECD) have given me opportunities to develop both my knowledge and a variety of perspectives on my parenting, my children's biopsychosocial development (and my own), and the impact and interrelationships of phenomena from the level of individuals to the level of cultures. This knowledge (and at times, maybe even wisdom) has informed and inspired the way I think, feel, and act as a parent. And lastly, while I have several times been told by faculty members or their spouses that university life is not "relationship friendly," the sacrifices I have had to make thus far have not been too onerous. But having heard the warnings, it is a challenge that I strive to be mindful of.

∞

As I see it, there was my life before fatherhood (which could justifiably be denoted *BF* to mark how distinct it was in my history), and then there was my new life that began when two new lives entered my life. Suddenly I had a family of my own. *Suddenly* I was directly responsible for others besides myself. Although it did not dawn on me until later, I had just exchanged independence for dependents. (Looking back, this was the experience that other parents tried in vain to warn us about. "Enjoy your freedom now," they would say, as if the experience of pure independence or couplehood was a commodity that could be stored and then savoured later, like a fine wine or Scotch.) Like so many first-time parents, I had the barest comprehension of the social contract—*the familial contract*, if you will—that I had just entered into (e.g., see Goodman, 2005). Excitement and apprehension—two sides of the same emotional coin— were roiling inside me. Did I have what it takes to be a good father? What did that even look like? (For systematized accounts of fathers' uncertainty about their role, see Daly, 1993; Marsiglio & Cohan, 2000; and Shears, Summers, Boller, & Barclay-McLaughlin, 2006.) Could I provide for my new family's financial, emotional, and social needs? As my daughters age and begin needing more than I can provide, will I have the wisdom and wherewithal to help them find what they need by themselves? These crucial questions, and others like them, are not answered easily or with certainty. In my experience, they are answered only by an intention: "I give you my word: I will do my best."

My daughters have developmental milestones[5] that they achieve as the months and years go by. And as I write this, I realize that I do, too. Right now their milestones are within the physical, emotional, cognitive, and social domains. Mine, not surprisingly, are more restricted in breadth—mine are currently within the social and emotional domains. But my milestones are no less deep than theirs. The first developmental milestone of my adulthood was accepting that being a parent is, and will forever remain, the most important job I will ever have.

According to the Eriksonian notion of generativity (Erikson, 1950; Santrock, MacKenzie-Rivers, Leung, & Malcomson, 2005) and the more recent theoretical extrapolation, generative fathering (Hawkins & Dollahite, 1997), I have come to believe that this developmental milestone may mark the most significant turning point of my adult life. Generativity refers to an adult's willingness to cultivate and promote the development of others, whether it is one's children, community, or culture (Snarey, 1997). With regard to children, generative goals include helping them overcome their own psychosocial crises, thereby developing a strong sense of trust, autonomy (cf. SDT; Deci & Ryan, 2000), initiative, industry (or competence, as SDT terms it), identity, and intimacy (cf. SDT's concept of relatedness). Erikson's framing of "generativity versus stagnation" refers to a psychosocial crisis or crossroads, with self-absorption down one path, and a committed concern for others, especially future generations, down the other. Successfully resolving this crisis (once and for all or as many times as necessary) is the task of middle adulthood. The strength or "virtue" of generativity is caring; the vice of stagnation is "rejectivity," an indifference to others that is posited to lead toward despair in later life (Erikson, 1950; Snarey, 1997).

For me, my first developmental milestone as a father meant striving to learn patience and unselfishness—two virtues I have no natural gift for. But I strive now in a way I never did before, because I have a motivation unlike any other: I have two youngsters who are always watching and learning from me (cf. social modelling; Bandura, 1986). So when I need encouragement, as I often do as I strive toward mastery (or a higher level of generativity), I hear

Sydney Carton chanting mantra-like, in the spirit of self-determination theory, *It is a far, far better thing I do than I have ever done.*

∞

Choosing to go back to school after spending ten years as an employee and consultant in the social service sector was in some ways easy, but in others quite difficult. It was easy, since I felt burned out as an employee. The part of me that enjoys analysis, strategy, and theorizing was malnourished, while the part that enjoys real-world action was exhausted from overuse. The tacit message I kept hearing was "Go, go, go! There's no time to strategize. We need funding. We need action ... *fast!*" Leaving that environment to pursue my doctorate was an invigorating change of pace and space—mentally, emotionally, and socially. It was like a vacation.

Yet the choice to become a student was also profoundly difficult because I was drastically slashing my income. And when my income gets slashed, my family's income gets slashed. Like many parents—especially those who are or have been breadwinners—I felt pangs of parental irresponsibility at this (Christiansen & Palkovitz, 2001; Mundy, 2012), as if I were in gross breach of my parental duty to financially provide for my family. This feeling was only heightened when, a month after I was accepted into my doctoral program, my wife was invited to go back to school by the departmental chair of another university. Thus, by September 2010 we had three students in the house—me, my wife, and my kindergarten-age daughter. If anything, we hoped our actions sent a message to our children (via social modelling; Bandura, 1986) about the value of education, believing in yourself, and pursuing your dreams. In my more pessimistic moments I worried that we were simultaneously—more out of omission than commission—sending an unspoken message to our children about the necessity of financial planning.

I have no way to ultimately determine if I made the right decision, and if I ever do, it won't be for many years. But I was uplifted the day before my first class began when my four-year-old daughter gave me a handmade card. On blue construction paper she had drawn a picture of herself, her two-year-old sister, and me—all standing next to my new school. When I asked why the illustrated me had *SD* written on his shirt and hat, she told me it stands for Super Dad, and that she and her sister each have their own *S* because they are super, too. Inside the card, in big block letters it says, "I LOVE YOU. HABE FAUN AT SCOOL DAD." On that day I realized that, while becoming a student meant sacrificing financial security, my father–daughter relationships give me a richer kind of wealth (akin to the increased sense of paternal self-esteem, meaning, and purpose described by fathers in Goodman, 2005).

Within a month at school, despite the intentions I had expressed when I applied to my doctoral program, I was surprised that I was now focusing my studies on father engagement in ECD. When I applied to university, I had planned to undertake a critical investigation of the philosophical under-pinnings of social marketing. But at my first meeting with my advisors, they gently suggested that my plan was closer to a lifetime project than a PhD dissertation, and I would be wise to choose something more specific and thus more achievable in the short term.

"You've just spent five years in the social service sector promoting the importance of ECD," said one of my advisors. "Why don't you focus your social marketing research on that?" My other advisor nodded in agreement. It was true. I had just finished leading my second Understanding the Early Years initiative, a federally funded research, communication, and community development project whose goal was the evidence-based promotion of the importance of the early years to caregivers and professionals.

"But I want to study the forest, not stare for years at one particular tree," I groused in rebuttal. A long pause, then: "You're right. I don't want to be in the doctoral program for years and years. In fact, I can't. I don't have the luxury. I need to find the sweet spot between finishing too soon, without enough publications, and staying too long and running out of money."

"It's your choice, Kevin," said my one co-advisor. "It really is," said the other. "We're just trying to guide you toward what will be best for you."

And so, after giving myself a day to be disappointed, I listened to the voices of experience and changed the focus of my studies to something I knew well. Thereafter, every assignment I completed related in some way to father engage-ment, ECD, or both. On the plus side, my new focus helped me delve deeper into a subject than I had ever delved before. But on the minus side, my new knowledge put extra pressure on me, from my expectations of myself and from my wife's expectations of me (*Since you know so much about fathering, why don't you get your head out of that book and go see what your daughters are bickering about?*).

What did I know before I started my current academic journey and what have I learned along the way? The answers, when combined, were a little sur-prising and a little disappointing.

By serving for five years as research and community coordinator on two Understanding the Early Years (UEY) initiatives, I had access to a wealth of neighbourhood-, school-, and population-level data on the well-being of children, families, and neighbourhoods. It was my job to analyze, interpret, and communicate the research findings to parents, educators, politicians, and social service providers (Black, 2008, 2010). To do so effectively, I had to quickly learn the ECD literature and integrate it with our local data. On the job, I also learned the most common arguments used to promote social and economic investments in the early years. And since I took responsibility for creating the ECD-promoting materials (e.g., newspaper ads, posters, and booklets), not only for the projects I led but for several other UEY communities, I had a share of the responsibility for developing and propagating those arguments, too.

I therefore became familiar with the original *Early Years Study* (McCain & Mustard, 1999), as well as its companions (McCain & Mustard, 2002; McCain, Mustard, & Shanker, 2007). These were compilations of leading-edge evidence from developmental psychology, neuroscience, and economics, describing the link between a society's investments in ECD, children's earliest brain development, and outcomes such as educational attainment, socioeconomic status, and overall well-being in the adult years. The thesis of these and similar reports (e.g., Pascal, 2009a, 2009b) is that children's first experiences with their environment—initially mediated mainly through their parents, and later through other caregivers and peers—profoundly shape the development of the neural pathways that will govern everything from language, cognition, and movement to emotional maturity, social competence, and well-being. During the first two thousand days of life, which mark the most malleable developmental window in the human lifespan, trajectories are set that become harder to change as individuals age (McCain et al., 2007). These trajectories resemble the social gradients that one sees in analyses of Canada's National Longitudinal Survey of Children and Youth (Willms, 2002), in the literature on the social determinants of health (Raphael, 2010), and in the community-based research conducted by me and my former UEY colleagues. Although these trajectories do not determine the lifetime outcomes of every individual, at the population level these social gradients are remarkably predictable. Those children who start school behind their peers tend to remain behind that way. Knowing this, the Nordic nations of Europe invest the most in the early years as a percentage of GDP, and they reap the result: the lowest rates of child vulnerability and highest ratings for children's physical, mental, and social health (Hertzman, 2010). Here in Canada, we spend the least of all industrialized nations on the early years—only 0.25 percent of GDP (Denburg & Daneman, 2010; OECD, 2006). This is a major reason why Canada ranks twelfth among the twenty-one OECD nations for child health (Raphael, 2010; UNICEF, 2007). If we want better outcomes for children through all social strata, greater social and financial investments need to be made throughout society.

Those facts and that argument were my bread and butter at UEY and my personal motivation as a parent. What I did not learn until I left the social service sector and began my doctoral journey was this: there is a wealth of research showing that positive father engagement has beneficial short- and long-term outcomes for children, fathers, and their partners (Allen, Daly, & Ball, 2012; Palkovitz, 2002). Specifically, a growing body of research shows that children of highly involved fathers—that is, those who have high levels of play with, and caregiving of, their children—have a greater likelihood of developing strong cognitive skills (Mitchell, Booth, & King, 2009; Rowe, Coker, & Pan, 2004), more emotional maturity and less mental illness (Dubowitz et al., 2001, and Deutsch, Servis, & Payne, 2001), and greater social competence (Berna-dette-Shapiro, Ehrensaft, & Shapiro, 1996; Lieberman, Doyle, & Markiewicz, 1999) than children of minimally involved fathers. Conversely, research has shown that when fathers are minimally involved or absent from their child's life, negative outcomes such as academic difficulties, antisocial behaviour, and drug use have a much greater likelihood of occurring (Bronte-Tinkew, Moore, & Carrano, 2006; Painter & Levine, 2000).

Upon learning of this research, a question began to gnaw at me: Why hadn't I learned about the positive impacts of father engagement when I was working in the ECD sector? The literature may be imperfect, like all research into human development (Allen et al., 2012), but it should have merited men-tion. If I had not been both a father and a student, I do not think I would have noticed. And since I noticed, I needed to delve further. I found that father involvement—the formal term for the parenting provided by men, regard-less of biological relatedness and family configuration—is rising (Beaupré & Cloutier, 2006; Marshall, 2006). Moreover, based on current social trends in education, economics, and demographics, father involvement is forecasted to keep rising into the next decade—perhaps to levels above 50 percent (Samir et al., 2010). If and when this will occur is uncertain. What is certain is that the social context in which gender roles and parenting practices are located is already changing (Ball, 2010). However, child-focused institutions, such as ECD agencies, have been slow to adapt to the changing roles and expecta-tions of Canadian fathers. For example, a national survey of parents (Russell, Birnbaum, Avison, & Ioannone, 2011) revealed that few fathers feel supported within their communities; are comfortable within their local ECD agency; or are aware of the links between positive father engagement in the first years of life and the beneficial outcomes children experience later in life (Allen et al., 2012). Recognizing the problematic gap between fathers and ECD agencies, some organizations have begun piloting programs for fathers. However, these agencies are struggling insofar as their programs, services, and environments were designed using a "maternal template" (Palkovitz, 2002), which, although good for many (but certainly not all) mothers, tends to unintentionally exclude or simply fail to resonate with many fathers (Ball, 2010). Uncovering these details through erudition, as well as conversation with parent educators and ECD providers, allowed me to crystallize a research plan for my doctoral studies (and, I hope, well beyond) that should have both applied and academic benefits. For me, it was a delicious moment, where I was able to blend parenthood and scholarship into something worthwhile to both groups of people and both parts of myself.

∽

Among my academic cohort, my growing expertise in the study of father engagement and ECD is a constant reminder that I am a parent-student and thus something of an outsider. When my colleagues want to stay late and work on a group assignment, or simply go out for drinks, I say no more often than I would like to, because it is more important that I pick up my daughters from school, take them to swimming lessons, or any of a host of other family responsibilities that deserve my attention.

But my concerns about colleagues' perceptions of me pale next to the truly pressing challenge of being a student-parent. Foremost, there's the perennial question, was my decision to become a student wise? (*Am I harming my family's well-being? Will this gamble pay off?*) The fact that my wife and I are able to be students and maintain our home is a source of amazement for friends, neighbours, and, frankly, us too. But it is also a chronic source of stress. We are regularly searching for part-time work inside and outside of the academy. The jobs we perform help build our CVs and our professional networks, but the main reason we do them is to earn the income we need to pay our bills. And our bills are not for extravagances like trips or technology. Besides payments for food, utilities, and our home, the largest costs are for summer camps, dance lessons, Girl Guides, and soccer. But while working these extra jobs relieves our financial concerns for a month or two, they feed the nagging doubt that we are failing as students when we succeed at work. (*Shouldn't I be focusing my energy on the doctoral qualifying exam, journal submissions, and completing my various research projects?*) Oh, to be the self-absorbed student I once was, free to read, write, and do whatever I wanted whenever I liked.

Work–life balance is probably the most frequently invoked aspiration of working parents. But to me, this holy grail of parenthood seems more like the unreachable horizon than an achievable goal. Perhaps work–life balance is a phenomenon that falls within Daniel Pink's definition of mastery, as that which one can approach with focused effort, yet never fully reach—and which is all the more tantalizing because it possesses this elusive quality (2009, p. 127). I can easily recognize extreme imbalance, but what does true balance look and feel like? (*Am I fooling myself when I think I'm balancing school, work, and parenting, never mind other roles like husband, friend, son, and neighbour?*) Perhaps work–life balance is more state of mind than state of life,[6] and can therefore be answered only in the moment—that is, "Am I balancing right now?" Yet, if I'm going to support my children's development the way I want to, I must keep one eye on the short term while the other eye is envisioning the future (à la SDT's concept of intrinsic aspirations; Deci & Ryan, 2000).

Creativity, courage, resilience, leadership, care and respect for self and others—the qualities that I admire and wish for my daughters are not bought quickly but earned, and most importantly, valued, with effort and time (Deci & Ryan, 2000; Dweck, 1999). I believe that one of my roles as parent is to be an educator, which means I must focus on the etymological root of that word ("to lead out") and find ways to help my daughters find, nurture, and amplify the positive qualities existent within them. Building confidence, teaching fairness, encouraging generosity, fostering a problem-solving attitude—these are among the most challenging tasks I face as a parent, made even more difficult when I feel heavily stressed or otherwise inadequate. But then I remember: my children are not the only ones who are developing (cf. Erikson, 1950; Hawkins & Dollahite, 1997). *It is a far, far better person I must become than I have ever been before.*

Being a parent, or in my case a dad, is much more than a biological or legal fact[7]—it is a daily choice I make. Being a dad prompts me to try harder: to be less selfish and impatient; to be more generous and empathetic; to try my best—and sometimes fail—to model the qualities I admire (à la social cognitive theory; Bandura, 1986). I doubt I would have grown as much, as quickly, and in the same way had I not become a parent. I would not have had the motivation to take the risks and make the mistakes that are necessary for personal and parental development. And, knowing what I do about social modelling, if I don't take risks and make mistakes, how can I expect my daughters to do the same?

Being a parent-student is challenging, but it gives me benefits that other working parents do not have. One day in June, my youngest daughter and I had a grilled-cheese-and-tomato-soup picnic on the front lawn while the other children on our street were at school and the adults were at work. I was able to watch my youngest daughter sing in her kindergarten assembly, when few other parents were able to attend. I get to walk my daughters back and forth to school, talking in the morning about what they are looking forward to most, and then hearing about the best part of their day as we walk home. And the best part of my day is when my daughters spy me walking up the path to meet them after school, and come running at top speed with beaming smiles so that we can wrap hugs around each other before I accede to their pleas and give them airplane rides until I am too dizzy to continue.

Being a student-parent also has discernible benefits. First, every interaction with my children, their friends, and other parents is an opportunity to get insight into my area of study. Second, knowing the research on the beneficial outcomes of father engagement (Allen et al., 2012) motivates my parenting. Third, if the knowledge I glean from reading articles on parenting, father engagement, and ECD is not always practically useful, at least the act of reading is like a meditation on the topic of positive parenting, prompting me to be mindful and reflective (cf. SDT; Deci & Ryan, 2008) about my own fathering behaviour and goals. Fourth, my research interests, speaking engagements, and academic projects bring me into regular contact with both parent educators and parents. These help keep me up to date on research and practice. Finally, I experience my time and energy as more precious than ever before. If I only have a short period of time in which to study or write, then I have to make the most of it.

Of course, despite these benefits, the question, "Is being a student parent worth it?" is an itch that needs frequent scratching.

∞

One August afternoon, taking a break from writing this essay, I start browsing a tattered cookbook compiled long ago by my grandmother and her friends. I'm looking for my daughters' favourite recipe for butter tarts when a piece of folk wisdom catches my eye. *Never be too busy making a living that you forget to make a life.* It sparks my thinking. Are there better ways to make a living than being a student-parent? Instantly the answer arrives: most definitely. But are there better ways to make a life? That's more difficult to answer. I struggle with it for days.

Undoubtedly spurred to offer a response—if not an answer[8]—to my question, my mind makes a mash-up of my thoughts, the cookbook's grandmotherly advice, and the lyrics to some of the music I have been listening to while writing: John Lennon's "Life is what happens to you when you're busy making other plans," and B.B. King's aching declaration about his career, "It ain't no good life, but it's my life."[9] Why did these come unbidden to me? What's the common factor?

I think it is a belief in the value of experiencing awareness and choice. There may be much better ways to make a living *and* better ways to make a life. But here and now, being a parent-student is the best life for me. Every day I am exquisitely aware—sometimes painfully so—that this is the life that *I* am choosing. And that, for me, makes all the difference.

Notes

1 At that moment in the conversation that was so memorable to me, I was thinking of conscious coping strategies (e.g., see Carver & Connor-Smith, 2010) or unconscious defence mechanisms (e.g., see Vaillant, 1977).

2 Within my education, the importance of having a useful frame of reference with which to interpret phenomena was highlighted in many places. Moments that leap to mind include (1) learning about the notion of paradigms proposed by Thomas Kuhn (1996) and those inspired by his work; (2) the oft-stated imperative within academia to use theories as frames of reference because, among many reasons, they can be used to describe, summarize, and explain phenomena (e.g., the traditional account, Christensen, 1994; an interpretive argument, Sabatier, 2007; a pragmatic view, Epstein, 2008); and last and oldest; and (3) the compare-and-contrast method, and the importance of articulating a personal viewpoint, which were taught to me within high school essay composition, if not earlier.

3 Since it's been over twenty years since I used that video clip for a high school English presentation, I think I'm forgiven for forgetting the second line of Carton's soliloquy: "It's a far, far greater rest I go to than I have ever known" (Dickens, 1859/2003, p. 390). Being the parent of two children under the age of six makes the idea of having a great rest utterly laughable.

4 Similar to (1) my experience of parenting, (2) Pink's description of mastery as asymptotic (2009, p. 127), and (3) Deci and Ryan's (2000, 2008) description of autonomously motivated intrinsic aspirations is Carol Dweck's (1999) description of effort from a growth mindset (or incremental theory of ability): "Effort is one of the things that gives meaning to life. Effort means you care about something, that something is important to you and you are willing to work for it. It would be an impoverished existence if you were not willing to value things and commit yourself to working toward them" (p. 41).

5 Always amenable to holism and the idea of the "whole child," my study of developmental milestones began when I started leading my first Understanding the Early Years initiative. A significant amount of our data was derived from the Early Development Instrument (EDI), which is an assessment made by kindergarten teachers of each senior kindergarten student's "school readiness to learn" across five domains of proven school success: communication skills and general knowledge; emotional maturity; language and cognitive development; physical health and well-being; and social competence. The EDI was developed at McMaster University's Offord Centre for Child Studies (Janus et al., 2007). For more information, visit www.offordcentre.com/readiness/index.html. To see examples of children's developmental milestones, visit the website of the Nipissing District Developmental Screen (NDDS) at www.ndds.ca. Here, parents and healthcare professionals can access 13 different screening tools, each designed for a specific age between one month and six years. Developmental milestones for young children include skills and abilities from the physical, cognitive, communicative, emotional and social domains (mirroring the EDI's five domains). For example, according to the *18 Month NDDS*, it would be common for a child of that age to be able to pick up a cup and drink; use four or more consonants; stack several blocks; and show affection to family members.

6 My thinking on this topic was influenced by two significant experiences while working on my first "real job" after completing my undergraduate studies. While coordinating outcome studies at a mental health hospital, I would weekly assess clients' psychometric tests for such things as state versus trait anxiety and depression. This made me mindful of the difference between transient emotions and long-standing conditions. The second experience was the regular conversations with a Buddhist co-worker, wherein we would, at times, discuss such ideas as self-deception, impermanence, mindfulness, and detachment.

7 As I have written and said numerous times since beginning the latest leg of my academic journey three years ago, father involvement is the formal term for the parenting provided by men, regardless of biological relatedness and family configuration. This is inspired by the research commitments of Canada's Father Involvement Research Alliance (www .fira.ca), as well as prominent scholars in the field of father involvement (see Allen et al., 2012).

8 One of the benefits of becoming a student again is that it gave me structured opportunities for self-study of topics that have long interested me. An example of this is the workshop on postmodernism and poststructuralism that I volunteered to provide to my colleagues, as part of a class on the methodological foundations of various forms of qualitative inquiry. Having studied this topic, I would be remiss to propose a grand narrative to my own life. Instead, I'll settle for a little narrative—one that is consciously flexible, contingent, local, temporary, and open to doubt, change, and creativity (Alvesson & Deetz, 1996; Jackson, 2003; Lyotard, 1984).

9 The first lyric is from John Lennon's song "Beautiful Boy (Darling Boy)" from the 1980 album *Double Fantasy*. The second lyric is from the Willie Nelson song "Night Life," a live cover version of which was included on B.B. King's 1996 album, *How Blue Can You Get?*

References

Allen, S., Daly, K., & Ball, J. (2012). Fathers make a difference in their children's lives: A review of the research evidence. In J. Ball & K. Daly (Eds.), *Father involvement in Canada: Diversity, renewal, and transformation* (pp. 50–88). Vancouver, BC: UBC Press.

Alvesson, M., & Deetz, S. (1996). Critical theory and postmodernist approaches to organizational studies. In S. R. Clegg, C. Hardy, & W. R. Nord (Eds.), *Handbook of organizational studies.* London, England: Sage.

Ball, J. (2010). Father involvement in Canada: An emerging movement. *Childhood Education, 87*(2), 113–119.

Bandura, A. (1986). *Social foundations of thought and action: A social cognitive theory.* Englewood Cliffs, NJ: Prentice-Hall.

Beaupré, P., & Cloutier, E. (2006). *Navigating family transitions: Evidence from the General Social Survey.* Retrieved from http://www.statcan.gc.ca/pub/89-625-x/ 89-625-x2007002-eng.pdf

Bernadette-Shapiro, S., Ehrensaft, D., & Shapiro, J. L. (1996). Father participation in childcare and the development of empathy in sons: An empirical study. *Family Therapy, 23*(2), 77–93.

Black, K. (2008). *The Milton Understanding the Early Years Community Action Plan.* Milton, ON: Our Kids Network.

Black, K. (2010). *Malton on the move: Community Action Plan of the Understanding the Early Years Initiative.* Mississauga, ON: Peel District School Board.

Bronte-Tinkew, J., Moore, K. A., & Carrano, J. (2006). The father–child relationship, parenting styles, and adolescent risk behaviors in intact families. *Journal of Family Issues, 27*(6), 850–881.

Carver, C. S., & Connor-Smith, J. (2010). Personality and coping. *Annual Review of Psychology, 61*, 679–704.

Christensen, L. B. (1994). *Experimental methodology* (6th ed.). Toronto, ON: Allyn and Bacon.

Christiansen, S. L., & Palkovitz, R. (2001). Why the "good provider" role still matters: Providing as a form of paternal involvement. *Journal of Family Issues, 22*, 84–106.

Daly, K. (1993). Reshaping fatherhood: Finding the models. *Journal of Family Issues, 14*(4), 510–530.

Deci, E. L., & Ryan, R. M. (2000). The "what" and "why" of goal pursuits: Human needs and the self-determination of behavior. *Psychological Inquiry, 11*, 227–268.

Deci, E. L., & Ryan, R. M. (2008). Self-Determination Theory: A macrotheory of human motivation, development, and health. *Canadian Psychology, 49*(3), 182–185.

Denburg, A., & Daneman, D. (2010). The link between social inequality and child health outcomes. *Healthcare Quarterly, 14*(Sp), 21–31.

Deutsch, F. M., Servis, L. J., & Payne, J. D. (2001). Paternal participation in child care and its effects on children's self-esteem and attitudes toward gendered roles. *Journal of Family Issues, 22*, 1000–1024.

Dickens, C. (2003). *A tale of two cities.* London, England: Penguin Classics. (Original work published 1859)

Dubowitz, H., Black, M. M., Cox, C. E., Kerr, M. A., Litrownik, A. J., Radhakrishna, A., … Runyan, D. K. (2001). Father involvement and children's functioning at age 6 years: A multisite study. *Child Maltreatment, 6*, 300–309.

Dweck, C. S. (1999). *Self-theories: Their role in motivation, personality and development.* Philadelphia, PA: Psychology Press.

Epstein, J. M. (2008). *Why model?* Paper presented at the Second World Congress on Social Simulation, George Mason University, Fairfax, VA.

Erikson, E. (1950). *Childhood and society.* New York, NY: W. W. Norton.

Goodman, J. H. (2005). Becoming an involved father of an infant. *Journal of Obstetric, Gynecologic, and Neonatal Nursing, 34*(2), 190–200.

Hawkins, A. J., & Dollahite, D. C. (Eds.). *Generative fathering: Beyond deficit perspectives.* Thousand Oaks, CA: Sage.

Hertzman, C. (2010). Social geography of developmental health in the early years. *Healthcare Quarterly, 14*(Sp), 21–31.

Jackson, M. (2003). *System thinking: Creative holism for managers.* Toronto, ON: John Wiley and Sons.

Janus, M., Brinkman, S., Duku, E. Hertzman, C., Santos, R., Sayers, M., & Schroeder, J. (2007). *The Early Development Instrument: A Population-based measure for communities.* Retrieved from http://www.offordcentre.com/readiness/pubs/2007_12_FINAL.EDI.HANDBOOK.pdf

Kuhn, T. S. (1996). *The structure of scientific revolutions.* Chicago, IL: University of Chicago Press.

Lieberman, M., Doyle, A., & Markiewicz, D. (1999). Developmental patterns in security of attachment to mother and father in late childhood and early adolescence: Associations with peer relations. *Child Development, 70*(1), 202–213.

Lyotard, J.-F. (1984). *The postmodern condition: A report on knowledge.* Manchester, England: Manchester University Press.

Marshall, K. (2006). Converging gender roles. *Perspectives on Labour and Income, 7*(7). Retrieved from http://www.statcan.gc.ca/pub/75-001-x/75-001-x2006107-eng.pdf

Marsiglio, W., & Cohan, M. (2000). Contextualizing father involvement and paternal influence: Sociological and qualitative themes. *Marriage & Family Review, 29,* 75–95.

McCain, M., & Mustard, F. (1999). *Early Years Study: Reversing the real brain drain.* Toronto, ON: Publications Ontario.

McCain, M., & Mustard, F. (2002). *Early Years Study three years later: From early child development to human development.* Toronto, ON: Founders' Network.

McCain, M., Mustard, F., & Shanker, S. (2007). *Early Years Study 2: Putting science into action.* Toronto, ON: Council for Early Child Development.

Mitchell, K. S., Booth, A., & King, V. (2009). Adolescents with nonresident fathers: Are daughters more disadvantaged than sons? *Journal of Marriage and Family, 71,* 650–662.

Mundy, L. (2012). *The richer sex: How the majority of female breadwinners is transforming sex, love, and family.* Toronto, ON: Simon & Schuster.

Organisation for Economic Co-operation and Development. (2006). *Starting strong II: Early childhood education and care.* Paris, France: Author.

Painter, G., & Levine, D. I. (2000). Family structure and youths' outcomes: Which correlations are causal? *Journal of Human Resources, 35*(3), 524–549.

Palkovitz, R. (2002). Involved fathering and child development: Advancing our understanding of good fathering. In N. Cabrera & C. S. Tamis-Lemonda (Eds.), *Handbook of father involvement: Multidisciplinary perspectives* (pp. 119–140). New York, NY: Routledge.

Pascal, C. (2009a). *An updated and annotated summary of evidence: A compendium to* With Our Best Future in Mind. Retrieved from http://www.ontario.ca/en/initiatives/early_learning/ONT06_018865

Pascal, C. (2009b). *With our best future in mind: Implementing early learning in Ontario.* Retrieved from http://www.ontario.ca/en/initiatives/early_learning/ONT06_018865

Pink, D. H. (2009). *Drive: The surprising truth about what motivates us.* New York, NY: Riverhead Books.

Raphael, D. (2010). The health of Canada's children. Part I: Canadian children's health in comparative perspective. *Paediatrics and Child Health, 15*(1), 23–29.

Rowe, M. L., Cocker, D., & Pan, B. A. (2004). A comparison of fathers' and mothers' talk to toddlers in low-income families. *Social Development, 13,* 278–291.

Russell, C. C., Birnbaum, N., Avison, W. C., & Ioannone, P. (2011). *Vital communities, vital support: How well do Canada's communities support parents of young children?* Retrieved from http://www.phoenixpembroke.com/ sites/default/files/Vital_Communities_Vital_Support_Phase_One_FULL_REPORT.pdf

Ryan, R. M., & Deci, E. L. (2000). Self-determination theory and the facilitation of intrinsic motivation, social development, and well-being. *American Psychologist, 55*(1), 68–78.

Sabatier, P. A. (2007). The need for better theories. In P. A. Sabatier (Ed.), *Theories of the policy process.* Cambridge, MA: Westview Press.

Samir, K. C., Barakat, B., Goujon, A., Skirbekk, V., Sanderson, W., & Lutz, W. (2010). Projection of populations by level of educational attainment, age, and sex for 120 countries for 2005–2050. *Demographic Research, 22,* 383–472.

Santrock, J. W., MacKenzie-Rivers, A., Leung, K. H., & Malcomson, T. (2005). *Life-span development* (2nd ed.). Toronto, ON: McGraw-Hill Ryerson.

Shears, J., Summers, J. A., Boller, K., & Barclay-McLaughlin, G. (2006). Exploring fathering roles in low-income families: The influence of intergenerational transmission. *Families in Society, 87,* 259–268.

Snarey, J. (1997). Foreword: The next generation of work on fathering. In A. J. Hawkins & D. C. Dollahite (Eds.), *Generative fathering: Beyond deficit perspectives* (pp. ix–xii). Thousand Oaks, CA: Sage.

UNICEF. (2007). *Progress for children: A world fit for children statistical review.* Retrieved from http://www.unicef.org/progressforchildren/2007n6/

Vaillant, G. E. (1977). *Adaptation to life.* Boston, MA: Little, Brown.

Willms, J. D. (2002). Socioeconomic gradients for childhood vulnerability. In J. D. Willms (Ed.), *Vulnerable children: Findings from Canada's National Longitudinal Survey of Children and Youth* (pp. 71–102). Edmonton: University of Alberta Press.

PART FOUR

Ongoing Negotiation in Academia

Navigating Role Conflict
in Pursuit of an Academic Career
A.k.a. "You will get used to it"

Jane E. Barker

Work–Family Role Conflict

According to recent estimates, women make up about a third of the full-time teaching faculty at Canadian universities. I am part of that third, and as a fifty-one-year-old associate professor I am just over the median age (forty-eight) for associate professors across Canada (Statistics Canada, 2012). I find this somewhat comforting—I am "on track" with my career. I am also a mother of two young children. As with most people, I find myself in various roles in my family and at work, and sometimes the requirements of these different roles result in a type of role strain. Role strain has been described as "an on-going stressor that is linked to the expectations of a social role or roles" (Elliot, 2008, p. 159). Role conflict can emerge as a type of role strain when competing roles are highly disparate (DeMies & Perkins, 1996) and perceived as being of similar importance (Gilbert, Kovalic Holahan, & Manning, 1981). So, from a traditional perspective, a woman like me may experience role conflict and stress as she tries to balance the contradictory demands inherent in the role of mother and that of an employed person (DeMies & Perkins, 1996; Gilbert et al., 1981; Guendouzi, 2006).

Whether employed or not, women typically face the same kinds of household chores associated with their role as mother. Employed mothers may spend less time on chores, but there is no decrease in the range of household responsibilities that they face (DeMies & Perkins, 1996). Moreover, these tasks are not considered optional. Women's perception is that they are an obligation that must be performed in order to keep the household running (DeMies & Perkins, 1996). Like women in other fields, female faculty members have indicated that they do more of the housework than do males (Baker, 2010; Biernat & Wortman, 1991; Elliot, 2008), and female academics report that they experience more academic and family stress than do their male counterparts (O'Laughlin & Bischoff, 2005).

While male and female faculty experience similar levels of role strain, there is a definite difference in the source of that role strain (Elliot, 2008). Male faculty's strain is more likely to be found in conditions of work, while female faculty identified family conditions as the primary source of role strain (Elliot, 2008). Specifically, for the male faculty members, the only family factor to increase their strain was if their wife/partner had trouble finding work outside the home. Female academics, on the other hand, reported more strain if they had children under eighteen years of age, had difficulties finding childcare, and were responsible for more housework (Elliot, 2008). The result of this research study resonates with me on a personal level. While there are certainly other aspects of my life that are stressed by the rigours of my work, having two children and negotiating childcare on a daily basis for the past thirteen years has certainly been a primary concern for me, and as such, I have chosen to focus on it in much of this narrative.

The Early Academic Years and the Challenge of Childcare

My first daughter was born during a six-year stint when I worked in the "real world," on hiatus from life in academia. In 2003, when she was three years old, I was hired into a tenure-track position at a small northern-Ontario university. The teaching load was 3/3, and the class times were already scheduled. There was a definite sink-or-swim mentality in my department regarding new faculty. Luckily, I am quite buoyant. In that first year, ten- to twelve-hour days spent in my office at the university were the norm, and sixteen-hour days were not unheard of. I was usually there at least one day of every weekend and I was exhausted a good deal of the time. While my husband and I were negotiating the changes that came with a new city, a tenure-track position for me, and a new job search for him, my daughter was also exposed to some significant changes as well. My mantra to her was "You will get used to it." This has become a constant phrase in my parenting repertoire, and likely a reflection of my own guilt at being unable to fully meet the demands of my role as mother as I strive to excel in my work role. Interestingly, in an examination of employed mothers' experiences of guilt, their descriptions of guilt were predominantly that it had a "strong, repetitive, everyday character" and most often revolved around responsibility related to their children (Elvin-Nowak, 1999, p. 73). Guilt stemming from role conflict has been hypothesized to be the result of reacting to the role conflict at an emotional rather than cognitive level (Gilbert et al., 1981). This makes sense to me intuitively. I know that I must make sacrifices with respect to mothering in order that my career can progress.

I understand this at a cognitive level, but my emotional reaction is not in line with this, and the guilt that I experience is quite similar to that described by Elvin-Nowak (1999) in that it seems to be focused on my maternal role, is ever-present, and is all-encompassing. It is this guilt that I try to assuage when I tell myself, or my children, that we will have to "get used to it."

Throughout the early years of my academic career, my energy was focused on two things: doing what I needed to in order to attain tenure, and raising my child, which included securing daycare for her. With tenure, the rules were clear. The requirements for tenure were laid out in various policy and procedural documents. Finding a good daycare was not so straightforward. I have a personal bias (likely based on my work in the criminal justice field) that I did not want my child in a home-based daycare (this was one thing I would not get used to). I wanted a licensed group daycare, with lots of staff on site with their police checks successfully completed, and parents dropping in throughout the day.

In the first year of my appointment, my daughter was in three different licensed daycares. While I put her name down on several waiting lists, the first daycare that she attended for several months was located at the other end of town because there was no waiting list. It was pretty apparent why. At pickup time, many of the kids were standing behind a chain-link fence, peering out at the parking lot. I still feel guilty about leaving her there. I do not think she or I ever got used to that one. The second daycare was wonderful. It was located on campus, and it had a two-way observation mirror where parents and guardians could watch the kids whenever they wanted to. It was staffed by early childhood educators and college students majoring in early childhood education. The sole problem was that it was open only from September to April. So, once the academic year had run its course, I was faced with finding a third daycare to send her to. By this time, her name had made its way up the waiting list and I managed to get her into a large licensed daycare. This was another transition, and another "you will get used to it" speech ensued. My daughter stayed there for the summer and then returned to the campus daycare in the fall, where she stayed until the daycare was closed permanently by the college[1] administration later that year (it took a while for both of us to get used to this).

In the meantime, my husband was unable to secure employment in his field and had to take on a night job. When the teaching schedule for my second year came out, it included a night class. I recall that I was asked at the time if I was okay with this, and although I really did not want to teach a night class, I felt that I could not say no. Similar sentiments by women academics have been noted in the literature (Palepu & Herbert, 2002; Ward & Wolf-Wendel, 2004). I was a very junior member of the department and was not yet tenured.

So, I was faced with having to find a daycare that was open until 10 p.m. My daughter would need to attend one daycare for the day and another for the night. I told her "you will get used to it." Since there were no licensed group daycares in my city open that late, I was forced to look for a home-based licensed daycare. It was time for me "to get used to" this, and get over my fears and anxieties about my child being left alone with another adult. I managed to find a home-based daycare that was used by a colleague, and with her glowing recommendation, I made the decision to place my daughter there on Tuesday evenings, for what seemed like twenty-four very long weeks. Suffice it to say, my anxieties around this were quite high. I was relieved at the end of that academic year when the night class finished, and I have actively avoided teaching a night class since then.

When my daughter got older, I was able to send her to day camps in the summer, thus giving her a break from the monotony of attending the same daycare that she went to after school every day. I sent her to day camps when she was younger, signing her up strategically so that every week of the summer was accounted for. I am still surprised at the reactions of those neighbours, friends, or even relatives who really did not understand why I needed daycare in the summer, since they were like most people (students included) who were under the impression that university professors did not work over the summer!

My daughter went to overnight camp for five days when she was six years old (people asked me if she was old enough to handle it, and my response was that yes, she was, and that she would "get used to it"). And over the years, she has. Her time at stay-away camp increased to two, three, and then five weeks. Now that she is fifteen, she spends her entire summer at camp and absolutely loves the adventures that she has there. Clearly, going to camp is something she did not have any difficulty getting used to.

The Decision to Have Another Child

I was acutely aware of the timing of this decision. I did not yet have tenure, nor was I in a position to put pregnancy off until I did. It has been said that "biological and tenure clocks have the unfortunate tendency to tick loudly, clearly, and at the same time" (Ward & Wolf-Wendel, 2004, p. 28). This was certainly my experience. The reality was that after spending my twenties and early thirties in grad school, I emerged with a PhD and not much of a social life. I entered the real world, met my husband in my mid-thirties, and had my first child less than a year after we were married. So, there I was, having returned to academia and survived my first year of teaching, frantically trying to get my research agenda in order and engaging in as much service (both at the university and in the community) as I could, in the pursuit of preparing as strong a case for tenure as possible. Not unlike other women academics (Ward & Wolf-Wendel, 2004), while all this was going on I was ever so cognizant that my eggs were not getting any younger. I remember speaking to a close friend about how it just was not the right time to have another child, I did not have tenure, we were not making a lot of money and so how could I afford another daycare bill? My friend, being the good friend that she was, bluntly said, "There is never a good time to have another child." And with that, I realized she was right. My husband and I made the decision that we would have one more. I became pregnant and we decided that this child would be our last, since I was going to be the other side of forty when the baby arrived.

꒰

There are institutional structures and personal financial exigencies that have had an impact on decisions that I have made with regard to taking maternity leave. Lack of institutional support in academia for marriage and family has been noted in the literature (Baker, 2010). There are reports that women academics' perceptions are that universities offer them less support for balancing work and family than they do for male academics (O'Laughlin & Bischoff, 2005). While I do not believe that I was consciously aware of having this sort of perception at the time, I am aware of it now. My youngest was born in the fall of 2005. I vividly remember going in to speak to the chair of the department very early on in my pregnancy (far sooner than most pregnancy guides would recommend) because I wanted to give him the heads-up that I would not be available to teach in the fall, and that he would need to make plans in order to accommodate my absence. He was relieved to hear that I was pregnant because he was afraid that I had taken a position somewhere else. My decision to take part of my leave prior to my due date in order that I might return for the beginning of the next academic term fits with an observation in the literature that some women try to juggle their leave around the academic terms (Baker, 2010). I realized that I would need to be back in December to prepare for January classes, and this meant that I would actually be back at work seven weeks after my second daughter was born. I was able to assure the chair that I would be available to teach during the winter term as I was not planning on taking more than seventeen weeks of maternity leave. This may seem like an odd number of weeks, but it is here where the institutional structure (and my own financial exigencies) had a direct impact on my decision process. The university where I worked would top up the employment insurance maternity leave amount for only seventeen weeks. Since I was the primary breadwinner, I had no choice but to come back to work early. Interestingly, I was later informed by a colleague who had been at the university for twenty-plus years that I was one of just a handful of faculty that she was aware of to have had a child and taken a maternity leave. I was curious, and decided to ask Human Resources if they could confirm this. According to their records, I was the third assistant professor and the fourth maternity leave by faculty (one person took two leaves) at the university since 1994. Given the lack of family-friendly policies at institutions of higher learning, this observation is not particularly surprising (Baker, 2010; O'Laughlin & Bischoff, 2005; Palepu & Herbert, 2002).

Reactions of Administration and Colleagues to the Realities of Role Conflict

When it comes to role conflict, it is not just the daily worries of childcare that are of concern to me. In some instances, I have felt that other committee members or chairs of committees are oblivious to the realities of those of us with childcare responsibilities when they suggest meeting in the evening, or worse, on weekends. My observations are not unlike those noted by Baker (2010), who reported a lack of awareness on the part of one department's scheduling of departmental seminars at a time when sole-parent faculty members could not attend. I often wonder why I need to remind people that those of us with children may need to make arrangements for childcare if a meeting is scheduled in the evening. The last time I reacted negatively to a weekend meeting, I was given the "Why aren't you a team player?" look. This kind of experience certainly can result in a perception of a lack of institutional support for balance of work and family, as has been noted in the literature (O'Laughlin & Bischoff, 2005; Palepu & Herbert, 2002).

In other situations where I find my role as a parent could conflict with my role at work, it has not. For example, I have a reasonable dean and he has approved my "special requests"[2] over the years to have my classes done by 5 p.m. so that I will have enough time to pick up my kids from daycare before it closes. Baker (2010) describes a similar situation where upon return from maternity leave, a female academic was scheduled to teach from 5 p.m. until 6 p.m. three times a week, and her daycare closed at 5 p.m. While I, and presumably the academic in Baker's (2010) paper were able to sort this out, others that I know have not been so fortunate. There have been some reports that women have not felt it was "safe" to ask for these kinds of accommodations (Palepu & Herbert, 2002).

The Realities of My Role Conflict

When children are sick, backup systems must be put into place. Luckily, my husband is able to take sick days to look after an ill child if I have to lecture, or am committed to a research meeting, or am engaged in service. I am fortunate that when I am not committed to specific times, I can work from home and care for a sick child. However, there are other situations that arise in which childcare places some limits on what I can do. Research has shown that women academics are more likely to note that being a parent resulted in less travel and less engagement in networking opportunities (O'Laughlin & Bischoff, 2005). This is certainly true in my case. When my children were younger I was not able to attend conferences out of town unless my husband took vacation time. Because he worked at night, in order for him to be available to look after the children, he had to book a vacation day. He has done this for me on numerous occasions, but at a cost to our family. Because he had a limited number of vacation days a year, if I went away for more than a few days to a conference or course, it would eat into what little family vacation time we had, which fed into my sense of guilt over family–work role conflict. This also extended to what I could feasibly do while on sabbatical. It was not an option for me to go away to do research while my children were young. I accepted this. I had to "get used to it."

I consider myself to be a feminist. I have always advocated for equality in relationships, and yet, when it comes to parenting roles, I find myself falling into a traditional pattern, where I, as the woman in a heterosexual relationship, take on the bulk of the responsibility for childcare. I can take some comfort in the fact that I am not alone here. This pattern has been noted in the literature, where inequality in the distribution of childcare responsibilities was seen in families of female academics (Biernat & Wortman, 1991). So, while I am the primary breadwinner, I am also the primary childcare provider. I find it puzzling that I cannot seem to let go of the role of primary caregiver.

Conclusion

There are so many wonderful aspects to life as a university professor. As a tenured associate professor, I can honestly say that I love my work—the teaching, the research, and yes, even the service. In recent years, as chair, I have found that I also enjoy administrative work. The pursuit of this career has its costs, though, as do many other professions. I have had to focus my energies on my work. I am curious about why more women are not represented in the higher ranks in academia (Canadian Association of University Teachers [CAUT],

2008). In Canada, if only one in four full professors is a woman, and only one in three associate professors is a woman (Statistics Canada, 2012), what is the reason for this? While it has been noted that "women's under-representation at the rank of full professor may be partly explained by the fact that women have entered the academic labour force in large numbers only recently" (CAUT, 2008, p. 3), I wonder if role conflicts are also playing a part, more specifically, if the direct and indirect responsibilities of parenting are having an impact on women's careers in the professoriate in Canada. This sounds like an interesting study to me; perhaps I will explore this.

Notes

1 The campus daycare was operated by a community college that shared the campus with the university.
2 At the university where I work, if an instructor needs to have classes scheduled in a particular way, for example, across two days for those who commute, this is considered a "special request" and must be approved by the dean.

References

Baker, M. (2010). Choices or constraints? Family responsibilities, gender and academic career. *Journal of Comparative Family Studies, 41*(1), 1–18.

Biernat, M., & Wortman, C. (1991). Sharing of home responsibilities between professionally employed women and their husbands. *Journal of Personality and Social Psychology, 60*(6), 844–860.

Canadian Association of University Teachers. (2008, March). Narrowing the gender gap: Women academics in Canadian universities. *CAUT Equity Review, 2.*

DeMies, D. K., & Perkins, H. W. (1996). "Supermoms" of the nineties: Homemaker and employed mothers' performance and perceptions of the motherhood role. *Journal of Family Issues, 17*(6), 777–792.

Elliot, M. (2008). Gender differences in the causes of work and family strain among academic faculty. *Journal of Human Behavior in the Social Environment, 17*(1/2), 157–173.

Elvin-Nowak, Y. (1999). The meaning of guilt: A phenomenological description of employed mothers' experiences of guilt. *Scandinavian Journal of Psychology, 40,* 73–83.

Gilbert, L., Kovalic Holahan, C., & Manning, L. (1981). Coping with conflict between professional and maternal roles. *Family Relations, 30,* 419–426.

Guendouzi, J. (2006). "The guilt thing": Balancing domestic and professional roles. *Journal of Marriage and Family, 68,* 901–909.

O'Laughlin, E., & Bischoff, L. (2005). Balancing parenthood and academia: Work/family stress as influenced by gender and tenure status. *Journal of Family Issues, 26*(1), 79–106.

Palepu, A., & Herbert, C. (2002). Medical women in academia: The silences we keep. *Canadian Medical Association Journal, 167*(8), 877–879.

Statistics Canada. (2012). Number and median age of full-time teaching staff at Canadian universities. CANSIM Table 477-0018. Retrieved from http://www5.statcan

.gc.ca/cansim/a26?lang=eng&retrLang=eng&id=4770018&paSer=&pattern=&st ByVal=2&p1=-1&p2=-1&tabMode=dataTable&csid=

Ward, K., & Wolf-Wendel, L. (2004). Fear factor: How safe is it to make time for family? *Academe, 90*(6), 28–31.

Engaging Academia as the Nest Empties

Timothy Sibbald

Within the field of education, graduate studies are typically preceded by a period of professional experience as a practitioner. As a consequence, many teachers pursue graduate studies after establishing their professional career, which frequently leads to issues around balancing family, career, and studies (Martinez, Ordu, Sala, & McFarlane, 2013). The way in which these demands are handled varies, and the focus of this narrative is to illustrate my own experience. I use a poststructuralist approach in understanding work–family balance issues (Dickerson, 2010) that also integrates aspects of a structural-functionalist framework (Charles, 2012; DeRosso, 1999). Overall, the use of these paradigms acknowledges a family culture where structures were perceived as real, while allowing for modern influences that were changing those perceptions. In my particular case, graduate studies entailed many online courses, which I treat as a form of telework (Standen, Daniels, & Lamond, 1999).

This narrative occurs over a period of slightly more than a decade (2002–2012), a period of "profound social changes" (Doucet, 2006, p. 8). This period began when I was thirty-five and had been married for thirteen years. My three children were older (ages six, ten, and seventeen) and all were in school. The family context when I enrolled in graduate studies is outlined below to establish the perceived structures and manifest functions (DeRosso, 1999). This provides the context for examining the poststructural evolution of parenting during graduate studies.

I have a blended family that began with a daughter aged five, but otherwise is based on a traditional heterosexual couple that met in their early twenties with less than two years' separation in their ages. My spouse and I are from long-standing nuclear families with many years of marriage, both in excess of forty years when I enrolled in graduate studies. Our approach to raising a family has been largely traditional and nuclear. However, my spouse and I felt we could make choices that were not necessarily consistent with a traditional nuclear family because of a social trend where "family relationships involving children become more diversified" (Ball & Daly, 2012, p. 4). The trend facilitated variances from traditions because of the diversification of family characteristics, which means we did not defy the position of privilege we held or the structural and ideological constraints (Krull, 2011) that bound us.

When my spouse and I completed our bachelor of science degrees, we got married. This brought a personal change, of course, because I had applied to graduate schools in other provinces the previous spring. The practicalities of balancing family and career meant deciding to continue my studies at teachers' college, rather than graduate studies, while my spouse financially stabilized the family by working. We were an example of an enabled family (Goldenberg & Goldenberg, 2000), and that set the stage for later career development in graduate school.

The teachers' college determined, geographically, where we lived. My spouse found work and, when I completed teachers' college, we remained in the city because of her employment. My spouse and I are from small families. Our parents lived over five hundred kilometres away, and the nearest family members an hour's drive away. This is to say that our family normally operates with little direct interaction with our extended families. Extended family had a minimal role on a daily basis, but visits occurred periodically.

In the early nineties, when I qualified as a teacher, I found work in industry because of the scarcity of teaching positions. I worked for a decade before making a complete transition into teaching in 2000. Staying abreast of computer languages and technology in industry entailed an ongoing effort (a manifest function of ongoing training toward sustaining a dynamically changing career). I upgraded continuously with considerable self-guided study at home, supported by a high internal locus of control (Michel, Kotrba, Mitchelson, Clark, & Baltes, 2011).

Two additional children were born into our family during the decade I worked in the private sector. Simultaneously, accomplishing the transition to teaching made me a full-time high school mathematics teacher. Industry had instilled the effort to stay abreast of changes and I sought opportunities to grow as a teacher. I pursued professional development and leadership training on an ongoing basis. The ongoing training, a manifest function, exceeded the pace of change in education and therefore provided an opportunity for growth beyond what is typical in a teacher's career. It is noteworthy that my spouse also contended with ongoing adaptations to her work and the children were somewhat aware of these pursuits as well.

When I entered graduate studies, the family included three children, with one having been included in the marriage. While formally a blended family, thirteen years of marriage made the distinction between a blended and nuclear family negligible. More importantly, all members of the family belonged to the differentiation-of-self end of Bowen's (Goldenberg & Goldenberg, 2000) conception of differentiation. Our oldest daughter lived in France for three months during a student exchange, and her exchange-student partner subsequently lived with the family for three months. Individuality became increasingly evident in the younger children, corresponding to the second oldest approaching the teen years. As the oldest daughter became more independent and autonomous (Swindler, 2010), the fusion exhibited by the children transformed into a dyadic structure. In many ways our family resembled our own parents' families with structured family meal times and well-established schedules. However, we both worked outside the home and contributed to domestic work, an important distinction that highlights a variance from tradition. While I may feel my spouse contributed more, it was not as extreme as traditional roles would imply. Looking back, the division of domestic labour lacks clarity and strongly resembles an "equality-difference dilemma" (Doucet, 2006, p. 26), reflecting a poststructuralist evolution of parenting identity that included determinations of equality and difference.

Master's degrees in education include a variety of completion options that facilitate a common policy that school principals complete their master's degree within a period of time of becoming a principal (e.g., U.S. Bureau of Labor Statistics, 2012). In my case, I did not require a master's degree and the choosing of a graduate program weighed options with the implications for parenting. It is noteworthy that my spouse did not have an equivalent opportunity to pursue graduate studies because her scientific field required face-to-face courses and extensive laboratory time. So, while the circumstance shows consistency with the notion of "patriarchal dividends accruing to men" (Ball & Daly, 2012, p. 9), a career choice made prior to marriage led to the inequity in opportunity. Consideration of whether to attend in person or using online courses was a key aspect of the available opportunities.

An onsite option at the teachers' college I attended had a rigid schedule that required classroom participation regularly two nights each week. This would place additional onus on my spouse to transport children to activities and events they engaged in, and that concerned us. In addition, the master's program extended beyond the foreseeable activities of the children, and direct conflicts could arise that would lead to my spouse being the only parent available to transport the children. Conceptually, this lens clarified the extent to which graduate studies might increase the inequity of division of labour

(Fudge, 2011); I desired to avoid becoming a "hardworking but unavailable figure" (Cowan & Bronstein, 1988, p. 346).

An alternative master's program at a well-known university (University of Toronto) could be completed with a large number of online courses. At the time, online courses were less common and there was little documentation; many details regarding the differences between in-person and online courses are better documented today (Braun, 2008; Cragg, Andrusyszyn, & Fraser, 2005). In the early days of online study, when this occurred, a dial-up connection and text interface were used, and it seems appropriate to draw a likeness to telework, a precursor to modern virtual work (Bailey & Kurland, 2002). This option allowed asynchronous engagement in classes from a home office, providing proximity and spatial separation of work and family (Hilbrecht, Shaw, Johnson, & Andrey, 2013). Using online courses complemented family schedules in the sense that online study did not have a rigid schedule and mitigated family interference (Higgins, Duxbury, & Lee, 1994; Jang, Zippay, & Park, 2012; Martinengo, Jacob, & Hill, 2010). The required workload appeared, at that time, feasible because the potential for interference with family decreases as children age (Allen & Finkelstein, 2014) and become more independent. It also complemented parental cooperation with my spouse because the telework (Duxbury & Halinski, 2014) style of the courses afforded flexible schedules. Within the confines of an increased workload, a high degree of control over the time used mitigated the level of stress (Fudge, 2011). Certainly, the amenability to spousal cooperation exceeded the traditional in-person program option.

Entering graduate school and using online courses coincided with the oldest daughter increasingly becoming autonomous. The early part of Duvall's stage of launching children (Goldenberg & Goldenberg, 2000) essentially describes her parental relationship. A month into my first graduate course, she made a planned moved two hundred kilometres away to participate in an enriched school program. She followed the program with a summer job working at a camp five hundred kilometres from home. The other two children lived continuously at home.

Assuming a conflict perspective (Shein & Chen, 2011) is common, given the combination of family, work as a teacher, and graduate studies. For example, the depletion argument says that I have a fixed amount of energy that is split between the three roles. However, my experience, contrary to the conflict perspective, entailed what Shein and Chen (2011) refer to as "enrichment." The three roles did not remain distinct, and blurring between them created benefits beyond the apparent fixed amount of energy. The most pronounced aspect occurred because graduate studies and the teaching role informed each other. Theoretical ideas provided different perspectives, making classroom interpretation more effective. In the other direction, some classroom or school events infused discussions in courses and provided timely professional development.

The same enrichment arose, though to a lesser extent, between the graduate courses and parenting. I had little formal knowledge of psychology, and what I learned in graduate courses facilitated interpretation of my own children. Shein and Chen (2011) refer to the recognition of applicability across roles as "awareness" and it was undoubtedly present. The benefit did not come as a guide for parenting, but increased course knowledge of some psychological perspectives helped avoid pitfalls within the heavy work–family commitment.

Similar to the positive view of multiple roles, McGonigal (2015) points out that "the sense of being alone in our suffering is one of the biggest barriers to transforming stress" (p. 165). Course discussions reduce the sense of being alone as a teacher and reveal issues others experience that cause a degree of suffering. The social forum of the graduate courses may reduce stress in the work role, an unintended consequence that can, to some extent, counter the increased workload.

Higgins, Duxbury, and Lee (1994) note that family demands decrease as children age and that should have facilitated my course of study. However, over the two years it took to complete the master's program, I miscalculated, a latent function (DeRosso, 1999), regarding the increase in the workload of the graduate program. The workload increased for two reasons: growing interest in courses that were becoming something of a coherent framework for education and an effort to complete the thesis component. As a part-time student, the latter would normally have been completed after coursework, but this would have required paying tuition for an additional year. The additional fee reflected a policy requiring continuous tuition combined with thesis research being conducted in a public school environment that was not available during the summer months. Spousal support undoubtedly addressed the additional domestic workload arising from the miscalculation. No alterations of the family structure arose, but some functionality shifted from me to my spouse to compensate for the thesis work. While reduced control over time (Fudge, 2011) and reduced internal locus of control (Michel et al., 2011) caused stress, we recognized that it would be of limited duration and therefore a temporary dysfunction that required coping as opposed to more drastic alternatives.

I completed the master of arts degree just prior to Christmas of 2005. At that point, the oldest daughter attended university, the middle child grew more autonomous in the middle of his teenage years, and the youngest child approached the teen years. For a couple of months we enjoyed a reduced work-load, but the desire to utilize what had been learned became apparent. That desire led to discussions about pursuing a doctorate. The discussions focused primarily on workload and the family impact of the master's, particularly the stress arising from underestimating the workload. The discussion led to a criterion of reducing my school teaching workload if pursuing a doctorate. This reflected the division of labour regarding the household environment becoming inequitable as the workload of the master's program increased.

I began my doctorate in the fall of 2006 and completed it in the summer of 2008. It included a research assistantship with a workload that effectively counteracted the reduction in my school-teaching workload but also reduced the financial impact to a very small amount. The use of online courses, again, left the overall structural and functional aspects of the family essentially unchanged from the involvement in master's courses. The program required a higher standard for engagement, but using a higher level of expertise, developed along the way, I achieved that engagement without causing too much conflict with family responsibilities (which Bailey and Kurland, 2002, noted among teleworkers). The expertise included time management, balancing multiple tasks, and, to the extent possible, having family, work, and graduate studies "work in accord" (Martinez et al., 2013). At the completion of the doctorate, university studies continued for our oldest child, and the middle child reached eighteen years of age and worked at a summer camp four hundred kilometres from home. He planned to attend college, where he would be fully independent. The youngest daughter, a teenager, demonstrated her competence with regard to differentiation-of-self. Completing my doctorate saw the resumption of full-time high school teaching and an overall reduction in workload.

My graduate studies experience, in my opinion, amounted to taking on a part-time job that allowed telecommuting. I continued with my regular career and involvement in the family. However, the addition of graduate studies represented telework that had all the advantageous features of telework: facilitated family–work transitions with minimal effort, flexible schedule, high level of autonomy, and mobility. The last requires some qualification because technology improved over the course of my studies to the point where courses could be continued while visiting relatives or, in one course, sailing on a cruise ship. My thesis advisor worked at a field centre rather than the main university campus. He taught online courses and routinely worked at a distance. He did not impose institutional ownership or a normative culture of the university or faculty (Brus, 2006). In terms of parenting, taking a part-time job perspective reflects the way graduate school represented an additional external obligation but within the scope of reduced hindrances than other forms of part-time jobs.

After defending my doctorate my oldest daughter pointed out that, if I found university employment, she might receive a tuition reduction as a dependent. I considered employment in post-secondary education, but positions worth leaving a fully tenured high school teaching position are relatively rare. The challenge of engaging in academia, without being in a university role, was exacerbated when online library journals, used during graduate studies, became inaccessible as the ivory tower closed the virtual door upon my graduation.

With my children aging and only one child remaining at home, there became a gap in roles. I increasingly had feelings of academic isolation and reflected that perhaps I should have invested the time with the children because the academic path essentially led to a dead end. In time, opportunities arose with limited involvement in research projects where I could facilitate the inclusion of schools in my geographical area. Additionally, an opportunity arose to teach part-time at the local faculty of education, which included library access. With one largely independent child at home, parenting became more of an orchestration of my daughter and me as to who would be home when. However, a fundamental change in the structure of the family, because of two children leaving home, made the original concern of conflict between a rigid schedule and multiple children obsolete.

In spite of the reduced parenting responsibilities and regaining access to academic resources, engaging academia included an untenable workload. The sustainability of the situation became increasingly doubtful and, more frequently, we ate dinners out to compensate for the workload. It is significant that the workload challenged me more than the workload of being a graduate student. The "enrichment" (Shein & Chen, 2011) between teaching high school and teaching pre-service high school teachers diminished. More often, events and lessons in high school infused my university teaching in a unidirectional relationship with relative rarity of transfer in the other direction. The consistency of the reduced enrichment supports the view that enrichment contributed to a lessening of the workload issue during the graduate school period.

At this point, an academic position arose that suited me. The location in northern Ontario, six hundred kilometres away, included a desirable opportunity for a lifestyle change. As I took on the position in academia, my youngest daughter entered her final year of high school. However, she planned on moving two hundred kilometres to an enriched school program for the second half of that year. We made the parenting decision, in consultation with our daughter, to maintain her opportunity to complete the half year without switching schools. This led to a temporary single-parent situation prior to my spouse joining me in northern Ontario.

As my narrative closes, I find it interesting that my entry into academia has corresponded to the emptying of the nest. Two of the children are still dependents and have the opportunity to realize reduced tuition opportunities; however, their independence appears to be taking them in other directions. The flexibility offered by academia defines workload rather than having a constantly high workload through the entire graduate studies process. Comparing workloads is difficult because the level of effort, beyond the basic expectations of academia, is largely dictated by the individual and motivated by the tenure process.

References

Allen, T. D., & Finkelstein, L. M. (2014). Work-family conflict among members of full-time dual-earner couples: An examination of family life stage, gender, and age. *Journal of Occupational Health Psychology, 19*(3), 376–384.

Bailey, D. E., & Kurland, N. B. (2002). A review of telework research: Findings, new directions, and lessons for the study of modern work. *Journal of Organizational Behavior, 23*, 383–400.

Ball, J., & Daly, K. (2012). Father involvement in Canada: A transformative approach. In J. Ball & K. Daly (Eds.), *Father involvement in Canada: Diversity, renewal, and transformation* (pp. 1–25). Vancouver, BC: UBC Press.

Braun, T. (2008). Making a choice: The perceptions and attitudes of online graduate students. *Journal of Technology and Teacher Education, 16*(1), 63–92.

Brus, C. P. (2006). Seeking balance in graduate school: A realistic expectation or a dangerous dilemma? *New Directions for Student Services, 115*, 31–45. doi:10.1002/ss.214

Charles, N. (2012). Families, communities and social change: Then and now. *The Sociological Review, 60*, 438–456.

Cowan, C. P., & Bronstein, P. (1988). Fathers' roles in the family: Implications for research, intervention, and change. In P. Bronstein & C. P. Cowan (Eds.), *Fatherhood today: Men's changing role in the family* (pp. 341–347). New York, NY: John Wiley & Sons.

Cragg, C. E., Andrusyszyn, M. A., & Fraser, J. (2005). Sources of support for women taking professional programs by distance education. *Journal of Distance Education, 20*(1), 21–38.

DeRosso, D. (1999). The structural-functional theoretical approach. Retrieved from http://www.wisc-online.com/Objects/ViewObject.aspx?ID=I2S3404

Dickerson, V. C. (2010). Positioning oneself within an epistemology: Refining our thinking about integrative approaches. *Family Process, 49*(3), 349–368.

Doucet, A. (2006). *Do men mother? Fathering, care, and domestic responsibilities.* Toronto, ON: University of Toronto Press.

Duxbury, L., & Halinski, M. (2014). When more is less: An examination of the relationship between hours in telework and role overload. *Work, 48*, 91–103.

Fudge, J. (2011). Working-time regimes, flexibility, and work-life balance: Gender equality and families. In C. Krull & J. Sempruch (Eds.), *A life in balance?* (pp. 170–193). Vancouver, BC: UBC Press.

Goldenberg, I., & Goldenberg, H. (2000). *Family therapy and overview.* Belmont, CA: Wadsworth/Thompson Learning.

Higgins, C., Duxbury, L., & Lee, C. (1994). Impact of life-cycle stage and gender on the ability to balance work and family responsibilities. *Family Relations, 43*(2), 144–150.

Hilbrecht, M., Shaw, S. M., Johnson, L. C., & Andrey, J. (2013). Remixing work, family and leisure: Teleworkers' experiences of everyday life. *New Technology, Work and Employment, 28*(2), 130–144.

Jang, S. J., Zippay, A., & Park, R. (2012). Family roles as moderators of the relationship between schedule flexibility and stress. *Journal of Marriage and Family, 74*, 897–912.

Krull, C. (2011). Destabilizing the nuclear family ideal: Thinking beyond essentialisms, universalism, and binaries. In C. Krull & J. Sempruch (Eds.), *A life in balance?* (pp. 11–29). Vancouver, BC: UBC Press.

Martinengo, G., Jacob, J. I., & Hill, E. J. (2010). Gender and the work-family interface: Exploring differences across the family life course. *Journal of Family Issues, 31*(10), 1363–1390.

Martinez, E., Ordu, C., Sala, M. R. D., & McFarlane, A. (2013). Striving to obtain a school–work–life balance: The full-time doctoral student. *International Journal of Doctoral Studies, 8*, 39–59.

McGonigal, K. (2015). *The upside of stress: Why stress is good for you, and how to get good at it*. New York, NY: Penguin Random House.

Michel, J. S., Kotrba, L. M., Mitchelson, J. K., Clark, M. A., & Baltes, B. B. (2011). Antecedents of work–family conflict: A meta-analytic review. *Journal of Organizational Behavior, 32*, 689–725. doi:10.1002/job.695

Shein, J., & Chen, C. P. (2011). *Work-family enrichment: A research of positive transfer*. Rotterdam, The Netherlands: Sense Publishers.

Standen, P., Daniels, K., & Lamond, D. (1999). The home as a workplace: Work–family interaction and psychological well-being in telework. *Journal of Occupational Health Psychology, 4*(4), 368–381.

Swindler, J. K. (2010). Fathering for freedom. In L. S. Nease & M. W. Austin (Eds.), *Fatherhood-philosophy for everyone: The Dao of daddy* (pp. 86–96). Malden, MA: Wiley-Blackwell.

U.S. Bureau of Labor Statistics. (2012, March 29). *Occupational outlook handbook: Elementary, middle, and high school principals*. Retrieved from www.bls.gov/ooh/management/elementary-middle-and-high-school-principals.htm

Juggling Fatherhood, Child Disability, and Academia
John Beaton

I can recall in the fall of 2008 preparing myself to become the department chair for a January 1, 2009, start date. I was both excited and nervous as this was a significant responsibility for me, especially since I had just received a promotion to associate professor. In addition, it was still early in my academic career, just in my seventh year, and I was only thirty-seven years old. However, I had lots of support from staff and faculty to take on this role in a department that was struggling a great deal at the time, and no one else was willing to step forward. I was also a little apprehensive about how to maintain a healthy work–family balance, which was important to me, with three young children and with my partner, Anna Marie, working full-time.

I have always been an involved father (as was my father), changing diapers, getting up in the middle of the night to bottle-feed babies, coaching soccer, doing homework after school, cooking meals, playing tickle monster, et cetera. My partner and I have always shared all child-rearing tasks in our home as we both work full-time. I was the only male in my department and college at the time who had taken a parental leave, not just one but two parental leaves. In my department (Family Relations and Applied Nutrition), faculty are predominantly women (many mothers), so there was support for me to take a parental leave. I am not sure if this would have been the case in a male-faculty-dominated department and a different academic discipline.

Throughout this chapter, I will rely briefly on the theoretical tenets of symbolic interactionism and masculinity identity to interpret my understanding of my experiences of being a man, a responsible father, and a productive academic. According to symbolic interactionism theorists, emphasis is placed on how people make meanings about their experiences and subsequent actions and interactions with others (Blumer, 1969; Daly, 2002). Through these experiences and interactions, men develop identities in terms of what it means to be a man, a successful worker, and a responsible father. Masculinity theorists would argue that men are given many powerful societal messages about ways in which they are to define themselves, act, and feel, and who they are to be in this world in relationship to others (Connell, 2005). Fathers particularly make their own judgments about their positive parental successes based on expectations and observations of others (Doherty, Kouneski, & Erickson, 1998; Pleck & Masciadrelli, 2004). According to Palkovitz (2002), men's identities have an opportunity to grow and develop through their positive experiences of being an involved father over the course of time.

My first parental leave semester was in 2004 after our second child, Johnny, was born, and prior to having tenure. I still strongly felt during this leave period the need to work on publishing articles, as I was untenured. I also felt a sense of responsibility to supervise my ongoing graduate students, and to continue with collaborative projects that I had committed to with other faculty outside my institution. For most men, we feel a need to contribute and produce at work. It is difficult for us to say no or that we cannot complete a work task. We also think that we are somewhat invincible and that we can juggle many tasks at one time (Connell, 2005). As men who want both to be successful at work and to be responsible fathers, we believe we can do it all, much as mothers in the workforce have been doing for decades. Technically, when you are on any type of leave, human resource policies clearly state that no work is required, but I know among my faculty colleagues work continues. It just made sense for me to take the parental leave as my partner worked for a U.S.-based company from our home and had only six weeks of paid parental leave.

As a result of policy changes over the last five years at our institution, a male faculty member is entitled to two semesters of parental leave and is paid 95 percent of his salary if he is the primary caregiver for the child. These policies did not exist for many of my senior male colleagues when their children were born. Even though there are now policy changes for men to take parental leave, it often takes time for cultural messages to shift about gender roles. As much as expectations about gender and parenting roles have shifted over the years and become more flexible for men to be full-time parents at home, men still perceive strong messages that it is important for them to provide for their families through paid work (Doucet, 2004). There are also still significant messages about men taking parental leave; research suggests that parental leaves are predominantly taken by women, and men may take a parental leave if mothers are not interested or eligible, depending on the culture of support at their workplace and potential loss of income (McKay, Marshall, & Doucet, 2012).

So I had Johnny in one hand and my computer in the other hand for most of the day during my first parental leave in 2004. To this day, Mariana and

Johnny regularly tease me that Daddy parents with his computer in one hand most of the time, and performs childcare and household tasks with the other hand. I am not sure that I would have taken parental leave if my partner had the opportunity to do so; I probably would have felt that she should have the first option to take the leave and that I needed to produce more at work, especially prior to tenure. I would have been nervous about what my colleagues would have thought about my competency and dedication to my job if I did not take parental leave out of pure necessity and the sense of opportunity for our family. As men we deeply care about other people's opinions about our work identities (Connell, 2005), particularly our identities as a provider, partner, and parent (Pleck & Masciadrelli, 2004). In my department, I imagine my colleagues would have thought what a responsible father and partner I was by taking parental leave when my partner could not, which of course positively supported my identity as a responsible father and partner. I know some of my women colleagues have intentionally waited to have a child until after tenure, even if they wanted to have a child earlier. In 2004, I was entitled to two semesters of parental leave, yet I just did not feel that I could take that much time away from work, so regrettably I took only one semester. I often heard of the mothers in our department who had taken parental leave still being involved in a number of work projects while on leave and trying to decide how many semesters of leave to take. To this day, I do not know of any other male colleague at my institution who has taken a parental leave, let alone prior to having tenure.

In 2007, I took two semesters of parental leave when our third child, Joey, was born, out of pure necessity for our home, and I did not feel as much pressure to produce as I was now tenured. I also was better at saying no to graduate supervision opportunities and ongoing collaborative research projects. I did not have enough hands to juggle my computer and three young children while my partner worked full-time. In addition, perhaps I was more comfortable now in my identity as a man, father, and worker, and I was less concerned about what people at work thought of me taking another parental leave. Palkovitz (2002) argues that over time men mature and develop through being fathers, and fatherhood provides an opportunity for identity transformation. To my knowledge there are only two other women faculty members in the history of my department who have more than two children. I can think of only three other fathers in our entire college who have at least three children. Unfortunately, I am not sure there is a culture of support at universities for women to have more than two children; it seems much easier for men to have more children, as they are not carrying the child during pregnancy and potentially taking multiple full-year parental leaves.

My department colleagues have always been supportive of the time I have taken with my children, but I still worried how taking lots of time with my family was affecting my career and how my colleagues viewed my capacity and competency. I can remember having coffee with the dean in the summer of 2008, and having to convince him that it would be okay; I could handle being department chair for five years and still be heavily involved in the lives of our three young children. I felt fortunate to have an academic job that was flexible, and I believed my strong time management skills would allow me to maintain a solid work–family balance. After all, I had always worked hard and completed what I set out to accomplish in my academic career while being significantly involved in my children's lives. Each day (including weekends) I would work early in the morning before the children woke up, and in the evening after the children went to bed. My laptop basically slept with us.

Despite being aware of this work–family balance issue potentially shifting with being a department chair, I was confident that I could maintain a healthy work–family balance with the support of my partner, the department, and the college dean, and juggle all the multiple balls in my life. I had juggled work and the birth of three children without many problems, at least in my own mind. I also prided myself in being a dedicated father. Furthermore, my research interests were in the area of responsible fatherhood, and I was an experienced therapist with lots of ideas about effective parenting and work–family balance. Little did I know at the time that my work and family life would change dramatically just four days before assuming my new role as department chair.

I remember December 28, 2008, clearly; however, this is also a day that I often try to block out of my mind as it is just too painful to remember. In addition, I was hesitant to share the following story openly in this chapter. As men we do not tend to show the emotionally vulnerable side of ourselves, let alone share it in a public form like this chapter. We are given powerful messages about being strong, stable, and emotionally controlled (Connell, 2005). If it is difficult for me to share openly about a painful parenting experience and I am a family therapist in the Department of Family Relations, I can only imagine how difficult it would be for another male faculty colleague in another academic discipline to share about work–family balance issues or parenting struggles. My partner, Anna Marie, and I were on our way to a holiday party at her family's home in late December 2008, with our three children, Mariana (seven), Johnny (five), and Joey (sixteen months). We were concerned about our youngest son, Joey, as he was not developing how he should be in terms of walking and verbal responsiveness, but this was our third child and we were well aware that our other two children and many other children developed differently. However, something was not quite right with Joey; my partner knew it well before I did or the doctors. That particular day in December Joey was not feeling well, but we decided to go to the holiday party anyway. When we arrived at the party, about an hour's drive from our home, Joey was cranky and feverish, and all of a sudden I heard screaming from the other room—Joey had turned purple, was shaking, and appeared not to be breathing. I ran and grabbed Joey and gave him CPR. The paramedics came and they took him to the hospital. It turned out that Joey had had a febrile seizure. The doctors said that he would be fine, febrile seizures were fairly common, and told us not to worry. Well, we continued to worry, and over the next six months Joey continued to have fainting spells, where he would hold his breath and have "mini seizures." Finally in the fall of 2009 we got the pediatrician to refer us to a specialist as Joey was not walking, nor did he have any verbal language at age two.

In October 2009, we were about a month away from his appointment with the specialist and something happened that was easily the scariest day of my life. Joey had a long grand mal seizure that seemed to me to last forever, and they had four people in the emergency room watching over him closely for hours. They had to intubate him. I thought he was going to die that day. He was flown by helicopter to another hospital, where he stayed for a week in the children's intensive care unit and received lots of tests. This was a very long week, and of course there was so much going on at work at the time, as this was my first fall semester as chair. I can remember being on my cellphone with the dean and my secretary every day, trying to make some decisions that at the time seemed important to me. Of course, in retrospect none of these decisions were that important. Even though no one at work expected me to work at all, I definitely expected myself to work and it helped to pass the long hours in the hospital waiting for the never-ending tests to be completed and for the results to become available. Even during times of family crisis, it is difficult as men to let go of our need to perform at work. In some ways, work provides a safe haven when things at home are in crisis. Work is familiar, and we can still fix things that have visible and concrete outcomes, whereas parenting struggles and health issues are often unfixable and invisible. It was determined that Joey had a very rare genetic disorder, creatine transporter deficiency syndrome (severe autism and epilepsy). Anna Marie had thought this for months, but no doctor believed her or would test Joey for this rare disorder, and I probably was in some sort of denial hoping that Joey would not have this type of severe, chronic, and debilitating disorder.

Upon reflection, I am not sure that I know of another faculty member in my department or college who has a young child with a severe special need. There are definitely faculty members in my department and college with children who have various degrees of mental and physical health struggles. At the time of Joey's diagnosis, I still did not fully appreciate how parenting a special needs child would dramatically influence both my family and work life. It probably took me eighteen months to completely figure out and accept this. Parents of special needs children often reflect on how parenting a special needs child is more stressful than a "normal" developing child. It can be particularly difficult for fathers of special needs children to deal with these issues, as there is so much uncertainty and unpredictability with parenting a child with special needs (Beaton, Nicholas, McNeill, & Wenger, 2012). As a man and father, I desperately wanted to fix Joey for myself, my partner, and my other two children. Obviously, I could not fix Joey with a rare genetic disorder. The story of how Joey's diagnosis significantly affected our family life is for a different time and venue.

In March 2011, I had to indicate to the dean that I would not be able to complete my five-year term as chair and that I would like to finish after three years in December 2011 (it ended up being three and a half years, until July 2012). I can remember what a difficult decision this was for me to make at the time. I worried about what people in my life both personally and professionally were going to think—that I couldn't "finish the job." I cannot recall many instances in my life where I have said, "I could not finish it" or "I could not fix it." As men, we are not conditioned to say, "I cannot fix it" or "I have failed." The work–family balance struggles were too much and I needed help. I still worry about this decision to a certain extent. Even though I have subsequently had tremendous support from dean(s), faculty, and staff colleagues, I wondered what my colleagues actually thought of this decision to not complete my five-year term. This is where the combination of work–family was just too much and I could no longer juggle all the balls. At least in my mind I was dropping balls, or my computer, and my life was completely out of balance.

I can remember going home many days emotionally drained from work, and not having much in the emotional tank to give to my family. Of course, my three young children still had lots of my time, but they could not understand why Daddy was more tired in the evenings and on weekends. There was less wrestling or playing tickle monster. I can recall being at home many nights physically present but definitely emotionally absent. I was giving my best energy at work, and I did not have enough quality energy to give at home. This had never been an issue for me before having our third child (with special needs) and becoming department chair; perhaps it was much more of a problem and I just did not recognize it. There came a tipping point in my life when I was not meeting my own expectations at both home and work; this is not a comfortable feeling. This is very difficult for men, the sense that you are not meeting expectations in two significant spheres of life: home and work (Connell, 2005). Even if I was receiving feedback at home and work that I was doing well, I knew this pace of life could not last and that sooner or later I would be "found out" as not performing how I should be.

As I think about my work future, I worry about how did that decision to not complete a five-year term as chair may affect my selection for another administrative role. I am not sure my colleagues will believe that I can balance work–family issues with three young children, one of them being a special needs child. And to be honest, I am not sure I can do it either. This is not something that I am used to thinking related to my work or family life: "Will I be able to get it done?" I imagine many other faculty have the thought, "Will I be able to get it done?" even if they are not parents; however, the academic culture does not provide many opportunities to share our failures and worries about work capacity and parenting issues. Yet, I have actually experienced lots of freedom and peace with the notion that sometimes I might not be able to get it done, and that is just fine.

As I reflect on my experiences of juggling work and family, I imagine my female colleagues who are mothers in my department have often felt that they cannot get it all done. Interestingly enough, I am not sure that in my Family Relations and Applied Human Nutrition department we have had explicit conversations about this juggling act. We may talk about how we are very busy at home and work and are supportive of work–family balance, but we certainly do not talk about how we cannot do it all and/or that we have failed in this balance. Maybe my female colleagues are having these discussions among themselves, without me? I am certainly not having these conversations with other men who are fathers at work. I think as academics, particularly parents, when we cannot juggle all the primary balls in the air, of teaching, service, and research, we make a conscious or unconscious decision to let one of those balls fall. Yet, we certainly do not talk about which ball we are letting slip. We are just hoping that it will not be obvious at performance assessment time. I cannot imagine that these conversations are occurring frequently about work–family balance struggles in other departments, if they are not happening in our department.

I am currently the tenure and promotion floater for our college, which means I am a member of all five departments' T&P committees for the college. There is definitely empathy for parents and understanding that parents will take parental leaves; however, in the long run the expectations are still the same for tenure and promotion and performance assessment. It is easy to forget at promotion time that someone took a one-year parental leave two years ago or has two children and that this might affect his or her total production.

I am really not sure how the "parenting factor" could be accounted for during tenure and promotion time. I do believe it would be unfair to my colleagues who are not parents to even consider the parenting factor during these tenure and promotion discussions. Perhaps we already unconsciously expect more from our colleagues who do not have children, and less from those faculty who do have young children.

I have almost accepted now that until my three children are much older I will not be able to thrive in all three areas of academic life (teaching, service, and research) with dramatically increasing student enrolments, less faculty and staff, increasing expectations with technology, and the pressure at work to do more with less, especially since Joey will more than likely be with us for our entire lives and requires lots of hands-on daily care. Being an academic and the parent of a special needs child is something that is also unique, and something I would like to explore in the future with other faculty who are in this situation. We are very thankful that Joey has not had a seizure for over three years, and that he attends school almost every day. Of course, he will always have significant challenges and requires lots of daily care. Joey is a blessing to us, and he reminds me every day when I leave for work and come home what is truly important to me. I am now consciously striving for "good enough" at work, and very good at home. I am not sure that I will ever obtain full professorship, which was never that important to me. However, I may never have the opportunity or capacity for another administrative role, which I would very much enjoy; I am still working on accepting this reality. I am also not sure how being good enough at work will affect my next performance assessment. Yet, I would never give up the privilege of being the father of our three beautiful children, Mariana, Johnny, and Joey. My heart goes out to some of my colleagues who I know desperately wish they had even one child, let alone three. Parenting and being an academic is a challenging juggling act and also a tremendous privilege.

References

Beaton, J. M., Nicholas, D., McNeill, T., & Wenger, L. W. (2012). The experiences of fathers of a child with a chronic health condition. In J. Ball & K. Daly (Eds.), *Father involvement in Canada* (pp. 190–204). Vancouver, BC: UBC Press.

Blumer, H. (1969). *Symbolic interactionism: Perspective and method.* Englewood Cliffs, NJ: Prentice-Hall.

Connell, R. W. (2005). *Masculinities.* Berkeley: University of California Press.

Daly, K. J. (2002). Time, gender, and the negotiation of family schedules. *Symbolic Interactionism, 25*(3), 323–342.

Doherty, W. J., Kouneski, E., & Erickson, M. (1998). Responsible fathering: An overview and conceptual framework. *Journal of Marriage and the Family, 60*(2), 277–292.

Doucet, A. (2004). It's almost like I have a job, but I don't get paid: Fathers at home reconfiguring work, care, and masculinity. *Fathering, 2*(3), 277–303.

McKay, L., Marshall, K., & Doucet, A. (2012). Fathers and parental leave in Canada. In J. Ball & K. Daly (Eds.), *Father involvement in Canada* (pp. 207–223). Vancouver, BC: UBC Press.

Palkovitz, R. (2002). *Involved fathering and men's adult development: Provisional balances.* Mahwah, NJ: Lawrence Erlbaum.

Pleck, J., & Masciadrelli, B. (2004). Paternal involvement by U.S. residential fathers. In M. E. Lamb (Ed.), *The role of the father in child development* (4th ed., pp. 222–271). New York, NY: John Wiley.

Hopeful Intrusions
Moments as Both a Dad and a Professor

David Long

Memories, like life, are never experienced linearly.[1]

I have many wonderful memories of experiences I shared with my dad, and over the course of my life I have grown to appreciate the delightfully unexpected ways he expressed his quiet humbleness, his trustworthy and disciplined work ethic, and his charmingly Irish sense of humour in our relationship. I have particularly treasured my dad's "way of being my dad" during the fifty years we have played golf together, for one of the first life lessons he taught me is that you truly see who a person is during a "simple" round of golf. Dad grew up with his mom, dad, and two sisters in the quaint Northern Ireland town of Newtonstewart, which also happens to be the setting for many of the golf and life stories he has shared with me over the years. Dad excelled in school, and in 1954 at the age of twenty-two he graduated with honours in engineering from Queen's University in Belfast. It quickly became clear that there were very few decent employment opportunities for recently graduated engineers in Northern Ireland, and so within a few months of graduation Dad set off with a friend for Canada. Fortunately, the luck of the Irish was with him, for within two years he had secured a stable and good-paying position with a major oil company. He soon met a young immigrant woman from Huddersfield, England, named Eileen Hardcastle through his work, and within five years we had become a family of four living what undoubtedly appeared to be an idyllic, middle-class Canadian family life in the suburbs of Toronto, Ontario. Dad had always been an avid and talented golfer, and I still feel a warm sense of delight every time I remember the first time he put a golf club in my hand at the age of five. Like many young boys, my childhood friends and I wanted to be just like our dads since they appeared to us to "have it made." Of course, the countless experiences and conversations I have shared over the years with my own dad, other dads, and especially my own children have taught me that there is much more to the life of a dad than meets even the most imaginative sociological eye.

Growing up in a loving and economically stable family in a safe, suburban neighbourhood allowed me to live a relatively carefree childhood. While I remember my friends and I playing grown-up war games and the like, it's hardly surprising that I don't recall any specific "growing up" experiences that prepared me to know what it would mean or feel like to one day be a dad or a university professor. However, I have become increasingly aware over the past twenty-five years that two rather simple life lessons have informed both my experience and my "critically hopeful" perspective on the relationship between these two central areas of my life. My mom, who loved most everyone she met, taught me the first and I believe most important lesson in life by showing me how listening respectfully and compassionately to others enables us to understand and respond to their lives in hopeful ways. Strangely enough, I received the second life lesson through the writing of C. Wright Mills, who wrote in *The Sociological Imagination* (1959) that

> scholarship is a choice of how to live as well as a choice of career; whether aware of it or not, the intellectual worker forms his or her own self in working toward the perfection of craft; to realize personal potentialities, and any opportunities that come his or her way, such a person constructs a character which has as its core the qualities of the good workman. What this means is that you must learn to use your life experience in your intellectual work: continually to examine and interpret it. In this sense craftsmanship is the center of yourself and you are personally involved in every intellectual product upon which you may work. (p. 54)

I came across this quote while writing my honours undergraduate thesis and immediately identified with Mills' wonderfully humanizing invitation to engage the relationship between my everyday life and my scholarly work in a critically reflexive way. Over the years I have grown to appreciate the many ways that inviting these two lessons into my personal and professional relationships has inspired me to creatively engage the question "What gives people hope?" in both the fathering and academic areas of my life.[2] The most basic answer for me to this question is that people experience hope when we know we are loved and when we express love to others. Given that love has most often come to me in unexpectedly awkward[3] moments, I have come to view such moments as *hopeful intrusions*.

Before describing my experience of a number of these intrusions, a brief comment about how I view this telling of my story.[4] I recognize that most sociologists seek to cultivate a relatively abstract and empirically generalizable understanding of human social life.[5] While the following account may shed light on certain similarities and differences between my experiences and those of other male professors with children, I am not attempting to provide a theoretical template that could be generally applied to the parenting experiences of male sociology professors.[6] The following account is, rather, a highly personal and theoretically storied glimpse into my own experience of being a dad and a university professor. I begin with a brief reflection on the early development of my academic disposition.[7]

Bourdieu Was Partly Correct[8]

Each time I look back on the circumstances of the first twenty or so years of my life, I can't help but think how remarkable it is that I became a university professor. I was raised from the age of two to twelve in the large urban centre of Toronto, though my parents separated when I was nine. My mom, who had grown up in a small hamlet in England before immigrating with her mother to Canada at the age of seventeen, increasingly experienced serious health problems due to the emotional, physical, and financial challenges of living and working as a single parent with two children in a fast-paced and largely unsupportive urban environment. Mom soon decided along with our stepfather, Biff, that it would best for her health and our family's well-being if we moved to a small house in rural central Ontario. Community life on the sparsely populated Sixth Concession of Rawdon Township was friendly and cooperative, and so I spent my teenage years living and working with people whose lives naturally ebbed and flowed with the changing of the seasons, the growing and harvesting of crops, the raising and slaughtering of animals, and regular gatherings to support one another and celebrate community. My extended family of friends along the Sixth Concession helped me to understand that farming was not simply a form of work that kept a roof over people's heads and food on their tables; farming was the life and consciousness of their families and community. People in this community thus never spoke of work–life balance, for the all-encompassing and perpetually demanding world of family farming *was* their life.

Aging and social change happen, of course, and within a few years of us moving into the area, more and more long-time residents of the Sixth Concession sold their farms to people from the city and retired to the nearby small town of Stirling. Just about every transplanted Torontonian was a hobby farmer at best, and so it was common for them to seek work in town and lease their large tracts of land to the farmers in the area who were young and interested in growing their farming operations. What I know now but only sensed back then is that the collective commitment to honouring the integrality[9] of work and life had been gradually eroded by the new landowners' commitment to pursue their own individual interests and by their work–life separation. My experiences on the Sixth Concession predisposed me to hear and apply the wisdom of Mills' words to my scholarly world, for I had seen and felt what can happen when people separate the work they do from their everyday lives.

It also happened that my decision to attend university benefited from the wisdom of a rather unlikely source. Although my stepfather, Biff, read extensively despite having had to quit school in grade seven to help support his working-class, single-mother-led family, I know for certain that he never read anything written by Pierre Bourdieu. Nonetheless, it was during a casual conversation on "my folks'" front porch one humid central-Ontario afternoon in early August 1977 that Biff helped me to understand the significance of pursuing my university education. I had always enjoyed and for the most part succeeded in most every area of school, and so in some ways applying to university seemed like a reasonable next step after graduating high school. However, the adults in the working-class and farming environments of my childhood and youth had shown me that one could live comfortably if one worked hard and lived in a strong, supportive community. I nonetheless sensed that university might well be part of my future, so I requested that my acceptance be deferred in order for me to make some money to pay for my education as well as to take a deep, mind-clearing breath after fourteen years of formal schooling. The decision over which university I might eventually attend was fortunately straightforward, as the good people of Wilfrid Laurier University were the only ones to wish me well and say that they hoped to see me for orientation a year from September.

What I regarded as decent employment experiences for recent high school graduates were fairly hard to come by in my relatively small high school town of Belleville, Ontario. And so it was that a bit of social capital[10] good fortune happened my way when my best friend's dad put in a good word for me with his railroad supervisor for one of four new positions on a "bridges and buildings" work crew.[11] I was invited along with ninety-six other applicants to write a grade twelve high school equivalency test, and we were told that the available positions would be offered to those who received the four highest scores. Almost every applicant I spoke with on the morning of the test recognized the obvious incongruity between the labour jobs we were applying for and the means by which the successful applicants were to be filtered and selected. Still, I was thankful for the opportunity to get paid decent money to dig ditches and repair bridges for a year while taking a break from school. I scored well on the test and accepted their offer to work in one of the four "toil-and-sweat" positions. Our gang worked ten-hour days on the main line across south-central Ontario for the next year. I visited Mom and Biff occasionally throughout the year, and on one visit toward the end of the summer I told Biff that my supervisor wanted me to stay and had offered me a promotion to foreman. When I mentioned to him that I was considering accepting the offer and working for another year, he looked at me and said, "Davey, don't be stupid." I asked him what he meant, and he told me that going to university would give me something he never had in his life: choice.

I tell this story at the beginning of each and every school year when I meet a new group of first-year students. I note that although Biff was unfamiliar with Bourdieu, he knew the social capital and upward mobility truth of what he was speaking to me about that day. I also note that he understood that despite his intelligence, his commitment to hard work, his good spirit, and his wonderfully insightful sense of humour, his lack of formal education had meant that he had failed to acquire the proper disposition and field of relations that would have enabled him to make certain kinds of choices in his life. Biff accomplished some remarkable things during his life despite his working-class roots and lack of formal education, including always helping to put food on our table and keep a roof over our heads by scouring the countryside and accepting whatever jobs were offered to him. He also built three solar-heated homes after reading a few library books and applying the lessons he had learned throughout his life at countless construction-related odd jobs. Biff nonetheless knew there were worlds of experience and possibility cultivated in university that were beyond his reach. The rather simple, fatherly wisdom that he shared with me on the front porch that afternoon was that he hoped I would choose the path that would give me far more liberating choices than he had ever had. Needless to say I listened to Biff's wise and caring words. I enrolled at Wilfrid Laurier in the fall of 1977, though as I note below it was not until the summer of 1984 that my experience of being a father as well as an academic began to dovetail.

Becoming a Fathering-Inclined Academic

My wife, Karen, and I met in a sociology of religion graduate seminar at the University of Waterloo in the summer of 1984, and we were married two years later on July 5, 1986. Our first daughter, Jennica, was born just over two years later, and we decided in the spring of 1989 as I was nearing completion of my dissertation that it would be a good move for our growing family if I accepted an offer for a tenure-track position in sociology from The King's University College[12] in Edmonton, Alberta. My department chair at Waterloo tried to convince me that it would be academic suicide to accept an offer to teach at a relatively small Christian university, but I was intrigued after my King's interview at the prospect of being part of a university in which professors and students were committed to "teach each other in all wisdom."[13] Tenure-track positions for sociologists in Canada were also few and far between at the time, and Karen and I agreed that our family would benefit from at least one of us having a steady income since she was three months pregnant and we were already caring for our twelve-month-old daughter, Jennica. I had also been awarded the inaugural Grant Notley Post-Doctoral Fellowship from the University of Alberta and was pleased when the dean of arts agreed to defer my award for one year so I could accept the tenure-track offer from King's. King's was also very accommodating, for the academic vice-president told me that that they would hold my position after I had taught for a year at King's in order to allow me a sixteen-month leave to take up my Notley Fellowship. I gratefully accepted both offers, and so Karen, Jennica, and I moved to Edmonton in 1989. We have now lived here for twenty-five years, and during that time my children, Jennica (twenty-five), Bethany (twenty-three), Sarah (twenty), and Kathryn (seventeen), have taught me something most every day about who I am and what it means to be a dad. This includes the times I have taken my children to work, for just about every time I have done so I have experienced their "hopeful intrusion" into my academically inclined world. The following incident is perhaps the most memorable of those intrusions.

I can't seem to recall my dad having talked to me about his work when I was young, though I will always remember the joyful and nervous sense of anticipation I experienced the day he invited me to join him on his company's "bring your kid to work" day. Perhaps in part because I had felt quite insulated from my dad's work, I decided that I would openly share my work life with my children. I have always felt wonderfully affirmed whenever my kids have shown interest in my work, and so I made sure to invite them to come with me to King's every once in a while. One of those days in particular remains quite vivid in my memory. It started as other weekdays often did with much laughter and silliness around our breakfast table. While both Kathryn and Sarah were at first excited when I told them they would be coming to work with me, three-year-old Kathryn told me as we were leaving home that she was a bit scared about being with so many big people. I remember assuring her that it would be fun and that "Daddy would take care of her," though I also remember sensing that it was not going to be a usual day in the classroom for me and my students.

The three of us left in good time to get to school well ahead of my first class at 9:30 a.m. The drive to work was more pleasant than usual since Kathryn and Sarah's joyful renditions of "The Wheels on the Bus" and "If You're

Happy and You Know It" were far more entertaining than the traffic reports and predictable radio fare I was used to hearing. I could feel our anticipation growing as we got out of the car and made our way across the parking lot to the main building along with a number of students. Our relatively small campus and wisdom-focused approach to university education breeds a mutually respectful, communal sense of familiarity among students and faculty, and as we walked across the parking lot two students who were in my first class of the day introduced themselves to Sarah and Kathryn and asked them if they were excited about coming to work with their daddy. They both said they were, and I felt a warm smile grow inside me as one of the students, whose name was Jane, told Sarah and Kathryn that their dad was her favourite professor in the whole school. Jane then asked Sarah what it was like having a daddy who was a doctor, and after looking slightly perplexed for a moment Sarah said, "Oh no, my daddy's not a doctor, though he's really good at making us feel better when we get hurt or sick." She then proceeded to tell Jane and her friend a rather graphic story about how I had held a washcloth on her head and told her everything would be all right one night when she "threw up a whole bunch in the toilet." We all shared a good laugh, and none of us could anticipate that we would experience the "truth" of Sarah's words less than an hour later.

As a bit of a pedagogical aside, I have always enjoyed teaching and learning along with the students in my classes. I understand well Bourdieu's (1991) insights into how and why most formal educational settings in general and universities in particular are characterized by relations of power, symbolic violence, and dominance. However, I'm much less inclined than Bourdieu and other critical theorists to stress the oppressive ways that power plays out its hand in university classrooms, for I have always sought to cultivate an open, honest, mutually respectful, and challenging dialogue of discernment in my classes (Long, 1995). I have never shied away from engaging students and colleagues in hard and sometimes quite personal discussions, and the relatively small classes at King's are ideally suited to cultivating exchanges that invite students and professors to learn from one another's experiences, insights, and questions (Long, 1992). I see the students in the classes I teach as whole people who deserve respect and dignity, and I do my best to treat them that way.

Even though King's has a communal feel and I am fairly at ease with students both inside and outside the classroom, the academic disposition that Bourdieu speaks of runs deep in most every interaction at most every university. Fortunately, over the years my children have taught me how to help them to feel at ease in "strange" public settings, and so I have always kept a few toys and colouring books in my office to keep them or other parents' children

playfully occupied. I was thankful that Kathryn and Sarah immediately settled into their surroundings by playing with their favourite toys, for I like
to spend a bit of time organizing my thoughts before class. I view sociology
in a thoroughly practical way, and so I regularly tell my students that I am
committed to our class discussions being as relevant to their lives as possible.
I have always viewed teaching as a means to challenge and enable students to
learn to ask their own "good" questions and to understand where their questions come from and what this says about them (Long, 1998). I encourage
them to ask whatever questions come to mind about Marx or Durkheim or
Smith or Bourdieu and to know that they are more than welcome to debate
and argue with the ideas of others. I also make it clear that learning to "argue"
with others in university includes learning how to pay serious and respectful
scholarly attention to others' ideas. Hence the importance I place before I enter
the classroom on having the main threads of my thoughts and a few concrete
examples from everyday life as clear in my mind as possible.

It was now 9:15 a.m. so the three of us packed up my notes, as well as a
snack, a few small toys, and a colouring book for each of the girls. We arrived
in the classroom of twenty students, and I set Sarah and Kathryn up beside
me at the front of the room, which was arranged with eight rectangular tables
joined at the end to make a square. The course was a senior seminar in the
sociology of marriage and family, and that day we happened to be covering
"theories of parenting." I introduced Sarah and Kathryn and told the students
that we were sharing a day at Dad's work. The students introduced themselves,
and after Sarah and Kathryn were settled in with their toys and colouring
books, the students and I began our discussion of how and why theories of
parenting in Canada and other Western societies have changed dramatically
over the past one hundred years. We were quite engaged in the discussion
when all of a sudden there was a high-pitched scream from across the room.
Sure enough, there by the door was my three-year-old, Kathryn, screaming
and crying loudly with her hand firmly stuck in the VCR! I was scared that she
would hurt herself if she tried in a panic to pull her hand out of the machine,
and so I quickly made my way to the door while saying to the class, "Excuse
me for moment, it's time for me to be Dad." I rushed over, and after we freed
Kathryn's hand from inside the machine I excused us and took her and Sarah
for a bit of a walk and to get a treat. Kathryn eventually calmed down and said
it would be okay if we went back so I could teach, and once we settled back in
the students and I engaged in a lively discussion of how theories develop and
why sociologists make sense of parenting the way we do.

Thanks to Kathryn's VCR experience, the students had seen me being
forced to step out of my professorial disposition to attend to the needs of my

child. As a vulnerable human being, Kathryn had been "the crack that lets the light come in"[14] to our academic habitus. I felt her pain and knew her fear as soon as I heard her cry of distress. I also recall feeling slightly self-conscious at first about relaxing my academic pose,[15] though the reactions of my students helped me to see that they expected me to care for my daughter. Kathryn's "awkward moment" of vulnerability and need to be immediately cared for humanized the somewhat taken-for-granted formality of our classroom and my professorial disposition. Her *hopeful intrusion* had also brought life to our academic conversation about love by simply trusting that I would care for her and make everything all right. Indeed, it has been experiences such as the one I had with Kathryn that day that have made me increasingly grateful for the many times and ways that my children have awkwardly and hopefully intruded into my academic world. As the following vignette suggests, I have been fortunate to experience similar intrusions by the dads I have worked with in the course of my community-engaged research.

The Humanizing of My Academic Disposition

I have always been committed to the scholarly pursuit of new knowledge, though one of the fundamental goals of my research and scholarship has long been to challenge and enable government as well as human service agencies to develop policies and programs that offer positive support to males in all their diversity (Long, 2004, 2008). King's faculty adopted Boyer's (1990) expanded models of scholarship in the mid-1990s, which has meant that I and a number of other faculty members have received strong institutional support for our community-engaged research.

My commitment to engaging and supporting dads in and through my research informed a conversation I had during my sabbatical in December 2012 with a King's sociology graduate who had taken up a position as a drop-in support worker for homeless people at a local community services centre. We were discussing her work and some of the needs of the people at the centre when it occurred to me that some of the men might appreciate being part of a support group that invited them to simply share their stories. Heather was enthusiastic about the idea, and so I asked my Elder friend Harry if he would be interested in helping me to organize and facilitate the group. I have long known the value of men sharing their own stories and listening to the stories of other men, and so Harry and I decided that we would simply ask the men in the group to share positive stories in response to the question I had posed to dads during the course of my sabbatical, which was, "What have you learned from your children?" We held our first group in January 2013 and provided the twelve participants with fresh-baked bannock and refreshments.

The circle is sacred to Aboriginal people, and so we had arranged the chairs in a circle in the middle of the centre's basement boardroom. Harry and I arrived after gathering a few participants from the upstairs drop-in centre, and as we entered the room we saw a fellow very loudly and rather obnoxiously "entertaining" people from his chair in the middle of the circle. Warren (a pseudonym) introduced himself to us, and it was obvious that he was quite intoxicated and revelling in the attention he was getting from a number of men in the group. We mentioned to him and others that the group was about to begin, and so he demonstratively pushed his chair backwards to the space beside where I was sitting. After I welcomed everyone and introduced myself and the purpose of the group, I passed the talking stick to Harry and he began to tell a story about how one of his daughters had taught him a lesson about the meaning of love during her adolescence. The warm bannock was on a table directly behind Warren and me, and when I tapped him on the shoulder to ask if he would like some bannock he put his finger up to his mouth and slurred quietly, "Shhh, I'm listenin' to the story." The sacred circle of dads, it seemed, had already begun its work in Warren.

The stick moved around the circle until it arrived at Warren, and he immediately shared in a surprisingly vulnerable way a moving story about a dilemma he was facing with his nineteen-year-old "daughter."[16] He told us that she had asked him if he would be willing to stand up for her at her wedding ceremony since her adoptive dad had said that he was unwilling to support her getting married to another woman. His eyes teared up as he explained that he didn't want to dishonour the relationship between her and her adoptive father, but he was confused about what to do since he loved her. Everyone in the circle encouraged him to know that whatever he decided she would know that he loved her. Warren passed me the stick, and after thanking him for sharing his story I began to tell mine. I shared how I had learned about love late one night as I was comforting my very sick daughter, and after I finished my story I started to pass the talking stick to Harry. As I was doing so Warren sat straight up in his seat and said, "Hey, wait jus' a minute." He pointed to a young female nursing student who was sitting beside me "observing" the group, and as he did so he slurred rather loudly, "Hey Angel [which serendipitously happened to be her name], what about you? Whass your story? Everyone in the circle has a story, and you're in our circle so we wanna know whass *your* story?" The student was taken aback but accepted the stick from me and began sharing how she obviously wasn't a dad, but she did have a dad and their relationship hadn't been very good for some time. When she said that she just wished he would love her and accept her for who she is, Warren immediately jumped in and said, "Hey Angel, maybe the same goes for your dad. Maybe he just wants you to love him for who he is, 'cause love gotta kinda work both ways, ya know what I mean?"

The group sat in silence for a moment after experiencing Warren's wonderfully hopeful intrusion into not only Angel's life but ours as well. Just prior to starting the group, Harry and I had briefly discussed whether we should allow Warren to take part, and we both knew the moment he uttered those words to Angel why we had decided to do so. We had honoured all the people who were part of our circle, and this had enabled everyone, including Warren, to be open to giving as well as receiving hope. The awkward, loving moment that Warren and Angel shared had taught us all that loving, hopeful relations between "men and their children" are possible anytime and everywhere. Despite the lesson my mom had taught me about listening respectfully, compassionately, and open-mindedly to others, I admit that I had not expected to learn something meaningful from Warren that day. I was grateful in the end for his vulnerability and wisdom, for he had helped me to realize how challenging it can be for even the most fathering-inclined of academics to learn anything outside of what our concepts, categories, and theories predispose us to see. His hopeful intrusion had stripped away layers from the "manner" in which I had thought about and related to him. The loving circle of homeless dads, it seemed, had also begun its work in me.

Concluding Remarks

> In academia, ... an art historian, on being stirred to tears by the tenderness and serenity he detects in a work by a fourteenth-century Florentine painter, may end up writing a monograph, as irreproachable as it is bloodless, on the history of paint manufacture in the age of Giotto. It seems easier to respond to our enthusiasms by trading in facts than by investigating the more naive question of how and why we have been moved. (de Botton, 2009, pp. 27–29)

My twenty-five years of fathering and being personally involved and professionally engaged with other dads have taught me that the lives of dads are rarely as they appear to be. Certainly I have long recognized the benefits of discovering and discussing the sociological patterns in the lives of dads. However, I am convinced along with de Botton of the deep importance of attending to the underlying "naive" questions of dads in any and every social circumstance. I have found that doing so has invited us to understand how and why we as dads experience the social patterning of our lives the way we do. It has also helped us to see how and why our way of "being dad" in socially patterned circumstances can be challenged and transformed by the often unintentional and delightfully awkward moments we share with others. My intention in this discussion has thus been to share a personal and theoretically storied glimpse into my experience of being a university professor and a dad. I noted that I have embraced the challenge of C. Wright Mills and Pierre Bourdieu to be mindful of the personal and professional biases in my teaching and research. I also noted my continuing commitment to emulate my mom's openness to engaging in respectful, compassionate listening in my personal and professional relationships. Lastly, I shared how I have learned to see certain experiences that I have had with my children and with the dads I know or work with as *hopeful intrusions* in the personal and professional areas of my life. While on the one hand I am learning that such intrusions can expose when and how I am academically disposed to see as well as communicate in impersonal and overly abstract ways,[17] I am also learning that such moments help me learn how to teach as well as craft my sociological stories in ways that engage and honour people as whole human beings (Long, 1998, 2008).

I have long agreed with Mills, Bourdieu, and others who call on sociological storytellers to be theoretically critical, empirically disciplined, and humbly reflexive in our intellectual work. Part of my interest in providing a theoretically storied glimpse into my experiences as a dad and a university professor has therefore been to highlight the benefit of inviting our whole selves into our sociological storytelling. However, over the past twenty-five years I have also become convinced that we sociologists need to learn how to tell hopeful stories that convey a sense of urgency.[18] My children, students, and the dads I have known personally and engaged with in my research have helped me learn this on an almost daily basis. Their hopeful intrusions into my personal and professional life have humanized my academically inclined, sociological "way" of engaging the relations between men and their children. They have also helped me to appreciate that the hopeful intrusions of others into my personal and academic life teach me ever-deeper meanings of what it means to love and be human. And that is the kind of a radical vision for sociology that presents me with a proper sense of both urgency and hope.

Notes

1 Aitken, 2009, p. 154.
2 I also engage the question, "What hinders people from experiencing hope?" in all my research, though I am convinced that there is more benefit to prioritizing the question, "What gives people hope?"
3 I have borrowed this term from Aitken's (2009) thought-provoking, poststructural analysis of the "awkward spaces" of fathering. Aitken views individual human identity as always partial, hybridized, and nomadic, and so it is that the "awkward moments" that

dislocate us from such hardened, ideological categories as "father," "professor," and "son/daughter" make something else—something different—possible in our relationship with (an)other (p. 56).

4 See Doucet (2007, p. 63) for a thoughtful discussion of the importance of engaging stories and narratives in sociological research.

5 I recall a colleague responding to my question, "Why do sociologists seem so afraid to use the word love?" by telling me that there is little room in an empirically focused discipline such as sociology to explore something as unreliable and immeasurable as love. As the following account suggests, I continue to respectfully disagree.

6 While I sympathize with Aitken's (2009, pp. 30–31) critique of the empirically driven grand sociological narrative that simply "domesticates" fathering by focusing on the converging responsibilities of mothers and fathers, his sweeping dismissal of fifty years of sociological research indicates his lack of familiarity with the extensive literature that engages the wonderfully layered and relationally complex lives of men in general and fathers in particular.

7 I am thinking here of the development of one's disposition in light of Bourdieu's (1986) concept of *habitus*, which he viewed as a dynamic social context involving the conscious and unconscious actions of "free"-thinking individuals and the structures of their interactions. Although some critique the vagueness of Bourdieu's concepts of field and habitus, they have heuristic benefit in that they capture well Bourdieu's understanding that the conscious and unconscious social behaviours of human beings are at times rather structurally predictable and at other times not. Although Bourdieu did not write at length on the implications of humans engaging in a variety of fields of interaction and thus "living and moving" in more than one habitus, it is clear that doing so contributes to an ongoing interweaving and transforming of our dispositions.

8 I say "partly correct" because Bourdieu's (1979) class-based analysis of the social reproduction of student dispositions focused on the privileged ways that students raised in an upper-class environment develop the language, manner, and gait necessary for educational success. It would seem, then, that I ended up doing well in school and eventually becoming a university professor "despite" spending my preadolescent years in a working-class, immigrant neighbourhood in Toronto and then all my teen years among a community of farmers, most of whom had not graduated from high school.

9 See Wilber (2003) for a discussion of the concept of integrality as essential wholeness.

10 Bourdieu (1986) defines social capital as "the aggregate of the actual or potential resources which are linked to possession of a durable network of more or less institutionalized relationships of mutual acquaintance and recognition—or in other words, to membership in a group—which provides each of its members with the backing of the collectively-owned capital, a 'credential' which entitles them to credit, in the various senses of the word" (p. 249).

11 Work on a "B&B" gang was physically demanding and monotonously predictable as it involved either digging tunnels through concrete-like southern Ontario clay to install steel culverts so water could pass freely under the tracks or replacing worn-out, three-hundred-pound creosote-soaked railroad ties that supported the tracks on bridges.

12 Alberta's use of the term "university college" is distinct in Canada, for it is used to identify a small number of degree-granting liberal arts universities in the province that are faith-based and largely funded by members of a supporting constituency.

13 I recognize that many academics at "secular" universities dismiss faith-based scholarship and university education for a variety of reasons, though the most common reason I have come across has been based on the erroneous assumption that faith-based scholarship is simply one more means by which people who take the spiritual dimension of the human condition seriously seek to bolster their religiously dogmatic views of life. That

this assumption is erroneous has become more and more clear to me thanks to the very diverse ways in which my King's, Aboriginal, and other like-minded colleagues have challenged and invited me to cultivate a critically hopeful view of social life that honours people as whole human beings. It has also always struck me as rather "interesting" that I have come across a good deal of closed-minded (i.e., secularized) dogma in the lives and work of many of my non-religious colleagues.

14 A well-known line from the chorus of Leonard Cohen's 1992 song "Anthem."

15 One of my favourite lines from Mills' *The Sociological Imagination* is "To overcome the *academic* prose you have first to overcome the *academic* pose" (p. 219).

16 Many Aboriginal people in Canada view their family in extended, community-oriented terms, and so it is common to hear individuals referring to their brothers, daughters, grandmothers, etc., even though they may not be immediately blood related.

17 While Mills (1959) cautioned academics on their use of academic prose, his point was not to dismiss the value of developing abstract concepts and engaging in critical theoretical analysis. Rather, his concern was simply that academics not take their academic prose for granted and that they commit themselves to communicating with others in clear and succinct ways.

18 When asked by a journalist when he knew a song he had written was "his," Leonard Cohen responded by saying that it is when the song gives him a sense of urgency. As soon as I read Cohen's words I thought we would do well to demand the same of all current and future sociological storytellers.

References

Aitken, S. (2009). *The awkward spaces of fathering*. Burlington, VT: Ashgate.

Bourdieu, P. (1979). *The inheritors: French students and their relations to culture*. Chicago, IL: University of Chicago Press.

Bourdieu, P. (1986). The forms of capital. In J. Richardson (Ed.), *Handbook of theory and research for the sociology of education* (pp. 241–258). New York, NY: Greenwood.

Bourdieu, P. (1991). *Language and symbolic power*. Cambridge, MA: Harvard University Press.

Boyer, E. L. (1990). *Scholarship reconsidered: Priorities of the professoriate*. Princeton, NJ: Carnegie Foundation for the Advancement of Teaching.

de Botton, A. (2009). *The pleasures and sorrows of work*. New York, NY: Random House.

Doucet, A. (2007). *Do men mother?* Toronto, ON: University of Toronto Press.

Long, D. (1992, Spring). Liberal arts and the love of bureaucracy. *Dianoia, 2*(1), 43–50.

Long, D. (1995). Sociology and a pedagogy for liberation: Cultivating a dialogue of discernment in our classrooms. *Teaching Sociology, 23*(4), 321–330.

Long, D. (1998). A radical teacher's dilemma. *Teaching Sociology, 26*(2), 112–115.

Long, D. (2004). *Not for men only: Enviroscan of services for men in Edmonton*. Edmonton, AB: MenInc. Press.

Long, D. (2008). *All dads matter: Towards a socially inclusive vision for father involvement initiatives in Canada*. Toronto, ON: Father Involvement Research Alliance.

Mills, C. W. (1959). *The sociological imagination*. New York, NY: Oxford University Press.

Wilber, K. (2003). *Excerpt C: The ways we are in this together—intersubjectivity and interobjectivity in the holonic Kosmos*. Retrieved from http://www.wilber.shambhala.com/html/books/kosmos/excerptC/intro-2.cfm

A Bridge Too Far? The Elephant in the Ivory Tower
Parenting and the Tenure Track

John Hoben

During a casual conversation about the current state of the university, I once jokingly asked one of my favourite law professors if he ever thought about how many elephants it took to build an ivory tower. While he did laugh, my sardonic comment was meant to drive home the fact that universities have become deeply inequitable institutions that impose some very real costs on those who work within them—costs that include broken relationships and neglected families. As Silva and Pugh (2010) point out, it is vitally important to "challenge any inclination to romanticize parenting—and mothering in particular—and [to] reveal the structural inequities that frame experiences of care" (p. 605).

While parenting choices disproportionately affect women (Austin, 2010; Manchester, Leslie, & Kramer, 2010; Mason & Goulden, 2002), they also have a distinct impact upon males, particularly those who take on non-traditional parenting roles (Dunn, Rochlen, & O'Brien, 2013; Sallee, 2012). As Sallee (2012) found in her study of parent scholars in three American universities, "many men worried that being an involved father indicated that they were not serious academics, or worse, were not fulfilling their role as breadwinner" (p. 799). Although women do undoubtedly face many more obstacles, gaps in the literature suggest that it is also worth mapping the role of men in non-traditional parenting roles as a means of examining the gender expectations that frame the institutional experiences of families where one or both parents are negotiating the conventional tenure track. As Hill, Nash, and Citera (2011) point out, "with more than half of children in the U.S. born into homes with two working parents, work/family balance is no longer just a 'woman's issue' but has become a family issue" (p. 113). Unfortunately, as Sallee (2012) emphasizes in her study of male American academics, this is an increasingly common story, with male academics fearing the stigma associated with taking time off to parent or to take advantage of institutional supports (p. 799).

Given the close relationship between parenting choices and gender, sexual orientation, race, class, and broader issues of generational equity, what is desperately needed is a sea change in the way universities view parents struggling to pursue academic careers with young families. Undeniably adjunct and non-tenure-track roles, often held by parents, particularly mothers, are undervalued. Yet, fortunately, there is a growing groundswell of support to bring equity to these spaces based on the conviction that "these vital academic positions must be made fairer—offering equal pay for equal work, benefits, office space, and support—to reflect the expertise and, yes, the flexibility they bring their institutions" (O'Connor, 2009, p. 6). By sharing my own parenting narrative, I hope to play some small role in encouraging a broader dialogue about the needs and struggles of beginning career academics—including males—in today's university. Perhaps in this way we can collectively engender a more equitable and tolerant institution that invests in aspiring scholars rather than treating them as disposable source material for the ready accumulation of publication credits, patents, and research funds.

My Own Story: Scholarship as a Guilty Privilege

Elephants are creatures of memory who possess a kind of uncanny, improbable dignity. More valuable than ivory perhaps is this lesson in how we can aspire to a sort of lumbering grace despite the incessant everyday afflictions that seem to serve as life's primary mode of instruction. My own story is a reflection on my own search for dignity as an aspiring scholar faced with many of the all-too-common fears, joys, and frustrations of a male parent working and studying in today's rapidly changing university.

My uncle, who had become a father while still a teenager and who went on to attend medical school late in life, once told me there is never a "great time" to have kids and so you might as well look life square in the eye and figure out what it is that you really want. He was right about that. Our first daughter, Sophia, was born one week after I finished my comprehensive PhD exams. My wife and I had decided to have children in our mid-thirties since she very much wanted to start a family and felt time was "running out." I worried about the timing of our decision as I had just received a three-year SSHRC research fellowship and knew that search committees did not often look favourably on any gaps in a candidate's research or publishing record. However, as my partner pointed out, if we deferred the decision to have children, circumstances were unlikely to be much more favourable after graduation when I would face the daunting challenge of finding an academic position.

Having already completed a law degree and practised law for a couple of years, I decided she was right. Since she was a self-employed physician, however, she could not afford to take much more than a couple of months' maternity leave, meaning that I was tasked with looking after the newborn while she returned to work. Fortunately, I still was able to write, but the pace was exhausting and my work suffered. Like O'Connor (2009), I felt that despite our best intentions, "my plans to introduce a baby seamlessly into my career now seem ridiculous" (p. 3). Understandably, as Mason, Goulden, and Frasch (2009) note, "in the eyes of many doctoral students, the academic fast track has a bad reputation—one of unrelenting work hours that allow little or no room for a satisfying family life" (p. 1). I found that for the most part such fears were well founded.

In many ways, today's academy has failed to recognize the complexities of changing family structures and the need for practical measures to promote diversity within the family unit, and even within the university itself. Rather, "upon close evaluation, we continue to find that many of our work/family policies remain based on the 'traditional' family with a male breadwinner and a stay-at-home mom—a clearly outdated model" (Hill et al., 2011, p. 113). Even though I often felt judged by my friends for my unconventional gender role, the truth is that it made economic sense for us and also enabled me to both pursue my vocation of choice and spend more time at home. In short, I was both lucky and privileged since I had options, whereas countless others are victims of circumstance through no fault of their own.

A related factor contributing to my unease was my decision to leave the practice of law to commence doctoral studies. Law was a high-status profession that was well paying and thus fit well with the traditional picture of the male breadwinner. Even though I recognized the flawed nature of those gender roles, I also could not help but feel self-conscious about being the male stay-at-home father without any immediate employment prospects. I remember being asked by one of my wife's colleagues, who was troubled to learn that the town would be losing a valued doctor, why I simply didn't just "get a real job." Apparently, my academic research failed to meet the unspoken criteria of what constituted legitimate work. As Dunn, Rochlen, and O'Brien (2013) point out, "psychological theories and empirical studies have underscored the idea that people respond negatively toward women and men who violate traditional gender norms" (p. 5). It wasn't until I received a well-paying PhD fellowship that I felt like my decision was one that made sense in the eyes of our blue-collar extended family members and the status-driven professional communities to which we both belonged.

Although I had a close friend who also had children during her doctoral studies, few of my fellow students or even faculty members were having children. I worried about this continually as a young PhD student trying to gain entry into an increasingly competitive job market. Perhaps it is surprising that many graduate students simply elect not to have children (O'Connor, 2009). Since my wife works full-time in a demanding profession, we also were fortunate to have the support of grandparents, as well as the financial security her work provided. This means, of course, that we are also less likely to move away from these forms of support or my wife's practice. As Baker (2010) points out, mobility is often a factor that influences tenure and promotion possibilities for academic parents, particularly if the family unit has deep attachments to place due to one or both partners' employment or family ties. Unfortunately, "graduates who believe that they lack geographic mobility may search for local jobs and find only contractually-limited teaching positions with few promotional possibilities, given the hiring preference for external candidates in many universities" (Baker, 2010, p. 2).

Baker's (2010) comments underscore the complexity of parenting and childcare arrangements when coupled with some of the internal institutional dynamics of universities. In other words, despite calls for change, "the academy continues to operate under the assumption that the ideal worker has unlimited time to give to work … a role that few will be able to fulfill" (Sallee, 2012, p. 799). With the birth of our second child, Norah, three years after our first, I once again found myself at home looking after a young infant, teaching sessional courses, and struggling to finish a thesis. To compound matters, neither of our infants seemed to sleep, meaning that quite often both of us were exhausted to a point beyond anything we had ever experienced, even though I had pulled many all-nighters trying to make court-filing deadlines and my wife had worked many gruelling twenty-four-hour hospital shifts.

Fortunately, all ended well. After completing my doctorate in five years and nearing forty, I decided not to pursue a postdoctorate since I wanted to remain close to my family. I instead found a good job as a full-time educational consultant within the university. While this was work that recognized the value of scholarship and writing, it was still a staff position with fairly intensive teaching obligations that afforded little real time for academic pursuits. Ironically, these new positions are also a structural necessity in light of budget cuts and the outsourcing of teaching that many see as having fundamentally undermined the conventional tenure system (Whitson, 2012, p. 2).

However, to function as an academic outside of academia also meant that I was always stealing time. When I was writing or reading it was always time that I should have been spending at "real work," that I should have been devoting to being a better employee, a better husband, or a better parent. This meant a number of things: first, that I felt the work I was doing was inferior and so there was never any real satisfaction in any accomplishment. Second, it also meant that quitting the academic job hunt was always quite tempting. It is difficult to motivate oneself when one feels the guilt of taking time from the people one loves to devote to pursuing a goal that seems ever, frustratingly just outside one's grasp. As Austin (2010) emphasizes, "it is noteworthy that, with the overall societal shift in recent decades toward greater involvement of men in handling family duties, studies of early career faculty show that both men and women are concerned about balancing family and professional responsibility" (p. 29).

Managing Expectations for an Authentic Life

It would appear then that our academic institutions have become places where people are used up rather than valued. As Collini (2012) points out, what many contemporary reform movements within education fail to realize is that "economic activity is principally a means to something else, a way of amassing the resources with which to do things which have more interest and significance for human beings than economic activity itself does" (p. 110). Being careful not to become, in the words of one of my mentors, "part of the departmental furniture," I found it was increasingly difficult to negotiate an intensely competitive academic career ladder while making time for family life. In part, this is because children need to be nurtured rather than simply tended—they require emotional connection and *being present* in ways that are far more demanding than any research problem one might encounter in the academic realm. I am reminded of famed behaviourist John B. Watson, who is once known to have boasted that if he were to be given a "dozen healthy infants" and could control the manner and environment in which they were raised, he could "train them to become any type of specialist he might select" (Watson, as cited in Gewirtz, 2001, p. 23). But what Watson and his fellow behaviourists fail to recognize is that neither education nor parenting is an exact science since life, as our children remind us, is much more complicated. Just as parents and teachers have seen the failures of "a child psychology predicated on the adjustment of children to the existing social order" and an "order ideology of schooling," so too must we reject a similar logic of academic acculturation as we lobby for deep and meaningful change (Steinberg, 2011, p. 48).

In other words, I had accepted what Silva and Pugh (2010) term the "depleting model of parenting," the same model that dominates academic culture itself. However, since then I have come to appreciate the perspective of "scholars who emphasize the heavy costs of ... a 'depleting model' of care [and who] draw attention to the ways that the social contexts of childrearing, rather than parenting itself, are generative of economic and psychological strain" (Silva & Pugh, 2010, p. 608). Everywhere I look there are young academics striving to find a place in an academy that treats them like annoying strays that have to be driven away. Continuously living like that is psychically taxing and hardly represents a sound recipe for a well-adjusted and happy emotional life. "Sometimes," Lamott (1995) says, "you may find it useful to let your characters huddle in the wings without you, preparing for their roles, improvising dialogue, while you set the stage for their appearance" (p. 74). This is how I feel many days, like one of those nervous characters waiting for the casting call that never comes. How many children, I wonder, feel the same way about their absentee parents?

To be honest, I often worry that mine have—along with far too many others. As O'Connor (2009) points out, "over 65 percent of faculty positions are now part-time and non-tenure track appointments (Knapp et al., 2005), and women are disproportionately affected by this trend" (p. 1). Increasingly, for the current generation of academics-in-waiting, balance seems to be nothing more than a hopeful myth. As Austin (2010) emphasizes, "senior faculty members (especially those who had a spouse at home while the faculty member negotiated the early career years) sometimes do not understand the pressures on their early career colleagues to fit personal as well as professional responsibilities into their schedules" (p. 29). Rather, "life on the job market is an endless cycle of publishing, applying for jobs, failing to get interviews or offers, and publishing again" (Whitson, 2012, p. 1). This seems more like an exotic affliction than any viable career choice, and when children enter the picture and other career choices are available, it also inevitably begins to appear selfish and self-indulgent.

Part of the problem with higher education, perhaps, is that we have tried to separate educational problems from everyday life. As Kieran Egan (2002) points out, "there are no natural units of human behavior, except on a purely physiological level, because what we count as a unit—an action or event—is determined by the larger frame of meanings in which it plays a part" (p. 159). Human life is the primary "unit of education," one that for our purposes takes shape within the university, an institution that one hopes one day can more fully embody the ideal of an interdependent collegial community. Rather than treating entry-level academics as children who are best seen and not heard, this process of re-creation is also one that must be engaged in by healthy academic communities intent on investing in a shared future. As Guyas and Poling (2011) remind us, "as mothers, parents, partners, lovers, daughters, sons, friends, and acquaintances we might participate in many folding and unfolding performances of life that are never fully separate from scholarship and education" (p. 174).

Finding Love and Meaning in the Borderlands of Fragmented Spaces

However, more importantly, it is worth remembering that children continually startle us; they force us to awaken and to attend, as much as we can, to the present moment. As Manning (2008) evocatively states in her poignant reflection on working and living with a sick child, "most of my living occurred as I travelled through the borderlands of fragmented spaces" (p. 243). Despite the trials, as some scholars have noted, "existing literature suggests that having children also enhances adults' lives by improving their skills, awakening them to new emotional and cognitive capacities, widening their social networks, and deepening their sense of meaningfulness and purpose vis-à-vis their own and their children's lives" (Silva & Pugh, 2010, p. 608). When people feel continually insecure and off-balance, they lose the sense of continuity that is a vital part of the memory work needed to engender a sense of purpose and belonging.

Rather than viewing personal and parenting relationships as liabilities, we need a university that models itself more after the family and its relationship to the broader community, rather than one that strives to emulate the monastery, the boardroom, or the factory floor. Since "meanings are in people, not in policy" (Manning, 2008, p. 245), administrators need to try to take steps to make a concrete difference in the lives of academics with children who are striving to contribute to the institution and their discipline over the long term. There are, in fact, some low-cost, high-impact policies that can make a distinct difference in the lives of novice academics, including ensuring that adequate daycare services are readily available, providing professional development for staff and administration on the competing demands of academic life and parenting, and allowing more flexible schedules for teaching and committee work (O'Laughlin & Bischoff, 2005, p. 101). Stopping the tenure-track clock, providing mentoring by tenured peers, or reducing the teaching load for new parents are other examples of such supports, though they do not seem to be intensive enough or widespread enough to have the desired effect (Sallee, 2012). We also need to place a renewed emphasis on teaching and provide security (i.e., tenure) for educators rather than viewing teaching as a regrettable necessity that is an unfortunate hindrance to research.

Trying to make meaning from personal experience in what Aitken (2009) calls the "awkward spaces of fathering" is a difficult, ongoing endeavour that is compounded by the instability and insecurity all parents find within today's university. Of course, this conflict between institutional power and personal desire is nothing new. I remember sitting once by a fellow law school graduate after our call to the Ontario bar. We were both struck by the strange power the formal legal process held over our lives. As she put it, "Funny, isn't it? I have the exact same views and opinions that I had when I was a waitress, but suddenly because I am a lawyer they are supposed to mean something more." While such institutional contradictions can be jarring, there is some solace to be found in the realization that "experience is the medium of education [and] education, in turn, is the process of learning to create ourselves" (Eisner, 2002, p. 3).

Like my astute friend, and being wiser than academics, children refuse to neatly compartmentalize the world. They are immensely curious and love learning, and yet, they are also deeply concerned with making personal connections. As opposed to a world in which I was never quite good enough and was constantly trying to win approval, my children offer an unconditional love and the endless marvel of their transformative imaginations. Recognizing that "parenthood is both a central identity and an ongoing, interactive process" (Silva & Pugh, 2010, p. 606), I have come to gain a broader conception of what it means to live a successful life. By confronting us with the limitedness of academe's solitary monastic culture, parenting reminds us that there is another mode of learning that is essentially a "way of searching in order to see" (Eisner, 2002, p. 89) since as Eisner (2002) puts it, "having a need to say, one looks more intently" (p. 89).

Before the plan, we first need a reason to keep going, since this is what gives plans their animating vision. Although we live in a time when many public spaces are becoming increasingly subject to a narrow technical form of rationality, this is also, we must recognize, a choice. With parenting you start with the person before you; so too it is with teaching. The life of the mind is first and foremost the life of flesh and blood, of people living to question and to be stirred by passionate conviction. We live in a time of fear but also one replete with possibility; this is our hope and our way forward, to find meaning and solace in the simple act of care that transcends judgment. This is the wisdom of the child and the first lesson of parenting: any knowledge that does not enhance the value and dignity of human life is not worth having. Simply by attending and struggling perhaps we will find a new and better world, after our children pull us upwards into the forgotten tranquil space of surfacing.

Why even create stories? Sometimes it is simply a way of taking stock and reimagining our place in the world. At times when I write it is like falling down a well of wonder and remembering. As Anne Lamott (1995) urges us, "day by day you have to give the work before you all the best stuff you have, not saving up for later projects. If you give freely there will always be more" (p. 202). This is, she suggests, what our children demand from us as they reassure us that imperfection can be its own reward and a means of achieving a sort of clumsy, giddy grace—our lives like ever-widening circles spreading out from some hidden, unseen centre, this undying love at the mute stone's core.

Postscript

A lot has happened since I initially wrote this chapter. I recently obtained a faculty appointment nearly five years after graduating with my PhD. During that time I worked many sixty-hour weeks with a full-time job, a heavy sessional teaching load, and daunting publishing commitments. Looking back now, I regret putting my family second to my academic work. Now that my eldest daughter is eight years old, as I write this I feel not only a sense of failure and shame, but also resentment at a system that tries to convince us that this is the just and necessary price for admission into the academic monastery. It is, to borrow one of Plato's phrases, a "noble lie" designed to convince us of the wisdom of our own complicity. There is, I believe, another way that emphasizes collaboration and the need for sharing burdens. It recognizes that academic citizenship implies a duty to safeguard the institution's waning integrity by fighting against exploitation and degrading work practices wherever they might be found. Knowledge, we must remember, will always fail us if we ourselves lack the courage to love and the wisdom to dream, like a child, fearlessly and endlessly—never completely alone.

References

Aitken, S. C. (2009). *The awkward spaces of fathering*. Burlington, VT: Ashgate.

Austin, A. A. (2010). Expectations of aspiring and early career academics. In L. McAlpine & G. Åkerlind (Eds.), *Becoming an academic* (pp. 18–41). Houndmills, England: Palgrave Macmillan.

Baker, M. (2010). Choices or constraints? Family responsibilities, gender and academic career. *Journal of Comparative Family Studies, 41*(1), 1–18.

Bethman, B., & Longstreet, C. S. (2013, May 22). The alt-ac track: Defining terms. *Inside Higher Education*. Retrieved from http://www.insidehighered.com/advice/2013/05/22/essay-defining-alt-ac-new-phd-job-searches

Collini, S. (2012). *What are universities for?* London, England: Penguin.

Dunn, M. G., Rochlen, A. B., & O'Brien, K. M. (2013). Employee, mother, and partner: An exploratory investigation of working women with stay-at-home fathers. *Journal of Career Development, 40*, 3–22.

Egan, K. (2002). *Getting it wrong from the beginning: Our progressivist inheritance from Herbert Spencer, John Dewey, and Jean Piaget*. New Haven, CT: Yale University Press.

Eisner, E. W. (2002). *The arts and the creation of mind*. New Haven, CT: Yale University Press.

Gewirtz, J. L. (2001). J.B. Watson's approach to learning. *Behavioral Development Bulletin, 1*(1), 23–25.

Guyas, A. S., & Poling, L. H. (2011). Embodying parenthood in academia. *Studies in Art Education, 52*(2), 171–174.

Hill, M. S., Nash, A., & Citera, M. (2011). Parenthood in academia: What happens when there is no policy? *Wagadu, 9*, 113–139.

Lamott, A. (1995). *Bird by bird.* New York, NY: Anchor Books.

Manchester, C. F., Leslie, L. M., & Kramer, A. (2010). Stop the clock policies and career success in academia. *American Economic Review, 100*(2), 219–223.

Manning, L. D. (2008). Parenting and professing in cancer's shadow. *Women's Studies in Communication, 31*(2), 240–248.

Mason, M. A., & Goulden, M. (2002). Do babies matter? The effect of family formation on the lifelong careers of academic men and women. *Academe, 88*(6), 21–17.

Mason, M. A., Goulden, M., & Frasch, K. (2009). Why graduate students reject the fast track. *Academe, 95*(1), 11–16. Retrieved from http://www.aaup.org/article/why-graduate-students-reject-fast-track#.Uq0Q6qXhXWE

O'Connor, N. (2009). Envisioning a new parent track in academia. *On Campus with Women, 37*(3). Retrieved from http://www.aacu.org/ocww/volume37_3/fromwhereisit.cfm?section=1

O'Laughlin, E. M., & Bischoff, L. G. (2005). Balancing parenthood and academia: Work/family stress as influenced by gender and tenure status. *Journal of Family Issues, 26*(1), 79–106.

Sallee, M. W. (2012). The ideal worker or the ideal father: Organizational structures and culture in the gendered university. *Research in Higher Education, 53*(7), 782–802.

Silva, J. M., & Pugh, A. J. (2010). Beyond the depleting model of parenting: Narratives of childrearing and change. *Sociological Inquiry, 80*(4), 605–627.

Steinberg, S. (2011). (Ed.). *Kinderculture: The corporate construction of childhood.* Boulder, CO: Westview Press.

Whitson, R. (2012, May 23). #Altac and the tenure track. *The Chronicle of Higher Education.* Retrieved from http://chronicle.com/article/Altacthe-Tenure-Track/131935/

Baby Step by Baby Step
That Was the Way to Do It!

Michelann Parr

One step at a time.

    Baby step by baby step.

        There was no other way to do it.

            No shortcuts, no secret passages, no escape hatches.

Simply loving the slow process of learning, of growing, of becoming—

    Loving the work as it unfolded.

        Loving each achievement and each goal as they were reached.

        Taking time—doing the right thing.

Baby steps—that was the way to do it.

    Walking, running, balancing—

        Adjusting each step along the way.

        No misstep, no wasted moments, no regrets.

Always moving in the direction of my dreams—

    The believe of childhood,

        The do of academia,

        A balance of the personal and the professional.

Since I was a little girl (I am now fifty-two), I believed that someday I would teach at the university level. I was not entirely sure how I would get there or what I would teach, but I knew where I wanted to be, and I was willing to take the steps required to get there, even if they were baby steps. I walked and ran through my undergraduate degree at Nipissing, joined in my final year by my daughter, who taught me the true meaning of baby steps. As I crossed the stage in 1986, degree in hand, I could see her patiently waiting on the other side, and I knew that she was reason enough to slow down my pace and adjust my step—there was no other way to do it. I needed to walk, not run through academia.

I could have gone to graduate school right then, but I quickly realized that graduate school was not the right thing to do at that time—there were simply more important things to do, places to go, and people to see. I was a stay-at-home parent at heart. My children (two more followed within four years) were, are, and will always be my priority. I loved the time spent finger-painting, engaging in bedtime stories, building puppet theatres, and crafting spring gardens to call forth new life. Time spent with them as they were learning, growing, believing, and dreaming was irreplaceable, and in retrospect, I knew that I wasn't willing to miss a thing—that would have been my greatest regret.

I adjusted my steps, reconsidered my short-term goals, and moved forward with my family, always keeping some healthy part-time "academic and research" work on the side to keep my mind active and my foot in the door, never losing sight of the possibility of moving forward in academia at just the right time. What I know now is that the most significant learning, growing, and becoming I did was with my children—they are part of who I am, both in and out of academia. The learning that took place in those few short years was unprecedented. I came to love each achievement and each reached short-term goal, recognizing that I would get where I wanted to be, one baby step at a time.

As my son, my baby, took his final baby steps and learned to run, I returned to complete my bachelor of education (BEd).

Now let me say this …

I knew the right time would come for me to return to school. In my heart, I knew that teaching at the university level was not something I would ever give up or readjust. But I had never, ever intended to teach at the elementary level. Underlying my application to the Faculty of Education at Nipissing was a frustration at not being able to make a master's in psychology work. But there were just too many reasons why a BEd was the right thing to do—I wouldn't have to leave home for longer than a day, I could weave together what I would learn with how I was parenting, and my days and nights would parallel those of my children—we could do school together!

Surprisingly, once I started my BEd early in 1991, I never looked back. And once I started teaching, I realized that my BEd *was* the right thing to do. My children had led me baby step by baby step through learning and understanding of childhood development. They taught me about language, reading, and writing—all of which I loved as a parent, and all of which I now love as a university professor.

When my son went to kindergarten, I began to teach elementary education, reserving enough time to keep him home afternoons and continue parenting him in the way I had grown accustomed to with my daughters. As they all entered school full-time, I began teaching full-time, and I returned part-time to pursue my master of education, getting me one baby step closer to my goal. I readjusted my step—no longer did I envision myself teaching language learning within the field of psychology. Now I understood that what I wanted was to teach language and literacy—I wanted to teach educators how to teach children to read, write, listen, speak, view, and represent. I wanted to share with my teacher candidates the importance of painting with all the colours of the rainbow, engaging in daily read-alouds, building confidence, and crafting lifelong learning.

There was never a misstep, never a wasted moment, and never a regret.

In 1999, I graduated with my master of education, having kept myself active in teaching, researching, and taking time with my children. I worked my way through kindergarten to grade six, teaching a combination of English, French immersion, and special education, learning about the uniqueness of each learner and the multiple pathways each one takes to get there, realizing that there are rarely escape hatches from life and learning. I realized that baby steps were critical; we simply had to move children from where they were to where they could be with patience, persistence, challenge, and understanding. I knew that was what I was doing every day in the classroom and with my own children, but I also knew that I was not done yet. Although I had come to love the work I was doing, there was still something more that I wanted, more baby steps to take. The professional qualifications that I had pursued (French as a second language, religious education, early literacy intervention, and special education), while critical to what I was doing, simply left me wanting more. I came to trust that with patience, persistence, challenge, and understanding, I would find a way to pull it all together.

Sometimes opportunities arise when you least expect them.

In July of 2001, I accepted a one-year contract to teach language and literacy in the Schulich School of Education at Nipissing. I was not returning this time as a student, but as an assistant professor of language and literacy. Now, I brought ten years of professional experience and sixteen years of personal experience with me. While life was incredibly busy, I had learned to balance the professional with the personal in a way that kept me moving in the direction of my dreams. While I had adjusted my steps along the way, I had never lost sight of my goal. In July of 2002, I was offered a three-year tenure-track position with the expectation that I would pursue a PhD.

Now that was pressure.

Recognizing at this point that my children were teenagers and could afford to be without me for a day, I applied to graduate schools in the Toronto area. While I made it all the way through to the interview stage, I did not secure a spot. The following year, I reapplied; this time I broadened my search. I applied to McGill, a process that required a full research proposal, a faculty advisor, and an oral defence, just to be accepted. My application was successful. I completed my coursework during 2004–2005, commuting two days a week to Montreal (seven hours on a good day from North Bay) as I continued to teach full-time and was an active parent of three teenage children.

As I was pursuing my PhD at McGill, my daughters were engaged in undergraduate education at Nipissing—again, we were doing school together. Baby steps that had once begun in the hallways at home were now echoing in the corridors of the university. You do not quite realize how quickly time is passing until you look at how it is passing for others. As my first daughter was concluding her undergraduate degree, I was gathering data. And as I was finalizing my dissertation, my second daughter was learning APA style, and therefore was the perfect editor. Our learning became reciprocal and interwoven. Again, I realized that academia in my world was about balance and how I envisioned my personal and professional lives, the types of conversations that I had, and the relationships I sustained. In a sense, my work was never set aside and my family was always with me—we complemented each other well.

Early in 2008, I set my sights on the finish line—finally earning my PhD, some twenty-two years after my undergraduate degree. As I look back today, I wonder how I managed to pull it off. I have learned that we need to believe that we have the capacity to do what we have to do regardless of how complex. I count myself fortunate that I never had to make a choice between my personal and professional lives, and that I was able to move forward with my children, modelling a foundation of what I hope will be lifelong learning for them.

In academia, though, education is simply not enough. While a PhD is the gateway to tenure and promotion, education has to be supplemented with effective teaching, satisfactory service, and scholarly work. When I was first hired, I was given some simple but critical advice: "Never go to a conference unless you are presenting, write two peer-reviewed papers a year, and serve on one university committee a year. Oh yes, and keep those teaching scores up!" I was told clearly that "academia is characterized by the rule of publish or perish," so that is what I did. I had worked hard to get here—this was the direction of my dreams. I had taken many baby steps, and I viewed scholarly work as simply one more baby step to take—this was the *do* of academia.

I learned to make good use of my time, to re-envision my writing, sometimes my life, and my scholarly work in many different ways. What was once a comprehensive question now became a chapter or a peer-reviewed paper. The day-to-day coursework in which I was engaged became the foundation for a textbook. What was once just a picture book on my shelf became the stimulus for a chapter in my dissertation. What was a simple revision and edit became an opportunity to teach my children how to do it, tracking, accepting, and rejecting changes as necessary. The heartbreaks I encountered with children and families in my classrooms became my inspiration for research. What I experienced with my own children became insights into who I was as a researcher. What was active and critical reflection on professional practice became dialogue among colleagues, and opportunity for collaboration in research and writing. Balance was about seeing possibility and the connections among the many parts of my self—academic, personal, and professional.

And then because life is always unpredictable, there were more baby steps—literally.

September 2008—a grandson

    a bundle of possibility,

        a new balance to be found

            in a family of active academics.

Supporting, caring for, and nurturing my grandson were made possible by academia. I was not limited or bound by its confines, but instead freed. I taught, I met with my students, I fulfilled my service responsibilities, and I earned tenure and promotion to associate professor in the spring of 2009. As always, I felt that familiar tug of balance—wanting to ensure that in the midst of academia, he had time to just blow bubbles, tell stories, build blanket forts, and sing songs. And soon, just as I had watched my daughters do years before, I saw my son taking baby steps and adjusting his steps when necessary—as his son began to walk in the hallways at home, he began to walk in the corridors of the university.

Balance? Balancing personal and professional was quite literal with my grandson. He was often perched on my knee while I was planning or revising a presentation for class; he ate his cereal and milk as I checked my email; and he often played at my side as I marked. Balance was about my class ending at six thirty and my son's beginning at six thirty. It was about a three-and-a-half-year-old understanding the difference between his school and Daddy and Nana's school, and what he could do at home versus what he could do at school. It was about structuring a personal and professional environment where a child, a university student, and an academic could grow, take risks, and become the very best that they could be. Today, this is the balance we continue to seek.

Balancing the culture and activity patterns of a family

> Always with the expectation of becoming
>
> The very best we can be—
>
> Never a question of *if* but *when*

When I reflect on my journey today and the balance I have managed to establish, I realize that the motivation, drive, and forces that pushed me to succeed are grounded in a story I lived long before I ever set foot in academia. Understanding of my story comes through a sociocultural lens (Rogoff, 1990, 1995; Vygotsky, 1978; Wells, 1999) where human activities are rarely separated from their cultural contexts, most often mediated by a significant adult or two who nurture and support us as we grow and become, starting where we are and anticipating where we can be with a little guidance and a whole lot of modelling.

I was fortunate and privileged to grow up with a nuclear and extended family that not only possessed great *funds of knowledge* to share with future generations (González, Moll, & Amanti, 2005), but also established optimal conditions for learning both in and out of school. The knowledge, skill, and value learned at home formed a solid foundation for lifelong learning (Heath, 2010; Rogers, 2003; Taylor, 1997). From the time that I first began to walk, I was encouraged to take baby steps: to set my goals, develop personalized action plans, and then celebrate the reward of individual successes, no matter how big or how small. For as long as I can remember, this was not only made explicit in word, but also modelled in action.

At seventeen, my grandfather arrived in Canada from Italy with a dream and a drive to be the best that he could be. Self-taught in language, reading, business, and tailoring, just to name a few, he continually encouraged and supported his family in whatever endeavours could be envisioned. All four of his sons earned professional designations—this was part of the allure of Canada. Growing up in this extended family, we observed an active and determined process of continuous learning where so much of daily life and culture was shared. My grandparents worked alongside each other, learning from each other, in their many pursuits, often with a grandchild or two in tow to apprentice into the family practices of tailoring, gardening, or pasta making. And while they were often heard conversing, the Italian language was not passed on to their children and grandchildren. Learning in our family was just something we did; it was never a risk but always an adventure. In my grandparents' house, I came to experience and understand the impact of a supportive, encouraging, and sometimes humorous response and the impact of family on all we do and become.

My mother moved directly from high school to North Bay Normal School, where she gained her qualification as a teacher. For many years, she was the primary breadwinner in the family. Throughout this, my father pursued his passion as a musician and gained his high school equivalency. From there, he was off to North Bay Normal School, and finally entered the teaching profession. This freed my mom to pursue her passion as a stay-at-home parent of soon to be five children, of whom I am the eldest. While teaching, my father modelled lifelong learning by returning to school, completing a degree, and securing his principal's qualifications. My mom modelled the importance of following your interests and always seeking to learn something new—among the many classes I recall were pottery and stained glass; she kept her foot in the door by teaching occasionally as well as in adult and continuing education. Although we encouraged her to return to university, she never did. She always said that our successes were her successes, and she would proudly don our regalia to formalize her role in our education. This is now a family tradition and one that underscores Dewey's (1916) point that our social environments are educative to the degree that we share or participate in joint activity.

Engagement and participation in the activity of my parents' education I recall best as road trips—the long summer days when my mom would pack five of us into a station wagon so that we could go visit our dad in Sudbury (those were the days when university residency was a requirement). And then later, into my early teens, we made the same road trip, although in a different station wagon and a little bit longer, to Espanola, where both my parents pursued ordained and mandated vocations in the church. Family participation was not optional but was an expectation; my parents' learning was a cultural and social activity in which we were all engaged—modelling in action.

Today, I recognize that my brothers, sisters, and I (all now with professional degrees) grew up in an atmosphere of high but individualized expectations; praise, reinforcement, and encouragement to *be the best that we could be*; responses that prompted critical, independent, and reflective thought; and most importantly, modelling of continuous and lifelong learning on the part of both my immediate and extended family. We were encouraged to learn by doing, and it was consistently reinforced that the greatest mistake we could make was not trying; "can't" was not a word we accepted—it simply propelled us to work just that little bit harder to achieve our goals, even if that goal was learning how to water-ski, bait a hook, knit, or make the perfect thimble cookie. As a result, our response to challenges and setbacks was patient, forgiving, and intelligent, thus giving greater meaning to our successes.

Our process in so many ways was our product; our journey was the real destination. It was never *if* but *when* and *how* we would get there. We lived and acted "in a medium of accepted meanings and values" (Dewey, 1916, p. 344) and a social environment that was "educative in its effects" (Dewey, 1916, p. 26)—university was not an option but an expectation. We learned that there was nothing that we could not do if we set our minds and hearts to it—we learned to never give up on what we wanted most. We were apprenticed into our own learning, guided in social activity with significant others who supported and stretched our understanding of, and skill in, using the tools of our culture (Rogoff, 1990, 1995). We participated actively, owned the purposes and processes of learning, "[became] familiar with its methods and subject matters, acquire[d] skill, and [were] saturated with its emotional spirit" (Dewey, 1916, p. 26). Over time, we were encouraged to accept increasing levels of responsibility for our own learning, developing a sense of both self-efficacy and self-advocacy that would serve us well for a lifetime of learning (Lave & Wenger, 1991).

Intergenerational activities

   Cultural inheritances

      Lifetimes of learning yet to come

It is these same values that I now instill in my own children and grandchildren as they take their own baby steps into academia. While there were times I took to just be, I never lost sight of my direction. When I look back on the journey I have taken, I realize that to some, it is unconventional and demanding. To me, though, it is what it is, and I would not change it for the world. For many of us in the field of education, it is the norm. We teach, we gain practical expertise, some of us have children, and then we return to academia with professional and personal credibility and experience.

Today, I understand the awe-filled *believe* of childhood (both my own and that of my parents), and I am well positioned for the demanding *do* of academia. I know what it means to take baby steps—I live this philosophy every day. I never know whether today is the day I will move forward or take time, but I willingly accept both possibilities.

Having watched both their parents (now divorced) go through a similar process, my children have incredible respect for the balances required of those in academia, and they have willingly accepted the steps required to pursue graduate education, whether it is a master's degree or a PhD they have set their sights on. As they face each day, they demonstrate awareness that we take life—personal and professional—baby step by baby step, celebrating successes and achievements as they come, recognizing that each step gets us closer to our dream.

Me? I would not change a thing. I am who I am today because of all my experiences—personal and professional—one more, one less, and I would not be the same individual.

Baby step by baby step,

    there was no other way to do it

        a slow process of learning, of growing, and of becoming,

           walking, running, and balancing—

the believe of childhood,

    the do of academia,

        true balance of the personal and the professional.

References

Dewey, J. (1916). *Democracy and education: An introduction to the philosophy of education*. New York, NY: Macmillan.

González, N., Moll, L., & Amanti, C. (Eds.). (2005). *Funds of knowledge: Theorizing practices in households, communities and classrooms*. Mahwah, NJ: Erlbaum.

Heath, S. B. (2010). Family literacy or community learning? Some critical questions on perspective. In K. Dunsmore & D. Fisher (Eds.), *Bringing literacy home* (pp. 15–41). Newark, DE: International Reading Association.

John-Steiner, V., & Mahn, H. (1996). Sociocultural approaches to learning and development: A Vygotskian framework. *Educational Psychologist, 31*(3/4), 191–206.

Lave, J., & Wenger, E. (1991). *Situated learning: Legitimate peripheral participation*. New York, NY: Cambridge University Press.

Rogers, R. (2003). *A critical discourse analysis of family literacy practices: Power in and out of print*. Mahwah, NJ: Erlbaum.

Rogoff, B. (1990). *Apprenticeship in thinking: Cognitive development in social context*. New York, NY: Oxford University Press.

Rogoff, B. (1995). Observing sociocultural activity on three planes: Participatory appropriation, guided participation, and apprenticeship. In J. V. Wertsch, P. del Rio, & A. Alvarez (Eds.), *Sociocultural studies of mind* (pp. 139–164). New York, NY: Cambridge University Press. Retrieved from http://methodenpool.uni-koeln.de/situierteslernen/Teaching%20As%20Learning.htm

Taylor, D. (Ed.). (1997). *Many families, many literacies: An international declaration of principles.* Portsmouth, NH: Heinemann.

Vygotsky, L. S. (1978). *Mind in society: The development of higher psychological processes.* M. Cole, V. John-Steiner, S. Scribner, & E. Souberman (Eds.). Cambridge, MA: Harvard University Press.

Wells, G. (1999). *Dialogic inquiry: Towards a sociocultural practice and theory of education.* New York, NY: Cambridge University Press.

About the Authors

Jane E. Barker completed her BA in psychology at McMaster University and attended Queen's University for her MA and PhD in clinical psychology. Jane worked in a number of federal correctional institutions prior to joining Nipissing University in 2003. She is an associate professor and chair of the School of Criminology and Criminal Justice at Nipissing. Her edited textbook entitled *Women and the Criminal Justice System: A Canadian Perspective* has been adopted at colleges and universities across Canada.

Jennifer Barnett is an associate professor in the Faculty of Education at Nipissing University. Her research interests include educational law, the enactment of rules and policies in sociopolitical environments, and finding the underlying truths beneath the rules and laws of any organization, be it a family, institution, state, society, or culture. She is a strong advocate for the concept of individual voice in a community and supports notions of equity. In her spare time she enjoys reading and socializing with people who also believe that taking care of others is the best way to take care of oneself.

John Beaton is an associate professor in the Department of Family Relations and Applied Nutrition at the University of Guelph. He primarily has taught in the Couple and Family Therapy Program, training graduate students to be therapists. He is a clinical member and approved supervisor with the American Association of Marriage and Family Therapy. His teaching, research, and clinical interests are primarily in the area of parenting children with chronic health conditions and disabilities.

Ellie D. Berger is an associate professor of sociology at Nipissing University and an adjunct professor of sociology at Laurentian University. She is also chair of the Social Policy and Practice Division of the Canadian Association on Gerontology. She received a PhD in sociology from McMaster University, a master of science degree in public health sciences from the University of Toronto, and an honours BA in gerontology and sociology from McMaster

University. Her current research focuses on ageism, older workers, identity, gender relations, retirement, and work–family balance in academia. She is the author of the forthcoming book *Ageism at Work: Negotiating Age, Gender, and Identity in the Discriminating Workplace*. She lives in Toronto, Ontario, with her husband and two children.

Kevin Black is a doctoral student in public health sciences at the University of Toronto, where he is using metaphor elicitation to study the conceptual models that fathers use to understand and inspire their parenting. Additionally, Kevin is a part-time research and policy analyst in the Family Health Division of Peel Public Health, where he is focused on the social health of new parents and developing a policy surveillance and advocacy system for child and family health.

Kathleen M. Bortolin lives and works on the West Coast. She is currently an educational developer at Vancouver Island University in Nanaimo, British Columbia. Since writing these stories, she has earned her PhD, landed an academic job, *and* had another baby, thus continuing her journey as a mama scholar. She is grateful for both the balance and the madness that exist for herself as an academic mother. Her current research interests include incorporating Aboriginal ways of knowing into higher-education curriculum design and narrative inquiry in faculty development.

Tarah Brookfield is an associate professor, cross-appointed in History and Youth and Children's Studies at Wilfrid Laurier University. She is the author of *Cold War Comforts: Canadian Women, Child Safety and Global Insecurity* (Wilfrid Laurier University Press, 2012) and other articles and book chapters about Canadian women's political action, Cold War films, and the history of adoption. Fast-forwarding four years since this chapter was written, she is also the mother of Juliet, an amazing kindergarten student who is now an excellent sleeper.

Erin J. Careless is a doctoral candidate at Mount Saint Vincent University in Halifax, Nova Scotia. Her research explores the ways that stepmothers learn to navigate this role and its accompanying complexities, with a focus on their use of social media tools to do so. Erin teaches part-time at Mount Saint Vincent University in the Lifelong Learning Graduate Studies program, and in the Masters of Adult Education program at St. Francis Xavier University, where she is a contract faculty member.

Melissa Corrente lives in North Bay, Ontario, with her husband and two children. She is a PhD candidate at Nipissing University. Her dissertation explores the realities of parenthood and graduate studies. She enjoys teaching health and physical education courses at the university and loves to cook, exercise, travel, and spend time outdoors.

Stephen Czarnuch is an assistant professor, jointly appointed to the Department of Electrical and Computer Engineering in the Faculty of Engineering and Applied Science and the Discipline of Emergency Medicine in the Faculty of Medicine at Memorial University in St. John's, Newfoundland. Two areas of interest—human motion tracking and automated planning—form the foundation of his biomedical engineering research, which is situated at the intersection of engineering, computer science, medicine, gerontology, and rehabilitation science. Through his current research projects, he aims to develop intelligent medical devices that can support people suffering from the loss of cognition associated with dementia, and to objectively assess the efficacy of medical treatments, interventions, and rehabilitation. He is also the father of four amazing children, owner of a sweet and yappy dog, and partner to an amazing and inspiring wife.

Christina DeRoche has a PhD in sociology from McMaster University and is an adjunct professor at Nipissing University in North Bay, Ontario. Her research interests include children with special needs, childhood and adolescent mental health, and special education. Christina is raising her daughter with her husband, Michael.

John Hoben, LLB (Western), PhD (Memorial), is an assistant professor in Memorial's Faculty of Education. A non-practising lawyer, in 2007 he was awarded an SSHRC Canada Graduate Scholarship (Doctoral) to conduct a qualitative study of teacher free speech, which formed the basis for his recent book on teacher censorship. John's areas of expertise include post-secondary education, law, the sociology of law, narrative inquiry, and critical thinking.

Anita Jack-Davies is a workplace diversity consultant and academic who specializes in helping organizations plan and implement equity and inclusion measures aimed at maximizing employee expertise and performance. She is currently assistant adjunct professor in the Department of Geography at Queen's University. In 2011, Dr. Jack-Davies earned her PhD in education in the area of cultural and policy studies. Her dissertation examined teacher candidate perceptions of inner-city schooling in Canada through the lens of cultural geography. Anita's research interests include urban-teacher education, inner-city schooling, and workplace diversity and inclusion.

Sara L. Jackson is a lecturer at the Metropolitan State University of Denver's Department of Earth and Atmospheric Sciences. She has a PhD (2015) in geography from York University. Her ongoing research interests include political and cultural geographies of resource extraction in Mongolia and environmental justice issues in Colorado.

Amber E. Kinser is a writer, speaker, mother, and professor. As a professor of communication and performance at East Tennessee State University, Amber Kinser is an expert on the relationship between gender and communication. She explores the links between human interaction, gender, and living empowered personal and professional lives. Amber draws on feminist thought and activism, her doctoral training in family communication, and over twenty years' experience as a mother to explore how women who choose to mother can do so as powerful people. Her weekly blog, Thursdays with Dr. Mama, has been featured at the Museum of Motherhood (and is currently on hiatus so she can focus on her grant research about family meals).

Elizabeth Koblyk is an instructor in McMaster's Bachelor of Health Sciences program, career counsellor at the Michael G. DeGroote School of Medicine, and former assistant director of the Centre for Career Action at the University of Waterloo. She is also a regular contributor to the Careers Café blog at *University Affairs*.

David Long is a professor of sociology at The King's University. Two fundamental questions have animated David in both his teaching and the more scholarly aspects of his work during his tenure at The King's University since 1989: "What gives people hope?" and "What hinders people from experiencing hope?" His most current research project involves gathering stories from dads in response to the question, "What have you learned from your children?" Select publications in which David has engaged his views on teaching, research, and fathering include "From Lost Boys to Hopeful Men: Contemporary Rites of Passage and the Rediscovery of Community," in *Transitions* (Vanier Institute of the Family, 2012); *All Dads Matter: Towards an Inclusive Approach to Father Involvement Initiatives in Canada* (FIRA, 2008); "A Radical Teacher's Dilemma," in *Teaching Sociology* (1998); and "Sociology and a Pedagogy for Liberation: Cultivating a Dialogue of Discernment in Our Classrooms," in *Teaching Sociology* (1995).

Ilka Luyt has a PhD in education and teaches at Queen's University in Kingston, Ontario, and at Jefferson Community College in New York. Her research interests include online learning, rhetoric, and composition. She continues to raise two sons with an amazing partner.

Mildred T. Masimira completed her PhD at the University of Alberta. She also has a master's in women's studies from Texas Woman's University, and a BSC in family and consumer sciences from Solusi University in Zimbabwe. Her research focuses on families, women, and youth in vulnerable communities as they negotiate different cultural contexts through participatory practices. An immigrant herself and a mother, Mildred has first-hand experience of life away from her motherland, which feeds her passion for research with marginal communities. She sees herself as a bridge of sorts between the academy and community, fostering sustainable partnerships and resource sharing.

Sarah Milmine studied at McMaster University, completing a combined honours degree in religious studies and social work (2004), and later returned in 2009 to complete her master's in social work. She has worked in child welfare at various agencies in southern Ontario, most recently being promoted to a supervisory position. Sarah continues to remain connected with academia as a teaching assistant at McMaster University in the School of Social Work. Her research interests surround the overmedication of children in care, and how text influences practice in child welfare. She currently resides in southern Ontario with her partner, Robert, and dog, Walter.

Michelann Parr is the eldest in a family of five, mother of three (who range in age from twenty-seven to thirty-one), and grandmother of two (ages four and eight). She currently teaches language, literacy, and special education, at both the graduate and undergraduate levels, in the Schulich School of Education at Nipissing University in North Bay, Ontario. She has ten years' experience in elementary education, where she engaged in early literacy intervention, special education, and French as a second language. She credits her family with the forward vision of never if, but when, as well as the consistent encouragement to be the very best that she can be.

Sarah R. Pickett has a PsyD, is registered psychologist, and is an assistant professor in Counselling Psychology and chair of the Sexuality and Gender Education Committee in the Faculty of Education at Memorial University of Newfoundland. Presently, her research interests focus on sexuality and gender discourses as they relate to teacher education and educational environments, with an emphasis on K–12 school culture and climate.

Rose Ricciardelli is an associate professor in the Department of Sociology at Memorial University of Newfoundland. She has published in a range of academic journals, including *The British Journal of Criminology*, *Sex Roles*, and *Theoretical Criminology*. Her first book, *Surviving Incarceration: Inside Canadian Prisons*, released in the spring of 2014, explores the realities of penal living for federally incarcerated men in Canada. Her primary research interests include evolving conceptualizations of masculinity, and experiences and issues within different facets of the criminal justice system. Her current research looks at prison culture, desistance, and the coping strategies, risk perception, and lived experiences of prisoners, prison officers, and police officers. She is also the proud mother of four amazing little people and feels fortunate every day to be married to an incredible person.

Geoff Salomons is a PhD student in the Department of Political Science at the University of Alberta. His dissertation is focused on the intergenerational equity of Alberta's resource wealth governance from 1971 to 2006. He also makes a mean homemade lasagna.

Timothy Sibbald is an assistant professor in the Schulich School of Education at Nipissing University. His instruction and research foci are in mathematics education. This includes content and pedagogical innovations for teachers, teacher development, and research into classroom achievement structures in standardized testing results.

Lisa J. Starr is a former secondary school teacher, currently an assistant professor at McGill University in the Department of Integrated Studies in Education (DISE), and past president of the Canadian Association for the Study of Women and Education (CASWE). She completed her doctoral degree in Social, Cultural and Foundational Studies in the Department of Curriculum and Instruction at the University of Victoria. She received a master of arts degree in administration and supervision from the University of Phoenix while working overseas. Her teaching career led her from Canada to Pakistan, Kuwait, and Mongolia and created a passion for the study of the relationship between identity and culture, particularly in relation to educational effectiveness and school leadership. Her current research focus is the use of autoethnography in the study of leadership philosophy and practice.

Index

academia: access to library resources, 219; adjunct faculty status, 113–14; advantages of, 16–17, 25–26; ambiguous policies, 36–37; career of middle-class students, 245n8; conservatism of, 36, 52; corporatization of universities, 50; division of labour, 113; elephants in ivory tower, 247, 248; expectations from faculty on leave, 143–44; family policies, 63, 139, 143, 207, 208, 253; female professionals, 121; female students, 77–78; gender imbalance, 2, 32–33, 144–45, 203; generational changes, 51, 52; neo-liberalism and, 35–36; parenting studies, 7–8; publish or perish, 260–61; same-sex relationships and, 7; unequal treatment of women, 34, 127; university college in Canada, 245n12

academic career: administrative roles, 228, 229; baby steps of, 257–58, 259; benefits for employees, 63, 218–19; care for child with special needs and, 228–30; challenges of, 7, 8; child-free choice and, 79–80; childlessness and, 78; employment prospects, 219; expectations from faculty, 228; failure sharing, 229; geographic mobility, 250; maternity leaves, 144–45, 153–54; part-time instructors, 113, 252; poetic representation of, 257, 265; pregnancy and, 151, 170–71; reproductive health and, 62; short-term goals, 258; tenure-track positions, 50, 252, 260–61; time management, 261; ultimate priority of, 121–22; work–life balance, 226, 228, 250–51, 258, 261–62; workload, 219, 260; work schedule, 204, 210n2

academic mothers: academia as escape, 53; advantages of, 16–17; biological clock, 15–16; childcare, 37, 204–6; children in classroom, 97–98; colleagues' attitude to, 25; conflicting emotions, 41; day planning, 99–100; decision to have another child, 206–8; discrimination, 34; early career, 204–5; feelings of guilt, 18; feminist perspective, 101–2; financial considerations, 14; heavy workload, 34; identities, 98, 100, 101, 106; illness of children, 209; importance of research on, 37; interviews with, 33; job security, 14–15; maternity leave, 25; negative view of, 98, 101–2, 103; new brand of women, 102; positive gains, 105; sacrifices, 104; sense of autonomy, 104, 105; spousal support, 14, 26, 35; structural and institutional barriers, 19–21, 36–37; tenure clock, 15–16, 32; time away from children, 26; time management, 34, 35, 37, 99–100; work–family conflict, 17–19, 33–34; work schedule, 32, 33–34

academic prose, 246n15, 246n17
academic work: nature of, 92, 141
Acker, S., 33, 101
Aitken, S., 244n3, 245n6, 253
Anders, S. M., van, 62
anti-oppressive practice, 55
Anzaldúa, G. E., 118
Aoki, T. T., 106
Armenti, C., 101, 112
Austin, A. A., 251, 252
Austin, J., 96
"awkward moments," 234, 244n3

Baker, M., 208, 250
Barker, Jane, 8
Barnett, Jennifer, 7

273

Bartlett, A., 146
Bassett, R. H., 122
Bateson, M. C., 67, 70, 71, 73
Beaton, John, 8
Berger, Ellie D., 7
Birth of Biopolitics, The (Foucault), 109
Black, Kevin, 8
Blakeslee, S., 81
Blumer, H., 170, 171
Bortolin, Kathleen M., 8
Botton, A. de, 243
Bourdieu, Pierre, 236, 239, 244, 245n7–8, 245n10
Boyer, E. L., 241
Brown, B., 68, 73
Burke, M. C., 67
Butler, J., 82

Calder, G., 136
Careless, Erin J., 7
Carton, Sydney (character), 186, 189, 196n3
Chacon, R. M., 127
Charlene (Charlene Marilynn D'Angelo Oliver), 80–81
Chen, C. P., 216, 217
child-bearing: impact on career, 112
childcare: as cultural construction, 79; gendered imbalance, 33–34
childfree choice, 78–79, 80–81, 83
childhood development, 258–59
childlessness, 77–78, 79–80
children: enhancement of life, 253; father engagement with, 192; impact on parents, 254–55; with special needs, 228–30; unconditional love of, 254. *See also* early childhood development (ECD)
Children's Aid Society, 59, 60–61
Christensen, M., 122
Citera, M., 247
Clandining, D. J., 1
Cohen, Leonard, 246n18
Collini, S., 251
Collins, P. H., 127
Comer, D. R., 5
compassionate listening, 244
comprehensive exam, 94, 128–29, 133
Connelly, F. M., 1
Cooley, C. H., 24
Corrente, Melissa, 7
Coward, R., 2, 3, 5
Czarnuch, Stephen, 8

Daniluk, J. C., 105
Davis, Wade, 93
Davis-Manigaulte, J., 96
daycare selection, 205, 206
Deci, E. L., 186
DeRoche, Christina, 7
Dewey, J., 263
differentiation: conception of, 215
discourse: forms of, 131; of silence, 130
Douglas, S. J., 5
Dowd, N. E., 2
Drozdzewski, D., 51
Dunn, M. G., 249
Duxbury, L., 217
Dweck, Carol, 196n4

early childhood development (ECD), 187, 190–91, 192, 196n5
economy: formal *vs.* informal, 89–90
education as commodity, 35–36
education leave, 59
Edwards, R., 4
Egan, Kieran, 252
Eisenbach, B., 67
Eisner, E. W., 254
Elvin-Nowak, Y., 205
emotional geographies of academic parenting: caregiving, 44; feelings of displacement, 43–44, 45, 53; illness of children, 44–45; intergenerational relations, 42; pursue of education, 42, 46, 50–51, 52–53; relations with spouse, 46–47, 49; relocation experience, 49; sense of guilt, 18, 43, 47; "suburban mom" identity, 46; work–family balance, 43–44, 47–48, 52–53
employment: paid *vs.* unpaid, 89–90
enrichment experience, 216–17
Erikson, E., 188
Evans, Elrena, 160
Evans, P. M., 136

faith-based scholarship, 245–46n13
family: conception of differentiation, 215; continuous learning, 262–63; diversification of, 214; division of labour in, 215; education and, 56–57, 236–37, 263–64; gender roles, 56, 57, 82, 249, 250; grown-up children and, 216, 217; interactions with relatives, 214; intergenerational relationships, 261–62; parenting roles, 224; parents as model for children,

263; perspective of Aboriginal people on, 246n16; religious values, 57; supportive relations within, 263

family-friendly employers, 63

father and professor: "bring your kid to work" day, 238–39, 240; decision to attend university, 236; first employment, 236–37, 245n11; hopeful intrusions, 234–35, 241; life in urban and farming environments, 235–36; life lessons, 234; marriage, 237; post-doctoral fellowship, 238; relocation, 238; reminiscences of childhood, 235–36; stepdad's influence, 237; tenure-track position, 237–38

fatherhood: in academia, characteristic of, 3; awkward spaces of, 253; care for sick child, 226–29; developmental milestones, 188–89; emotional exhaustion, 228; engagement in childhood development, 187, 192–93; relations with children, 233–34, 236, 240, 242–43; research on, 2–6; social patterns, 243–44; sociological research on, 245n6; theoretical interpretations of, 223–24; uncertainties of, 187–88; work–family balance, 224. *See also* dad and professor

fatherhood and PhD studies: birth of children, 87, 89; career path, 88–89; caregiving, 91, 92–93; financial contributions, 89; gender roles switching, 91; housework, 90, 91–92; priority management, 92, 93; pursuits for education, 88–89, 91; relations with spouse, 87–88, 89; sense of perfectionism, 92; teaching job prospects, 88; time management, 91–92, 93

Feltey, K., 145

feminism, 37–38, 82, 110

feminist political economy, 87, 89–90

Fothergill, A., 145

Foucault, Michel: *The Birth of Biopolitics*, 109; on discourse and silence, 130, 132; on driving force of market, 113; on human capital, 110–11; on liberalism, 110

frame of reference, 185, 196n2

Frasch, K., 247, 249

friendship, 79

gender inequality at workplace, 55

generative fathering, 188

Gillespie, R., 77, 79, 80

Giroux, H. A., 114

Godderis, Rebecca, 145

Goulden, M., 247, 249

graduate-student-mothering: child sickness, 129; comprehensive exam, 128–29, 133; decision to start family, 125–26; discursive practices, 130; fatigue and pressure, 132–33; feminist exploration of, 125; fertility concerns, 125; formal accommodations for, 131–32; formal and informal strategies for, 133; identity, 126, 127; outsider-within framework, 127; racial-sexual stereotypes, 126; spousal support, 132; time away from family, 128, 132. *See also* journal of graduate student-mother

graduate studies: challenges for female students, 3–4, 77–78; comprehensive exam, 94, 128–29, 133; division of labour and, 215–16; family responsibilities and, 215–16, 218; funding, 120; generational shift, 52; international student experience, 119–20; online courses, 216; parenting and, 43, 67, 87, 213, 216, 217, 250; part-time job and, 218; perfectionism, 92; spousal support, 217; time management, 90–91; workload, 65, 120, 217

Grenier, R. S., 67

Guyas, A. S., 252

habitus: concept of, 245n7

Hall, S., 131

Hickey, A., 96

Higgins, C., 217

high school teaching, 214

Hill, M. S., 247

Hirakata, P. E., 105

Hoben, John, 8

Hodgetts, D., 41

homosexual parenting. *See* queer parenting

Hooks, B., 126

hopeful intrusions, 234–35, 241, 244

Hoschild, A., 3

human capital, 110–11

identity construction, 100–101

immigration experience, 233, 262–63

Jack-Davies, Anita, 8

Jiron-King, S., 122

Johnston, Sara L., 3

journal of graduate student-mother: anxieties of academic process, 68; bonds between spouse and child, 68, 69, 70–71, 72; breastfeeding experience, 69; emotions and vulnerability, 72, 73; importance of place in narrative inquiry, 71; main themes, 68; perception of university students, 70; positive aspects of being student-mother, 67; recovery after birth, 72; research work challenges, 72–73; role identity, 68, 72–73; social pressure, 72; spousal support, 68, 70, 73

Kane, E. W., 82
Kasl, E., 96
Kegan, R., 81
King, B. B., 195
Kittlestrom, A., 4, 5
Klocker, N., 51
Kuhn, Thomas, 196n2

Lamott, Anne, 252, 254
Lee, C., 217
Lemke, T., 112
Lennon, John, 195, 197n9
Lent, B., 141
Lewis, Magda, 127
life: definitions of, 195; societal perspective of, 81–82
Long, David, 8
Longhurst, R., 41
love: of children, manifestations of, 77–78; sociological research, 245n5
Luyt, Ilka, 8
Lynch, K. D., 66

making living *vs.* making life, 195–96
Mama, PhD (Evans and Grant), 137
mama scholars. *See* academic mothers
Manning, L. D., 253
Marotte, M. R., 2
marriage, 81–83
masculinity theory, 223–24
Masimira, Mildred T., 8
Mason, M. A., 247, 249
mastery: definition of, 193–94, 196n4
maternity leave: academic schedule and, 138, 207; access to benefits, 136–37; administrative policies, 138–39, 145–46, 153–54; child caring, 139, 140; expectations from women on, 135–36, 143–44; institutional perspective on, 142; justification for shorter leaves, 141–42; research activity during, 135, 137, 139, 140–43; studies of, 144; underemployment, 137; work–family balance, 136
Maushart, S., 79, 81
McCluksy, H. Y., 67
McGonigal, K., 217
McKittrick, K., 126
Mead, G. H., 168, 175, 180
Michaels, M. W., 5
microaggression, 158, 159
Mills, C. Wright, 234, 244, 246n17
Milmine, Sarah, 7
motherhood: in academia, negative view of, 102, 103; academic career and, 24, 130; aging and, 206–7; barriers of, 80; change of lifestyle, 58; as cultural construction, 79; discourse of, 131; feminist perspective on, 110; graduate education and, 4; myth of, 5–6; "new momism," 5–6; ownership of, 103; planning of, 138–39; research on, 2–6; as transformation of self, 73–74; value of, 98; in Western society, 77. *See also* academic mothers

narrative. *See* personal narratives
Nash, A., 247
nature: debates on value of, 93
neo-liberal culture, 109–10
neo-liberal education, 35–36

O'Brien, K. M., 249
O'Connor, N., 249, 252
Ollilainen, M., 144
Olsen, T., 122
online teaching and learning, 109, 113, 114, 216
O'Reilly, Andrea, 121

Palkovitz, R., 224, 225
Panofsky, R., 137
parental leave, 223, 224–25
parenting: academic opportunities and, 112–13; birth giving experience, 152–53, 167, 172–74; career expectations and, 229–30; changing norms of, 51; conversations about, 185, 196n1; as daily choice, 194; depleting model of, 251–52; exploration

of children's world, 186–87; familial contract, 187; further involvement in, 197n7; father–daughter relationships, 189–90; financial challenges, 153; gender roles, 2, 223, 224, 247; grown children and, 219; identity change, 110–11, 115, 254; as interactive process, 254; in North American context, 2; part-time work and, 111, 114; poetic representation of, 257, 265; positive effects of, 70–71; rewarding experience of, 194–95; self-determination theory of, 186–87; sense of perfectionism, 92–93; shopping, 163; small steps in, 265; story-sharing about, 1; studies of, 1, 2; trade-offs of caregiving, 93–94; as turning point in life, 185, 188; workforce organization and, 63

Parenting and Professing: Balancing Family Work with an Academic Career (O'Reilly), 121–22

parenting in academia: administrative policies, 151–52; career and, 42–43, 48–50, 63–64, 112–14, 176, 255; challenges of, 117–18, 121, 179–80, 181–82; children in classroom, 97–98; from a child's perspective, 117; conference trips, 163; consciousness of self, 175–77; daycare, 184; discourse of, 130; divide-and-try-to-survive approach, 175; emotional geographies, 42; emotions, 176, 179; external pressures, 182; goals and priorities, 177; guilt management, 182–83; husband's responsibilities, 165–66; identity change, 179, 180, 181; non-traditional role of father, 181–82; parents' self-awareness, 164–65, 168; personal balance, 178; pregnancy, 166, 169, 170–71, 172; pursue of education, 166, 169; relations with colleagues, 226; research work and, 174–75; sacrifices, 181; scholarly research on, 154; self-imposed rules, 182–83; social environment, 180; spousal relationship, 177–78, 181; stay-at-home-mom stereotypes, 179–80; strategies of, 166–67, 183; thesis defense, 169–70; time constrains, 180; traditional views of, 122, 123, 151–52, 187, 225, 226, 250, 252; work–family balance, 167–68, 170, 172, 176, 184

parent-students: caregiving, 120; challenges of, 117–18; conference attendance, 121;

degree completion rate, 123; disadvantaged position of, 118; employment prospects, 120; family support, 119; financial difficulties, 120; housework, 120; international students, 119; life–study balance, 123; personality change, 185; time management, 118, 120–21; work interruption, 122–23

Parr, Michelann, 8

part-time work, 111–12, 113, 114

perfect mother, 164–65

Perna, L., 36

personal narratives, 96, 235–36

PhD studies: financial challenges, 91, 189; friendship and, 65; impact of gender on experience of, 66–67; physical space of library, 71; pregnancy and, 65–66; pros and cons of, 51, 60–61; research on parents in, 67; selection of research topic, 190; spousal support, 60–61, 73; workload, 65

Phillips, S. P., 141

Pickett, Sarah R., 8

Pink, Daniel, 186, 193

Poling, L. H., 252

post-secondary education: business administration, 61; choice between career and, 59–60; educational problems, 252–53; employment prospects, 61; family influence, 57, 236–37; learning experience, 57; paid and volunteer work, 57–58; partner's support, 58; part-time labour force, 111–12; reproductive health and, 62; social capital and, 237; teaching assistantship, 59–60; work–life balance, 61

pregnancy: academic career and, 151–52, 170–71; graduate studies and, 65–66; relations with colleagues, 152, 171; sense of insecurity, 170

Pugh, A. J., 247, 251

Pulkingham, J., 137

queer parenting: academic career and, 149, 151, 157–58; benefits and costs, 156–57; comparison with heterosexual parenting, 155–56, 159–60; family planning, 149–50, 154, 156; fears to remain childless, 150; financial challenges, 153; lack of recognition of, 154–55; microaggressions, 159; parental leave, 153, 157–58; personal fulfilment, 160; public perceptions of, 158; relations between generations, 155; relationship building, 160

Quint V Boenker Preemie Survival Foundation, 174

Relph, E., 71
reproductive health, 62
Reynolds, Martin, 2
Ricciardelli, Rose, 8
Richardson, B., 141
Richardson, L., 96
Rochlen, A. B., 249
role conflict, 203, 208, 209
role strain, 203, 204
Rose, G., 44
Ryan, R. M., 186

Sallee, M. W., 247
same-sex couples, 149–51
Sandberg, Cheryl, 63
Savarese, R. J., 2
scholarship, 241, 245n13
self-determination theory (SDT), 186–87
sexuality, 81
Shein, J., 216, 217
Shields, C., 1
Sibbald, Timothy, 8
silence as discourse, 132
Silva, J. M., 247, 251
Slaughter, Anne-Marie, 2
Smith, C. S., 78, 79, 81
Smith, H. B., 78, 79, 81
social capital, 236, 237, 245n10
social work profession, 62–63
Sociological Imagination, The (Mills), 234
Sorcinelli, M. D., 138
Springer, K. W., 3, 4
Starr, Lisa J., 8
Stewart, D., 141
Stites-Doe, S., 5
Stolte, O., 41
storytelling, 241–43, 244
student-parent, 189–90, 193, 194–95, 197n8
Swanson, D. H., 3
symbolic interactionism theory, 223

Tale of Two Cities, A (Dickens), 186
technology in education, 114
tenure-track / tenured positions: decline of,

50, 252; expectations from, 35, 260–61; parenting and, 110, 112, 138, 247, 248
Theory of Margin, 67
transformative learning, 96
Trimberger, E. K., 79

Understanding the Early Years (UEY) initiatives, 190–91
Unger, P., 80

Van de Gaag, T., 137
Violich, F., 71
vulnerability, 73

Wallace, D., 159
Wallerstein, J., 81
Waring, Marilyn, 89
Warrick, G., 143
Watson, John B., 251
Weststar, J., 138, 144
women: bisexuality, 82; childfree choice, 78–79, 80–81; identities, 5; as mothers, 2; public perception of, 5; social concepts of, 79; traditional image of, 82
women in academia: administrative work, 209; decision to start family, 137–38; delay of motherhood, 58; discrimination, 4; emotions and feelings, 55, 203–4; growing number of, 102; housework, 203; main challenges of, 3, 4; popular perception of, 203; problem of equality, 2; scholarly literature on, 66–67; studies of, 3–4, 13, 31–32; success and sacrifice, 5; underrepresentation of, 210; women bodies, 126–27; work–family balance, 6, 209; work schedules, 138–39, 205–6, 208, 210n2. See also academic mothers
Women's Ways of Knowing, 115
work–family balance: academia career and, 226; caring for disabled child and, 228–30; commuting, 24, 26; conversations about, 6–7; health issues, 23; identity negotiation, 24; life course perspective, 23; poststructuralist approach, 213; relations with children, 26; spousal support, 26–27; timing for motherhood, 24
work–family role conflict, 203–4
work–life balance phenomenon, 193–94

Yorks, L., 96